The Gunfighter

The gunfighter was a product of his time and environment. He came from all parts of the United States: Hickok and Bat Masterson from Illinois; Allison from Tennessee; Longley from Texas; others from farther West. Today many of them stand tall and invincible in the eyes of Western readers. But what spelled the difference between the fast gunslinger and his opponent? Was he a legendary name because of his courage, speed, and accuracy, or was it because of the considerable degree of trickery and psychology in gunfighting?

We will probably never know who was the "best" gunfighter. But this definitive book explores in highly colorful detail all of the glorious legends and the true facts behind them.

A Signet Brand Western

More Westerns from SIGNET

Great Gunfighters of the West

Carl W. Breihan

1977 Edition,
Revised and Expanded

A SIGNET BOOK from
NEW AMERICAN LIBRARY
TIMES MIRROR

Published by
THE NEW AMERICAN LIBRARY
OF CANADA LIMITED

DEDICATED TO

Fr. Stanley, whose excellent
and authentic research on things
Western is a mint of information
for struggling writers

Acknowledgments

I WOULD LIKE to state my grateful appreciation to all those fine people who so willingly and ably assisted me in the compilation of this work. Their helpfulness and kindness took many a weary load from my shoulders and enabled me to locate data that otherwise might have remained hidden years longer. If I missed anyone, it is not intentional, believe me.

Special thanks go to the following for exceptional help beyond the call of duty: Fr. Stanley, whose research into the lives of the desperados of New Mexico is fantastic; Jack Demattos, a meticulous searcher of hidden facts regarding things Western; Colin Rickards, whose fine work with the characters of Tombstone is commendable; Barney Hubbs, dean of Texas lore along the Pecos, for his exciting help with the Clay Allison story; Jim Hastings of Yorkshire, England, who went out of his way to help with the Ben Thompson birthplace matter; W. H. Dodd, grandson of the man who succeeded Judge Roy Bean, for his notes and photos "West of the Pecos;" Ed Bartholomew, Texas word-slinger of good factual books about our old West; Joe Rosa, whose fantastic work dealing with the "Wild Bill" Hickok story is superb; Chas. Rosamond, whose knowledge of the Harrison, Arkansas, area is fantastic; Sgt. Wayne Montgomery, whose father and grandfather were personal friends of Bat Masterson and other noted Western characters; Velma Ater, grandniece of Bill Hickok; Raymond Thorp, whose own works about Doc Carver and the Bowie knife are outstanding; Southeastern New Mexico Historical Society; Texas State Library and University; Colorado State Historical Society and Library; *Pecos Enterprise;* Kansas State Historical Society; Oklahoma State Historical Society; Texas Rangers; Arkansas State Historical Society; *Frontier Times;* National Archives; Noah H. Rose; Kerry Ross Boren, Historian of Utah history and President of the National Association and Center for Outlaw and Lawman History, Logan, Utah; Bill Kelly, historian and author; Bob Mullin, expert on Billy the Kid lore; and many contemporary newspapers and historical societies other than those herein mentioned.

C. W. B.
St. Louis, Mo., 1976

Contents

The Guns They Used

WILD BILL HICKOK
Early in life—.45-caliber Deane-Adams English 5-shot.
At McCanles' killing—Colt's 1851 Navy.
With Buffalo Bill—Two Colt's Frontier model, silver-plated, pearl-handled and engraved.
Personal, 1876—Pair of Remington 1875 Army and two Henry derringers.
Killed Phil Coe with a Williamson derringer, model 1866.
Wore when killed—Smith & Wesson Model No. 2, 32-caliber first issue, tip-up.
Buried with Sharps rifle, 1852 model.

WILD BILL LONGLEY
Dance .44-caliber 1863 model.
Colt's Frontier 1873 Army model.

CULLEN BAKER
Colt's 1848 model, .44-caliber 6-shot.
Also carried at various times the Remington cap-and-ball percussion type revolver, and a percussion shotgun.

BAT MASTERSON
Colt's Frontier model 1873, 7½ in. barrel, silver-plated, pearl-handled and carved with Mexican eagle, marked "W. B. Masterson."
Also .45-caliber Colt's Peacemaker (1873).

HENRY STARR
Colt's Army .45-caliber (New Service model of 1909), walnut grip.

HENRY BROWN
Winchester 1873 model rifle, .44-.40 caliber. Sidearms usually were two Colt's single-action .45-caliber revolvers, 1873 Peacemakers.

BEN THOMPSON
A handmade English shotgun.
Also carried a single-action Colt's .45-caliber Frontier 1871 model (the Peacemaker), or the popular single-action Colt's Army .45-caliber 1873 model.

CLAY ALLISON
Colt's .45-caliber single-action Peacemaker (1873). Also a heavy-slugged double-barreled shotgun.

FRANK LESLIE
Colt's .45-caliber Peacemaker (1875).

The Gunfighter: Prologue

THE GUNFIGHTER was a product of his time and his environment. He came from all parts of the United States—Hickok and Bat Masterson from Canada; Allison from Tennessee; Longley from Texas; Henry Starr from Oklahoma Territory. Today many of them stand tall and invincible in the eyes of man and boy alike. But what spelled the difference between the fast gunslinger and his opponent? Was his name carved in the West's hall of fame because of his courage, speed, and accuracy, or was it because there was a considerable degree of trickery and psychology in gunfighting?

We probably never will know who was the best gunfighter of the day. There were no electric timers and in many cases the winner was the one who started for his gun first. Quick reflexes depend upon good health, both mental and physical. No one is at his peak every day—as in the case of Wild Bill Hickok, who took to carrying a shotgun most of the time because his eyes had gone bad. A little-known fact is that he was totally blind for a time, due to a disease he had contracted and for which he was treated at the Army Hospital in Rochester, New York.

Many circumstances contributed to the coming of the gunfighter. Never content to remain rooted in one spot very long, the gunman was always looking over the next hill, always on the go, and like water, he usually found his own level.

The gunman was known everywhere, whether a lawman or

an outlaw; his home was anywhere, along the cattle trails, in adobe dwellings, or in the dust-ridden towns of Wichita, Cimarron, Dodge City, Abilene, Caldwell, Hays City, and others of like reputation. Sometimes the gunslinger was a dashing poker dealer or perhaps the man behind the badge. In remote areas, where civil law had not yet penetrated, the gunman was the law. His story is the real story of the West, not so much because he brought progress and wealth, but because he represented the form of person and life that the Americans in the East wanted to believe existed in the West. The timeless allure of the West caught the breath of the Easterners, those who craved to swagger down a boardwalk in high heels and to display their guns and Stetson hats. The West was romantic to those who knew little or nothing of it. The lurid hack writers of the day played up the scene and made it colorful.

The heyday of the gunfighter, regardless of what category he fitted into, lasted from the end of the Civil War until about 1900. Usually he was a young fellow, recently returned from war duty in the Union or Confederate armies. Almost without exception he had learned the art of handling firearms even before he entered the war. When he returned he was an expert. He could draw his .45-caliber revolver from its holster, aim and fire it within split seconds. He had to know by instinct how to handle the six-gun and where to point it at the precise moment of squeezing the trigger. Without that exacting sense of direction he would soon be on Boot Hill.

Few scenes stir the imagination more than the picture of a dusty trail town street bordered by saloons, dens of vice, gambling casinos, with two intent men, hands poised over their holsters, advancing toward each other with deadly motives. The winner was the one who remained calm, took his time, and pulled the trigger just once. Such a shoot-out was not too common an affair, since a great many of the gunfights occurred in the saloons on the spur of the moment or sometimes even from ambush. An open gunfight was an exciting affair. Black powder was still in use, and often the gunfighter was enveloped in a weird cloud of dark smoke. Often if guns were fired at close range the powder burns might ignite a man's clothing and there were times when the victim literally burned to death.

The professional gunfighter never notched his guns. He let willing others keep count for him, and sometimes that number was greatly increased as time passed. By virtue of his record the gunman was a marked man. Seldom did the killing of an opponent settle anything—there were always others who wanted to try, be it a relative, friend, or merely a stranger who figured he was better than the top gun of the vicinity. The gunman had to watch every path for an ambush, note more details than the ordinary person would, and be cautious in his every move. He must sit with his back to the wall when playing poker. When Hickok failed to do this just once he was assassinated. Other great gunmen met the same fate because an ordinary gunfighter was afraid to tackle them—Billy the Kid Bonney, King Fisher, and Ben Thompson, for instance.

Some of the gunfighters possessed a blind courage. They were men born without knowing what fear meant, who thought they could master any living thing. Others were almost cowards. These depended upon a small reputation given them by their advantage over the ordinary man. Their kills represented the deaths of amateurs in the gunfighting game. Seldom, if ever, would they tackle a real professional. Many of them preferred an ambush, as did Billy the Kid when he killed Sheriff Brady at Lincoln, New Mexico.

A few of the noted gunmen had more than average intelligence, and usually possessed highly sensitive nervous systems. They faced the odds knowingly and willingly. Whether such a man was brave or simply driven on by will is a moot question. At any rate, he never was a normal individual. Only the best of them survived. Wyatt Earp, Bill Tilghman, and Bat Masterson lived to see the end of the gunfighters' era, and doubtlessly were happy to do so.

The Western novel and the movies have done much to distort the facts in regard to the gunmen of the old days, especially about the art of gun-fanning (in which the pistol is held at hip level, firearm jammed against hip bone to steady, muzzle pointed at target, trigger held back in firing position, the open left hand slaps the single-action banner rapidly with the outer side of the hand, which cocks and fires the pistol) and firing two revolvers simultaneously. True, many of the gunmen carried two weapons and could shoot equally well with either hand. However, in a gunplay they would alternate their fire or empty one revolver and then use the other, sometimes reverting to the "border shift" of throwing the loaded gun into their more efficient hand.

We know that Wild Bill Hickok carried weapons with the "dogs" (hammers of the pistol) filed off, but there is little record of him being an expert fanner. Almost all students of the era believe that gun-fanning never existed or could exist,

3

especially with single-action revolvers. Some of the old gunmen simply held their trigger tight against the guard and then fanned the hammer with no lost motion. But to hit a small target using the fanning method is almost impossible. It impairs the accuracy of the weapon to fan it, even though it also makes a single-action weapon almost as fast as a double-action gun. In a shoot-out, to fan a gun would be little short of murder. Pictorially, the fanner makes an exciting picture; in reality, gun-fanning would be suicide. Most old-timer gunmen, outlaws, and lawmen seldom used the fanning method. They usually relied on the truth that one bullet would do all the damage needed if it was put in the right place.

The majority of the Western gunfighters chose to carry their pistols in holsters, but Hickok seldom or never used them. He carried two pistols in his waistband, their butts pointing inward for a crossarm draw. Dallas Stoudenmire, the two-gun marshal of El Paso, carried his revolvers in special leather-lined hip pockets. He could draw those lethal weapons with amazing speed. At one time he killed three men while under the deadly muzzle of a scattergun. He killed the shotgun man first and then got the other two. The noted Ben Thompson was prolific with any method of drawing. He used them all—holster, waistband, hip pocket, and hideout gun. Legend has it that Ben was the inventor of the shoulder holster. Wes Hardin designed a vest with gun holsters in it. The vest was made of calfskin, with two holster pockets slanting outward from center to hipbones, and holding two pistols, butts pointing inward. To draw, the arms were crossed and the guns plucked out.

Many of the Western gunmen, however, seem to have fallen into the category of phychological maniacs. Perhaps a knowledge of applied psychology might have helped them. Many embarked on careers of violence because they suffered inferiority complexes. Once the gunman started on his smoky road there was no turning back. That road led straight to Boot Hill, and normally a gunman's speed and clever gunplay merely postponed the trip. Once he killed, he had to kill again and again to retain his reputation and to save his own life. Others sought him out, hoping to boost their own standing by killing the man who had killed so-and-so. Every man had his match. The question was: how long could he go before facing him?

It is morally wrong to make a hero of a killer. And yet frequently it is a thin hair that must be split in separating the killer from the professional gunfighter.

No killing can be justified; I am only trying to point out that in some cases it actually narrowed down to one thing in the old West—to kill or be killed.

The stories recorded herein are factual gatherings from musty old records, yellowing newspapers, historical documents, personal interviews, and grassroots research. The final judgment is left to each individual. The reader must judge from his own inner sense of value and justice just how these men rated and where they stand in the annals of their time.

.45-caliber Deane-Adams English 5-shot

1   Wild Bill Hickok

DURING THE YEAR following the close of the Civil War the name of a man flashed across the raw Western frontier like the descent of a shattered meteor. This man was "Wild Bill" Hickok, the enigma of the Border, who basked in the notoriety of his own imagination. The heat of this dubious fame was generated to gigantic proportions by the prolific pens of such contemporary thrill-writers as Ned Buntline, whose real name was Edward Zane Carol Judson, and Colonel George Ward Nichols of Boston, Massachusetts.

Quick to sense the keen interest of the eastern populace in the expanding West, such periodicals as *The Police Gazette* and *Harper's Weekly* climbed aboard the bandwagon and carried thrill-filled action stories of "the world's greatest scout and gunfighter." The tales were so fantastic and far-fetched that a number of hack writers must have been employed to grind them out. Hickok wanted to be fair with his public, and tried to some degree to live up to the reputation tailor-made for him. So the legends grew and grew until only the Greek myths could match them. Yet the true story of Bill has another hue, one that is not all glossy and bright.

William Alonzo Hickok—according to some the family Bible spelled it Haycock—Bill's father, was a deacon in the Presbyterian Church and was born December 5, 1801, at North Hero, Grand Isle County, Vermont, and passed away in 1852. He married Polly Butler in 1827 and they had six children: Oliver, born in 1830; Lorenzo, born in 1832; Horace, born in 1834; James Butler, born in 1837; Celenda, born in 1839; and Lydia, born in 1842. James Butler Hickok, later destined to become the fabulous Wild Bill, was born on May 27, in a town now known as Troy Grove, Illinois. It once had other names: Walnut Grove, Iowa, and Homer, and was in La Salle County, near the Little Vermillion Creek. There he remained until 1855, at first working on the family farm, later in a general store his father had opened after having had bad luck with farming.

From his boyhood days Bill disclosed a marked fondness for firearms; when fourteen years old he secured an excellent pistol by exchanging furs for the weapon. A short time later his father presented him with a first-class rifle. Very few books were obtainable in that part of the country. *The Life of Kit Carson* and *The Trapper's Guide* made such an impression on James Hickok's mind that he told his friends: "One day I'll beat anything that Kit Carson ever did or attempted!"

In 1852, just two days before the boy's fifteenth birthday, his father passed away. Bill helped the family by hunting for food while his brothers again operated the farm, work which the boy did not relish too greatly. Young Bill also hunted wolves for their bounty in order to supplement the family's meager income. From then until his death in 1876 Hickok lived a life filled with violence and strife.

Hickok fast became accustomed to the rough life on the frontier, and his first experience with violence came in 1855 when he was working as a towpath mule-driver during the construction of the Illinois and Michigan Canal. Young Bill got into a fight with a bully named Charles Hudson, beating the man so badly that he feared he had killed him. He did not linger in camp to learn the results of Hudson's injuries (the man recovered), but fled west to Leavenworth, Kansas, by steamboat.

Hickok arrived in Kansas sometime during the year of 1856, taking up residence with the family of John Owen, who had married an Indian girl. The homesite was at a place called Mill Creek, in Monticello Township, Johnson County, Kansas. He found work with a farmer named Williams, but, soon tiring of this manual labor, Bill quit his job and joined General James Lane's band of Free Staters. During those pre-Civil War days, bands of raiders from both Missouri and Kansas raided and plundered each other's territory, one side wanting Kansas admitted to the Union as a Free State, the

8

other wanting Missouri's sister state admitted to the Union as a Slave State. Two Kansas factions known as the Jayhawkers and the Red Legs rode into Missouri to plunder and to steal. Later during the Civil War these factions clashed with the notorious William Clarke Quantrill and his Missouri Raiders. Young Hickok joined the Red Legs, so called because they wore bright red leggings to identify themselves, and assumed the first name of his father, William.

There has been much discussion as to why Hickok was called Wild Bill when his name was James. However, this sobriquet was acquired while he was using his father's name, some claim. Many writers have claimed his famous nickname stemmed from his bravery and raiding at the Rock Creek Station affair, but such is not the case. There are two suppositions dealing with the situation, and either could be correct. During a riot while in Leavenworth, Kansas, Bill was instrumental in disposing of several men. But where others were content to vanquish an opponent, Bill was not satisfied unless he maimed the man. During this affair an excited woman spectator yelled: "Give him hell, Wild Bill!" If such be the case, his new name was born amid violence and death. On the other hand, it is claimed by some that a name attached to him, "Duck Bill," simply finally became "Wild Bill." If so, then his famous name was born amid ridicule and harrassment.

Hickok left Kansas in 1857, traveling with the wagon train of Lew Simpson, which was attacked by the same group of Mormons and Indians which had been responsible for the infamous murders at Mountain Meadows, Utah, in which all but seventeen children of the Captain Fancher wagon train had been ruthlessly slaughtered. This horrible affair occurred in September of 1857, the band being led by John Doyle Lee, bishop of Harmony, Indian agent to the Piedes, and Brigham Young's adopted son. Lee was later arrested and executed by a firing squad at the scene of the Mountain Meadows Massacre.

Later Hickok returned to Kansas, where, on March 22, 1858, he was elected constable of Monticello Township, also working a 160-acre farm he had filed a claim to in 1857. Bill built a livable cabin on his claim, and many of the old-timers stated he also did another thing ... he married a half-Shawnee Indian girl, Mary Owen, tribal fashion. Of course, no records of such an incident would have been kept, so it is anyone's guess as to whether it really happened. Bill's association with Jim Lane had caused many Missourians to resent his presence nearby. One night his cabin was burned to the ground. Hickok was not to be intimidated; he built another cabin. It also was burned to the ground.

Tiring of such experiences, Hickok hired out as a wagon driver on the Sante Fe Trail. During these jaunts from Missouri and Colorado and points in Kansas and Nebraska, Bill met the famous scout Kit Carson in Sante Fe, New Mexico, in 1859. Hickok must have had many exciting experiences as he drove stages over the Overland Trail for Russell, Majors, and Waddell and many an occasion to use his weapons. Unfortunately, these have not been recorded to any extent; consequently, there is little on record concerning this portion of his life.

In October of 1860, while Hickok was driving a team between Independence, Missouri, and Sante Fe, New Mexico, he had his famous fight with a female cinnamon bear at Raton Pass, New Mexico, in the Soccoro Mountain range. It has been recorded two ways: the bear was a grizzly; fear was a cinnamon. . . . Bill's partner, Matt Farley, driving his team a mile or so behind Hickok's wagon, said it was a cinnamon bear. In any event, the mother bear and her two cubs were blocking the road, much to Bill's anger. But he felt that his two pistols and his Bowie knife were ample protection against a mother bear. So, jumping down from his springboard wagon-seat, Bill approached within a short distance of the bears. He fired several times with his pistol, which only served to enrage the beast. The bear charged, grabbing Bill in a viselike grip. His only salvation was his knife. This he used to finally dispose of the animal. When Matt Farley arrived on the scene he found the bear lying across Hickok's body. His employers had Bill taken to Sante Fe and later to Kansas City, where he slowly began to recover from his terrible injuries.

In January of 1861 Hickok arrived at Rock Creek Station, Nebraska, on the Overland route, where he had been sent by his employers to do lighter work on account of his injuries. David Colbert McCanles was then in charge, and assigned Bill to work as a helper at the stables.

For some unknown reason McCanles disliked Hickok from the first. He took every occasion to humiliate the young man. He gave him various nicknames, one of which was "Duck Bill," due to Hickok's protruding upper lip. He would also seize Bill when there were crowds of men present, wrestle with him, and then throw him down. Bill could not do much about it, for his left arm was still disabled, and it was only with pain that he moved about at all. McCanles pretended that this was all in fun, but there was malice behind his every movement. He continued this course to within a few days of his death. Others claimed that Hickok was lazy and neglected the stock and that he and McCanles got into many arguments because of it.

Hickok's temper was far from even. He could not bear to be called Duck Bill. This fact was significance because little credit has hitherto been given to Jack McCall's story that he killed Hickok to avenge the death of his brother.

Near Rock Creek Station lived the widow McCall and her two small sons, Jack, twelve, and Andy, nine. They had recently moved to Nebraska from Kentucky. One day young Andy called to Hickok, "Howdy, Mr. Duck Bill."

Hickok flew into a rage and ran after the lad, striking him on the head with a hoe. The blow proved fatal.

"I'll kill you when I grow up!" cried Jack McCall. We all know how he lived up to that threat.

Nebraska Territory in 1861 had no real law, so Hickok was never brought to justice for his crime. Mrs. McCall made frantic efforts to have something done about Andy's killing, but with the whole country in heated discussion over the slavery question and civil war, not much attention was paid to her pleas.

On May 1, 1861, the stage company bought the East Rock Creek Station from McCanles, with payments to be made in several installments. Russell, Majors, and Waddell appointed Horace Wellman superintendent, with Hickok and one Doc Brink acting as hostlers at the station. McCanles moved to his ranch on the Little Blue, at the mouth of Rock Creek.

Although married to Mary Green, McCanles had a mistress living at the West Rock Creek Ranch, across from where Hickok was employed. Bill had become aware of the relations between McCanles and Miss Sarah Shull (also called Kate Shell) soon after his arrival at Rock Creek, and he kept informed as to the exact nature of the relationship. Taking advantage of what he knew, he made progress for himself in the good graces of the pretty woman. McCanles became suspicious of Hickok and in his furious jealousy devised a means to discover the truth. Afterward he regarded Hickok with a deadly hatred.

When McCanles moved to the ranch on the Little Blue, Miss Shull and a Sarah Kelsey lived for a while at the West Rock Creek Station, as companions for Mrs. Wellman; she was visited there by Hickok. McCanles had knowledge of his visits at once, and he promptly warned Hickok to keep away from Miss Shull and not to cross the creek to the West

11

Ranch under pain of death. Bill confessed to two of his intimate friends that there was no room in his heart for any woman other than Sarah Shull. He was always looking for her, hoping to see her, take her in his arms, have her for his own. It is probable that after she left Rock Creek, Sarah never gave Bill another thought. It was something he came to realize later, but it never changed him.

It was on the afternoon of July 12, 1861, that McCanles told Sarah Shull he was going to "clean up" on the people at the station. It is not known exactly what he meant by the expression. The stage company still owed McCanles money for the Rock Creek Station. Perhaps he meant he was going to get his money, perhaps that he meant to fight them. Yet the latter explanation would not agree with the record that the McCanles party was unarmed during the subsequent affray. McCanles was accompanied by his cousin, James Woods, and by James Gordon, an employee. He also took along his young son, Monroe, which bolsters the belief that the men were not armed. Certainly McCanles would not endanger the life of his own boy.

Apologists for Hickok claim the party was armed and that McCanles approached the station in a belligerent manner and demanded his money. Legally he had every right to evict the people there and to reclaim his property. The stage company had defaulted in its payment of the agreed sum at a stipulated time.

At the station the McCanles group met only the common-law Mrs. Wellman. She stated her husband was absent, that he had not returned from Jacksonville, where he had gone in an effort to get the money due McCanles. The visitor could tell she lied. At this point Hickok appeared on the scene. He pushed Mrs. Wellman aside and confronted McCanles. His appearance surprised and enraged McCanles, and must have had a sobering effect upon him, for he stopped to parley. The fact that McCanles believed Hickok elsewhere that day adds more credibility to the report that he was not armed. McCanles bore no killing hatred against the others at Rock Creek Station. He had threatened only Hickok.

"What in hell have you got to do with this?" he snapped.

"The station's business is my business," replied Bill, "and I don't intend to see you bully Wellman or his wife."

"My business is with Wellman, not you, and if you want to take a hand in it come on out here, and we'll settle it like men."

McCanles knew that Wellman was in the house, that Mrs.

Wellman's story was but a stall, and he was uneasy. Perhaps a weapon was aimed at him, covering his every move.

"Send Wellman out here so I can settle with him, or I'll come in and drag him out!" he shouted.

There was danger, he knew now, so he walked from the west door to the south or front door. From there he had a view of the interior of the whole house, except that portion shut off by a calico curtain. In the west room, the kitchen, was Sarah Shull—who later said she was two miles away at the time—and Sarah Kelsey, a stepdaughter of Joe Baker, who had been employed by McCanles.

McCanles stepped into the south doorway, from which position Wellman and Hickok were in sight. He did not attack them, and he could think of nothing better to justify his presence than to ask for a drink of water—which clearly was an excuse, for there was a bucket of water with a dipper in it two feet away. Hickok left Wellman, went to the bucket, dipped up a gourdful of water, and handed it to McCanles. Then he turned and walked stealthily back toward the curtain. McCanles had not really wanted water. He dropped the dipper and called upon Hickok to wait. Hickok ignored the request. He was soon behind the curtain, where he had every advantage. McCanles realized the danger in which he stood. Now Hickok called back to McCanles that if he came in to drag him out: "There will be one less son-of-a-bitch when you try that!"

It will never be known whether McCanles started in to drag Hickok out, for almost immediately a shot was fired from behind the curtain, and the bullet went through McCanles' chest. He staggered and fell backward in the yard. Notwithstanding his mortal wound, McCanles attempted to raise himself up, and was helped by his son Monroe, who had run to his aid.

"Run, son, run! Your life's in danger here! I'm a goner!" Hurry, get going now!" McCanles commanded the boy.

With that, young Monroe took off at a good sprint and disappeared in a nearby gully. Probably it was fortunate that he obeyed promptly, for he might have fallen another victim to Bill's blood-lust.

When Gordon and Woods heard the shot and saw McCanles fall, they left the barn and ran at full speed to the house. Woods attempted to enter by the kitchen door, which was the west door, where McCanles had first appeared. Gordon ran to the south door. Woods was mortally wounded when Hickok shot him twice with his revolver. As he collapsed in a patch of weeds, Mrs. Wellman, in an insane fit of hatred, grabbed a grubbing hoe and quickly killed Woods. Gordon came up just in time to see Hickok shoot Woods. He tried to make a run for it. Hickok fired, and Gordon fell to the ground. Rising, Gordon staggered into the woods, followed by Hickok, Wellman, Doc Brink, and a man named George Hulbert. They found the wounded man at the creek, where he was quickly killed with a shotgun blast.

On July 13 the dead were buried while Hickok rode to Marysville, Kansas, to confer with an attorney named Brumbaugh in case he would be tried for murder. We wonder what kind of cock-and-bull story he told this man.

It was often said afterward that James Butler Hickok killed nine of the McCanles gang of horse thieves who attacked the Rock Creek Station to steal horses for the Confederacy. This is absolutely not true. The whole affair was really McCanles *versus* Hickok, a showdown between the two. Both were men of destiny, strong, fitted to stand in the forefront of the frontier's advance—to take the lead of civilization into new lands. By his later courage, his intrepidity, his iron will, his marvelous personal achievement, Wild Bill won fame. By his strength of character and his tragic death, McCanles won fame. One was a knight of the Middle Ages, strangely out of time; the other a freebooter with the daring to take what he wanted regardless of the consequences. Both will live on in the pages of the West's history.

Many have questioned the record, which clearly depicts Hickok as a sadistic killer at the time of the Rock Creek affair. The official files are still intact in Nebraska, but were not located until many years after Bill was raised on his pedestal of fame. The still-existing records show that a complaint was filed, and was the first heard in Gage County, Nebraska Territory. It reads as follows:

Territory of Nebraska
County of Gage S.S.

The complainant and informant, LeRoy McCanles, of the county of Johnson, Territory aforesaid, made before T. M. Coulter, Esquire, one of the Justices of the Peace, in and for Gage County, on the 13th day of July, 1861, who being duly sworn on his oath says ... That the crime of murder has been committed in the county of Jones, and that Dutch Bill ... Doc ... and Wellman (their other names unknown) Committed the same. ...

J. L. McCanles

Subscribed and sworn to before me on the 13th day of July 1861.

T. M. COULTER,
Justice of the Peace

Upon this complaint Justice of the Peace Coulter then made out an order of arrest, which was served, and a record made and duly filed:

The warrant ... the within warrant ... came to hand this 13th day of July, 1861, at 2:00 o'clock p.m.
Served the within warrant by arresting the within Dutch Bill, Doc, and Wellman this 15th day of July, 1861.

E. B. HENDEE
Sheriff of Gage County
Nebraska Territory

Sheriff's Fee $5.00

Hickok (Dutch or Duck Bill), J. W. (Doc) Brink, and Horace Wellman were placed in custody on July 15, 1861, at Rock Creek Ranch, which lay six miles southeast of the present city of Fairbury, Nebraska. They were loaded into a wagon and driven to Beatrice, thirty miles away, and on July 18 their case was given a preliminary hearing, of which record still exists. Brink and Wellman were accused as accessories to the crime of murder. It might be mentioned that most chroniclers of Hickok's career have declared that Wild Bill never was arrested for a crime. This rather sets the record straight. Some have also claimed the prisoners were released by the Justice of the Peace on the grounds of self-defense. Also, not true. A Justice of the Peace Court cannot try a murder case nor can he release a prisoner charged with such a crime.

The prisoners were bound over for the Circuit Court, Judge Mason, but the trial never took place. The start of the Civil War and the quick departure of Miss Shull from the territory provided interruptions. All the same, the fantasy constructed from Wild Bill's performance as a gunfighter at Rock Creek is now seen for what it was. The famous fight was in truth a massacre. Hickok's stature is somewhat lessened. He decamped and left for St. Louis, Missouri, and never returned to the vicinity of Rock Creek, except once when scouting for the Union army.

In August, 1861, Hickok became a brigade wagonmaster

under the command of General John C. Fremont, in command at Fort Leavenworth. He seemed to take his work seriously and Lieutenant-Colonel Goerge A. Custer had this to say of Wild Bill:

> Whether on foot or on horseback he was one of the most perfect types of physical manhood I ever saw. Of his courage there could be no question. His skill in the use of the rifle and pistol was unerring. His deportment was entirely free from all bluster and bravado. He never spoke of himself unless requested to do so. His conversation never bordered upon the vulgar or blasphemous.
>
> His influence among the frontiersmen was unbounded; his word was law; and many are the personal quarrels and disturbances which he had checked among his comrades by the simple announcement that "this has gone far enough," if need be, followed by the ominous warning that, if persisted in, the quarreler "must settle with me."
>
> Wild Bill always carried two handsome, ivory-handled revolvers of large size. He was never seen without them. I have a personal knowledge of at least a half dozen men whom he has at various times killed, others have been seriously wounded—yet he always escaped unhurt in every encounter.

Custer being as great a showman as Hickok himself, this sounds like something the colonel would say.

Amazing yarns have been told of Hickok's service as a Union Scout and spy. The most famous include how he dashed through large bodies of Confederate soldiers or Quantrill guerrillas, laid half of them low, then managed to escape without a scratch; or how he crawled into the enemy camp, obtained information of the utmost secrecy, and returned unharmed to help win a major battle. It does not stand to reason that all that has been written about him could have happened. The odds against one man performing so spectacularly are too great. Regardless of his amazing proficiency or uncanny ability to handle weapons, he could not have escaped all the bullets supposedly fired at him during his Civil War escapades. Probably the most incredible of Bill's war exploits was his sharpshooting at the Battle of Pea Ridge, Arkansas, March 6–8, 1862. The Union forces under General Samuel R. Curtis were battling the Confederates under Generals Sterling Price and Benjamin McCulloch.

Hickok's commanding officer instructed him to find an advantageous spot overlooking Cross Timber Hollow and to pick off as many of the enemy as he could. Crawling to the protection of some heavy timber, Hickok began to fire at the Confederates. For several hours he picked off gray-clad soldiers until he had downed a total of thirty-six. By that time it seems the enemy felt they had a formidable sharpshooter taking heavy toll. General McCulloch ordered a charge against the hidden Union rifleman. But before the charge could become effective Hickok shot and killed McCulloch, demoralized his men, and was able to escape.

It was also during March of 1862 that Hickok met Susannah Moore, who later figured in the Dave Tutt killing. In March he also operated with John R. Kelso as a Union spy behind the enemy lines. Another famous spy worked with Hickok during the war. He was the scout and spy named Timothy "Big Jim" Courtright, later famous marshal of Fort Worth, Texas, and later still to be slain by little Luke Short in a framed duel. This writer is proud to own a tobacco or money pouch given to Courtright by Hickok during the war on Jim's birthday. It was made by an Indian woman from a part of Hickok's boot and a part of his fringed jacket.

There can be no question that Hickok risked his life daily for the Union cause, as did many thousands of other faithful men. Of course, Hickok was singled out to become the champion because of his glib talk, his expert way of making a mountain out of a mole hill, and his growing reputation as a fighter. Bill had no scruples worth mentioning. One day while he was riding through a small Missouri town an old man poked his head from an upstairs window and yelled: "Hurrah for Jeff Davis!" Hickok took a single shot at the man and killed him.

In July of 1864 Hickok had a run-in with three Federal soldiers in Phelps County, Missouri. According to legend, he dispatched all three within seconds and managed to secure one of their mounts, a beautiful black mare which he named Black Nell. The animal was well trained, acting upon orders to "fall dead" or to seek a suitable hiding place when the occasion demanded. This horse was one of Hickok's most treasured possessions, and when she died in Kansas City in 1869, her passing caused Wild Bill great grief.

During the Battle of Westport, Missouri, Wild Bill and Big Jim Courtright again carried on their spy activities behind the Union lines to good effect. Again their escape was made on horseback; even so, they were almost captured because it was later believed that Dave Tutt had betrayed them. In January of 1865 there occurred another event which was spawned from someone's vivid imagination. It was then that Wild Bill

17

was supposed to have slain Conquering Bear, a Sioux sub-chief who had been lured into Kansas on the promise of receiving large rewards to help the Union. Nowhere has this author been able to find whether Hickok was near the scene at the time Conquering Bear was slain.

A search of the Federal War Records and volumes of *The War of the Rebellion, Confederate and Union, 1861–1865* indicates that Hickok was a satisfactory scout for General Curtis, but nothing is recorded of his amazing escapes and his ability to outwit the enemy at every turn. Discharged from the service after General Lee's surrender in 1865, Hickok returned to Springfield, Missouri, but the welcome mat was not laid out as he had expected. In the *History of Greene County* we find that Hickok was unpopular with the citizens. There is one account which gives this picture of him:

> Duck Bill provoked trouble wherever he could. He had a room at the Lyons' House, where he delighted in terrorizing the guests by his bullying and swaggering ways. He was by nature a ruffian, soon to become a drunken, swaggering fellow who delighted, when on a spree, in frightening nervous men and timid women by riding on horseback on the sidewalks and into the saloons, hotels, and other public places on Black Nell.

The *Kansas City Star* carried the following uncomplimentary piece about Hickok.

> On one occasion a 300-pound foreigner, named Phillador, who operated a saloon on South Street in Springfield, rushed from behind the bar just as Hickok came riding through the swinging door of his place, grabbed the horse's bridle, and nacked him on to the sidewalk. Bill dismounted and came into the saloon, calling vile names at the saloon keeper, who drew a knife with one hand and slapped Bill's face with the other. Turning his back to Bill, he said, "Shoot me in the back, that is your way, but I'll kill you before I die."

It was in Springfield that Hickok had his fight with the man from Arkansas, Dave Tutt. Bill had been friendly with Dave's pretty sister, but when an old acquaintance of Bill's arrived in town he discarded Tutt's sister and made plans to romance the new arrival, Susannah Moore.

Susannah was friendly with Hickok, whom she had met previously, but suddenly the relationship was broken off and she became more interested in Tutt. This infuriated Hickok, who needed only an excuse to kill someone. Tutt knew this, but did not fear Bill's supposed reputation as a scout and gunslinger. On July 21, 1865, the two men clashed in the town's square. Rumor has it that Hickok and Tutt had fallen out over a card game and that Tutt had refused to return Hickok's watch to him, but the main reason was Susannah Moore.

Hickok and Tutt were seventy-five yards from each other when Tutt fired at Hickok, the bullet just missing Bill's head. Calmly Hickok rested his gunhand upon his left arm to steady it and shot Dave through the heart, immediately turning around and pointing the gun at Dave's friends, who appeared ready to take part in the matter but did not do so. The range of Bill's shot immediately placed him in the category of a cool and deadly marksman. These were not the quick-draw tactics for which Hickok has gone down in tradition. The authorities decided the slaying was justifiable, and on August 5 Hickok went free.

On September 13, 1865, Hickok lost his bid in the election for marshal of Springfield, coming in second with sixty-three votes. That same day Colonel George Ward Nichols arrived in Springfield, eager to find an exciting gunman or outlaw to provide a feature for *Harper's*. So far he had been unsuccessful. No deadly gunmen infested the West, it was too early. They were yet to come. Something would have to be concocted. The people in the East were accustomed to reading bloody accounts of the Civil War, and they wanted more in the same vein, regardless of how it was served up. Nichols decided that if he could not find the right man, he would create one. His opportunity came quicker than he had anticipated. One day when seated outside his hotel he noticed a tall, handsome man astride a fine mount. He later said the figure appeared more like that of a woman than of a man. His curiosity was genuinely aroused.

A former Union officer stationed at Springfield, Nichols had no trouble in finding out about Hickok. The hotel proprietor told him of the Tutt killing.

"Excellent!" cried the colonel. "Just what I need. See that we're introduced."

It was during the interview that was arranged that Hickok told the fantastic tale of wiping out, single-handed, the terrible McCanles gang of horse thieves at Rock Creek Station. The lurid and grossly misleading account was later published in *Harper's Weekly*, Vol. 34, February, 1867. Colonel Nichols introduced the article by saying: "I have checked care-

fully into the account and have interviewed eyewitnesses. ....
I am convinced this entire story is true."

What the colonel failed to mention was that in less than
five hours after the Rock Creek affair, S. J. Alexander, Secretary of State, and D. C. Jenkins, Member of the State Legislature, Nebraska, arrived there to investigate the affair.
Instead of ten dead ruffians, as told by Hickok, they found
three murdered men.

Overnight, Hickok was skyrocketed to fame. The great
New York Herald sent Henry Stanley to interview the "hero
of the plains." Rival newspapers and periodicals so twisted
and warped the facts concerning Wild Bill Hickok that it is
now impossible to tell where truth ended and fiction began.
Bill took full advantage of his popularity. He discarded his
buckskins and took to wearing corsets, a Prince Albert coat,
checkered trousers, silk waistband, and a flower-lined cape.
Again leaning to his feminine inclinations, Bill sported high-
heeled shoes and wore his blond hair long and flowing.

One of Wild Bill's most ardent admirers was Mrs. Custer,
wife of Lieut.-Col. George Armstrong Custer. It was chiefly
through her intercession that Hickok was appointed a deputy
United States Marshal in February of 1866, operating out of
Fort Riley, Kansas. His job was to work against the horse
thieves infesting that area. The official records show that he
did a good job of bringing in rustlers and army deserters,
sometimes battling it out with them.

During the years of 1867–8 Hickok was a scout for General Hancock in his campaign against the Indians, as well as
a scout for Custer's Seventh Cavalry. As a government
courier he risked his life daily in his secret treks through Indian country to obtain information for his commanding officer. Had the hack writers of the day stuck to facts about
Hickok, no doubt many interesting and true stories could
have been written, possibly more absorbing than those dished
out in fable form. Now no one knows what to believe, or
even whether to believe any of the accepted legend. There
seems to be no accurate account of Hickok's experiences during those two years, so most of the legend writers have based
their incredible stories about him on events supposed to have
happened in that short period.

We know that during that period Hickok met Moses
Milner, otherwise known as "California Joe." They became
good friends, Hickok counting Milner and "Colorado Charlie" Utter among his best friends. Another alleged incident
supposedly occurred on December 22, 1867, in Jefferson

County, Nebraska, when he was in search of better trapping grounds. En route to his destination Bill stopped off at a saloon for a drink. Five cowboys, seeing Hickok alone at his table, thought he would be a good target for some heckling. Bill paid little attention to the bragging cowboys until one of them threw a glass of whiskey into his face. The story as told is so ridiculous that it is no wonder no record exists of it. Hickok told the bartender to count to three, at which time the three men chosen to fight him would turn and fire, he doing likewise. In the fracas, it is said that Hickok killed Seth Beeber, Jack Slater, and Frank Dowder, with Bill being shot through the right arm. After receiving treatment for his injured arm, Bill is supposed to have ridden to Kansas City, taking seven days in which to make the journey.

What a story Bill could have told had he been present on November 27, 1868, when Custer attacked the Cheyenne camp of Chief Black Kettle in the snowswept valley of the Washita River. The dawn ripped alive to the brassy crash of the Seventh's marching song as thundering hooves crashed into the stunned camp. The grizzled chief Black Kettle spun and fell as a .52 caliber slug ripped through him. Death for him had waited four years since the dreadful day when Chivington had attacked the Cheyenne camp at Sand Creek, Colorado. At Washita an estimate of 103 Indians were killed— men, women, and children. At five below zero, the region, now western Oklahoma, was a white hell, with even the moon trying to find refuge behind the Antelope Hills. Bill was not there that awful morning, but California Joe was. At that time Hickok was snowed in on the Canadian River with the command of General William Penrose, later to be rescued by a party led by Buffalo Bill Cody.

Like a rolling snowball, the legends grew and grew. Soon Hickok began to tire of running messages for the government and decided to bask in his fame. On February 28, 1869, Hickok left his position as army scout, never again to return to that profession. He was at Fort Lyon, Colorado, at the time and decided to visit his home. While there he went to Mendota, Illinois, where he had his photo taken. He went to the studio of J. Blakslee to have his picture taken full length while dressed in buckskins, pistols, and a Bowie knife. In April of the same year he visited his mother for the first time in fourteen years. What a reunion that must have been. ... It was their last.

Everywhere he went the newspapermen followed and interviewed him. In the gambling houses of Topeka, Kansas City, and Leavenworth the crowds gaped in amazement at this "Eighth Wonder of the World." Men who hardly knew his name suddenly had known him all their life! Those who knew him slightly had been his neighbors at one time or another!

In May, 1869, Wild Bill swaggered into Hays City, Kansas, a rough-and-tumble town badly in need of law and order— civic virtues it had not acquired. The local politians prevailed upon Hickok to place his name on the ballot for sheriff of Ellis County. On August 23, 1869, Hickok was elected sheriff to fill an unexpired term. He also acted as city marshal of Hays. Bill displayed skill and cunning in his policing of Hays City, but there is no factual record giving any account of fast-draw shoot-outs and such exploits as the movies and contemporary writers would have us believe. Like the gunmen who followed him, Hickok devised all sorts of tricks to throw an adversary off balance or distract him for a fleeting second. He tried to seek out the little, unnoticed failings of his foe, thereby usually having the slight edge on his opponent.

On August 24th a man named Bill Mulvey, a notorious thug from St. Joseph, Missouri, rode into Hays City. After having a number of drinks at Drum's saloon, the badman commenced wandering around town, smashing windows and lamps in his wake. When Hickok arrived on the scene Mulvey was standing rigid, two pistols in his hands, daring anyone to take them from him. Then Bill did a strange thing; he backed off several feet, looked behind Mulvey, and called out: "Don't shoot him, he's only having a little fun." Mulvey turned, expecting to see a deputy at his rear. At the same instant Hickok snatched out a revolver and shot the man dead.

The most talked about killing by Hickok while in Hays City was the shooting of an all-around badman named Samuel "Jack" Strawhim on September 27, 1869. Apparently there was no personal animosity between Hickok and Strawhim other than that Bill had helped the marshal of Ellsworth, Kansas, round up the so-called desperado on several occasions when the man was creating trouble in that town. Also, it was a known fact that Strawhim had boasted that he would clean up Hays City, especially now since Hickok was marshal, and if Hickok got in his way, he'd kill him.

On the night of September 27, Strawhim entered Drum's saloon, looking for Wild Bill. Hickok saw his enemy, but made no motion to draw. Strawhim, thinking he had not been observed, pulled a pistol. Before he could fire, Hickok drew his revolver and killed him. Some reports claim that Hickok shot Strawhim before the latter had drawn. The news spread quickly. "Hickok had drawn with lightning speed and slain his adversary in a matter of seconds." Hickok was soon resting on his laurels. His reputation had preceded him to every place he stayed, and men who dared to face him did so nervously, the "Hickok reputation" weighing heavily upon them. This was a decided advantage to Wild Bill.

Hickok's career in Hays City came to an abrupt end on July 17, 1870. That afternoon a group of soldiers from Fort Hays came to town, visited Paddy Welch's bar, and then proceeded to become abusive and plain downright mean. Apparently the final outcome of the fracas came about after Wild Bill had thrashed the boisterous sergeant with his fists. One of the other soldiers lunged at Hickok, while others caught him from behind. Wild Bill was able to draw his pistol, and he killed Private John Kelly, who was behind him. His second shot wounded Private Jeremiah Lanigan, and the fight ended as quickly as it had started.

General Phil Sheridan ordered Hickok to be arrested, dead or alive. But the wily Bill had taken leave of Hays City some minutes after the fracas. He hid out at the cabin of Harry Pestana near Ellsworth until his slight injuries healed.

Spring of 1871 found Hickok at Abilene, Kansas, where he secured a room at the Alamo Hotel and became a regular customer at the gambling tables. Abilene had been without a satisfactory marshal since the death of the famed Tom Smith, the man who tamed the town with his bare fists. Smith had been waylaid and killed by two ruffians named Joe Hammer and Mac McConnell on November 2, 1870. News that Hickok was living at the Alamo reached the anxious ears of Mayor Joseph C. McCoy, whose duty it was to appoint a new marshal. Former Mayor T. C. Henry did not approve of Hickok, saying that Tom Smith was genuine and believed in law and order, while Hickok was a poseur and a killer.

Mayor McCoy noticed how the crowds gathered before the Alamo, anxious to get a look at the famous Wild Bill Hickok. And truly he was something to look at. He was as perfect a specimen of manhood as ever walked, and often dressed as a regular frontier dude. He was six feet two inches tall in his boots and was perfectly proportioned. He was wide-shouldered, lean of waist, with hands and feet as small as a woman's. His blond hair hung over his shoulders in uncut ringlets falling carelessly over his powerful frame. His blue-gray eyes were piercing, staring one straight in the face when in conversation, and his finely shaped nose inclined to the aquiline. His well-shaped mouth was partially concealed by a handsome moustache. McCoy was more interested in Hickok's guns than in his appearance. He finally was able to persuade the City Council to back him in offering Wild Bill a hundred and fifty dollars a month for his services as marshal of Abilene, Kansas. Hickok accepted the job on April 15, 1871, and a more sinister and deadly atmosphere of law enforcement very soon hung over the town. It was to be an exciting year for Wild Bill Hickok.

Abilene, Kansas, in July, 1871, was as tough as a western town could get. Since most cowtrails led to and ended at Abilene, it was there that the cowboys blew off the steam they had built up over the long, dry months on the cattle drives. There, too, was the notorious Bull's Head Saloon, owned by Ben Thompson and Phil Coe. Thompson and Coe were on the outs with Marshal Hickok because he had ordered them to remove an obscene advertising figure of a bull from in front of their saloon.

Along with the herds of Johnson and Carol came the notorious young gunslinger John Wesley Hardin. At Abilene, Hardin was requested by his employers to remain on to round up the strays. He agreed and was also quick in establishing his reputation in the town. The first night he and his boss went out and got into an argument with a police officer named Carson, who pulled his gun and ordered Carol to jail. Wes Hardin quickly covered him and promptly told him if he was looking for trouble to get Hickok and come back. The officer left, but did not return.

Thompson, a deadly enemy of Hickok, saw a situation which he might turn into a profitable shooting match. He told young Hardin that Hickok was passing the word around that he intended to shoot Wes in the back at the first chance offered. Hardin, however, refused to be goaded into a shooting match with Hickok on Thompson's unsupported word. He didn't seek out Hickok, but he didn't sidestep him, either. Despite a Hickok ordinance, issued on June 8, 1871, that guns were not permitted within the town limits, Wes Hardin wore his pistols everywhere he went. The saloon keepers and merchants complained to Hickok, and the marshal finally stopped Hardin as he was leaving a saloon one morning and ordered him to hand over his weapons. Hardin calmly pulled his pistols out and handed them toward Hickok, butts first. As the marshal reached for them, Hardin suddenly twirled the guns in his fingers, and Hickok was staring into the barrels. Wild Bill and the townspeople gathered around were frozen by Hardin's deftness. It was one time when Hickok had to back down. He slowly returned his guns to their holsters.

A number of the people in the crowd yelled at Wes Hardin to shoot Hickok down, for he was not popular with some elements in Abilene. Wes ignored the crowd and told Hickok he had heard the marshal was planning on gunning him in the back when the chance presented itself. Hickok denied the accusation, and the two men finally stepped into a private room in one of the saloons to talk things over. They parted friends, and a few minutes later Wes was in another saloon drinking. Later on an attempt was made to murder Hardin as he slept in his hotel room. Before dawn on July 7, Hardin heard someone unlock his door and creep into the room. Light was reflected from the blade of a dagger in the hand of his would-be assassin. Hardin always slept light and with a gun under his pillow. As his assailant approached the bed Hardin rolled to the floor and emptied his pistol into him. Wes Hardin never knew for certain who his assailant was, but years later in Huntsville Prison, Texas, he wrote a letter in which he accused Wild Bill Hickok of hiring the assassin. Strangely enough, no contemporary newspaper accounts carry this story. Also, the "road agent's spin," as it was called, was not new and not the invention of Hardin, as he also claimed; it had been used by outlaws in several states. It seems certain that Hickok should have been aware of it—and especially with his experience, it seems unlikely that he would accept surrendered weapons unless the man doing so was holding them by the barrels. There is no question but that Hickok did disarm Hardin, but the action was no doubt a peaceful and simple one. Hickok was already dead when Hardin's book appeared, so was unable to refute the statement.

Bill had the run of pretty women in Abilene, and the cause of his next trouble was another woman. His old flame Susannah Moore, from Springfield, Missouri, had come to Abilene to share a cottage with him. She bore no grudge for his killing of Dave Tutt. And on July 13, 1871, Wild Bill met Mrs. Agnes Mersman Thatcher Lake, who brought the Hippo-Olympiad and Mammoth Circus to the trail herd town. She fell hard for Hickok, but he was not interested in her advances. An attractive woman named Jessie Hazell, operator of an expensive bawdy house, caused Phil Coe and Hickok to fall out. Others claimed that accusations of bribery and fixed gambling wheels in the Bull's Head Saloon brought about the rivalry. As Fate would have it, again a woman was a factor in one of Hickok's gunfights. Things came to a head when Jessie Hazell moved her belongings into the expensive hotel rooms where Ben Thompson and Phil Coe lived. On October 5 Phil Coe announced that he was leaving for Texas and taking Jessie with him. This was another bitter pill for the proud and sensitive Hickok to swallow.

In the evening of that same day the jovial Texans were having a merry time celebrating their departure and Phil Coe's having found himself a loving woman. All this rankled with Wild Bill, who would have no part of the festivities. They found him at the Alamo Hotel, but he refused to go with them. After leaving Wild Bill the crowd went west on First Street to Cedar. A noisy dog got mixed up in the crowd and bit Coe in the ankle. The enraged Texan shot and killed the animal.

At the sound of the shot Wild Bill came charging from the hotel, wanting to know who had fired a gun.

Coe still had his weapon in his hand, and informed Bill that he had just killed a dog. Perhaps the sight of the pistol in Coe's hand unnerved Hickok. At any rate, he grabbed his pistols and the fight was on. The two men emptied their guns at each other. One bullet went between Hickok's legs and another over his head, knocking his hat off. One man in the crowd was killed and two were wounded. Hickok's last bullet hit Coe in the groin. He died of blood poisoning two days later. Had Coe been sober, no doubt Bill's career would have ended then and there. It was on this occasion that Bill also killed his trusted friend, Mike Williams (also called Jim Williams), who came running to assist him. Hickok thought some of Coe's friends had joined in the fight so he fired, and killed him. Hickok took the death of his friend very hard, and some said it was the first time they had ever seen him shed a tear.

This fight was the peak of Hickok's career as a gunman. Most people said he lost his nerve completely afterward. He took to carrying a sawed-off shotgun, a regular shotgun, and two pistols, as well as a Bowie knife in his waistband.

On December 13, 1871, the City Council of Abilene discharged Wild Bill Hickok as marshal, stating they had no further need of his services. To sum up Hickok's activities in Abilene we have the following report of Stuart Henry, brother of T. G. Henry, Abilene's first mayor:

Wild Bill's headquarters were in the palatial Alamo Saloon, only a block from our house. He gambled there as one visible means of support. The town trustees appointed

26

him marshal since no one else came forth.... The choice did not prove satisfactory to the citizens, still mourning the death of Tom Smith. Grave misgivings did they feel, for Hickok consorted entirely with criminals or the law-breakers, cheek by jowl with Texans and "badmen." He lived outside the civic center. The Abilene citizens regarded him as a desperado and aurgued whether "Texas Jack" surpassed him as a badman.

Smith's effective regime of disarmament the summer before, his almost perfect control, made Hickok's line of duty far easier than Smith's ... but since his interests and time were divided by gambling, he did not remain strict about the gun-carrying ordinance ... Residents gradually got accustomed again to the pistol-toting and the shots at night.

Wild Bill did not patrol Texas Street either on horseback or on foot. He stayed in the Alamo at his games. . . . The proprietor of the theater next door felt so uncertain of Bill's handling the town efficiently that he went to the expense of employing an officer for his own place (Mike Williams). If wanted, Wild Bill had to be looked up in the Alamo Saloon. He was not a trained police officer ... he did not fancy taking a culprit or offender to the Justice of the Peace to deal with. He acted only too ready to shoot down, to kill outright—conceptions of courts, the right of trial by jury, appeared to lie beyond his conscience or experience.... He did not see why as marshal he could not sit in public poker games ... so Texas Street simmered....

During 1872 Hickok left Abilene and went to Georgetown, Colorado, to visit his dear friend Charles Utter. He finally wound up in Kansas City, Missouri, where he lost all his money at the gambling tables.

Destitute, Hickok finally gave in to the offers of the Barnett's Wild West Show to appear on the stage for that company. On August 28, 1872, Hickok actually gave two performances at Niagara Falls, New York, much to the delight of the audiences. In March of 1873 it was reported in several newspapers that Hickok had been killed. He promptly wrote the editors stating that the story was false. Also, if desired, he would put in a personal appearance if they would pay all expenses incurred in so doing. With a bit of humor he wrote: "Ned Buntline has been trying for years to murder me with his pen."

In July of 1873 Buffalo Bill convinced Hickok that he should join his show, *Scouts of the Prairie*. However, Bill's eyes were going bad on him and he was nearly blind. Cody had always been a lukewarm friend of Hickok, but when Wild Bill actually needed help Cody threw him out. Wild Bill said: "I wish I had killed that son-of-a-bitch when I had the chance years ago."

Many persons have expressed disbelief concerning the fact that Hickok was going blind from a disease, probably gonorrhea. Yet the records show that he went to the medical authorities at Camp Carlin, Wyoming, to have his eyes treated. The report read, "Advanced glaucoma in left eye and soon would be completely blind." Bill also sought treatment for his ailment at the army hospital at Rochester, New York.

It certainly seems that violence of one kind or another followed Hickok wherever he went. Some was of his own choosing, some was not. In August of 1873 Hickok arrived in New York to begin work on the stage play devised by Buffalo Bill Cody. Even there he got into a fight with a hack driver who overcharged him. For that he was fined ten dollars. In November of the same year he got into a free-for-all brawl in Pennsylvania after a performance of *Scouts of the Plains*. On March 11, 1874, while in Rochester, New York, Hickok quit the show for some reason or another. Again he got into a fight, this time at Binghamton, New York, being fined several dollars as a result of it. In Sidney, Nebraska, it is claimed that Bill killed three men in a gunfight in Tim Dyer's Dance Hall. Although there appears to be no contemporary evidence to support this story, it is told by W. Frank "Doc" Carver, a dear friend of Raymond Thorp, who later wrote a book about Carver entitled *Spirit Gun of the West*. Thorp, also a dear friend of this writer and the man who wrote the introduction to one of my own books, *The Younger Brothers*, told me the same story. I see no reason for such reputable men to lie about such a matter.

On June 17, 1875, Hickok was in Cheyenne, Wyoming, taking up residence in Laramie County. It was in this state that his first real love affair bloomed, amid a display of bravery and violence. During a performance of a lion show conducted by the then-famous Lake Troupe, Bill leaped into the ring to rescue from the jaws of a maddened African lion Mrs. Agnes Thatcher Lake, who had known him in Abilene. Three well-placed slugs from his Colt .45 disposed of the king of beasts permanently. This incident must have caused Bill to realize something else, for on March 2, 1876, he said to the proprietor of McDaniel's Variety Theater in Cheyenne: "My eyes are getting bad. The best that I can do with them now is to see a man's form, indistinctly, at sixteen paces. My shooting days are over."

On March 5, 1876, Hickok married Agnes Thatcher Lake,

widow of William Lake, a famous clown of the day and a principal performer, with his wife, in the Spaulding and Rogers Circus. The marriage took place at the home of S. L. Moyer, where Mrs. Lake was staying while in Cheyenne, and the ceremony was performed by Rev. W. F. Warren of the Methodist Episcopal Church. Bill gave his age as forty-five, raising it with his usual chivalry, his residence as Laramie County, Wyoming; she gave her age as forty-two, her residence as Cincinnati, Ohio. Actually Hickok was nearly thirty-nine years old, the bride was fifty, having been born in Alsatia, Louisiana, in 1826.

"Parson," said Hickok to Reverend Warren, "this is one knot you will never be called upon to untie, for in a couple of months I am going to the Black Hills, and I don't expect to come from those hills alive."

After a two-week honeymoon in Cincinnati, Ohio, at the home of Mrs. Lake Hickok's son-in-law, Gilbert S. Robinson, Hickok departed via stagecoach from Ohio for the Black Hills. His wife was never to see him again. Arriving in St. Louis, Missouri, on May 17, 1876, Hickok agreed to guide a group of one hundred would-be miners to the Black Hills. En route, Hickok continually worried about his eyes, even trying target practice along the route of the stages he was guiding. His arm was fairly good and his actions were amusing to the passengers. Bill had only two cartridges left in each of his revolvers when the group was set upon by a band of five outlaws, led by Frank Culley, an old enemy. One by one, Bill disposed of four of the bandits. Then his guns clicked empty. Culley, close enough to hear the click of the guns, grinned gleefully in anticipation of shooting the great Wild Bill Hickok. He advanced on the stopped stagecoaches, leveling a sawed-off shotgun and ordering the passengers to get down. Culley's eyes left Wild Bill for only an instant, but that was the break Hickok needed. With all his strength Bill hurled one of his empty revolvers at the outlaw, hitting him on the head with the impact of a cannon ball, crushing his skull.

Later Hickok laughed as he brought to mind the words of Buckshot Roberts, the expert rifleman of New Mexico, who was killed by Billy the Kid's henchmen: "The only thing a sixshooter is good for is to throw at someone."

Shortly thereafter Hickok learned that Colorado Charlie Utter was in Cheyenne so he hastened to that point. On June 27, 1876, Hickok, Charlie and Steve Utter, and Joe Anderson left Cheyenne for Deadwood, South Dakota. Much has been said about Hickok's great marksmanship, but Colorado Charlie could shoot rings around him. Charlie could hit a dime a hundred feet away, nine times out of ten. Once, while riding on horseback through Hays City, he fired six shots from his pistol at a knothole in a telegraph pole, and all six bullets struck the knothole. Few men ever matched Charlie for marksmanship. On the other hand, Wyatt Earp claimed to have seen Hickok place six bullets in the letter "O" of a sign hanging about a hundred yards away. He said Hickok held his gun as almost every man skilled in such matters preferred to hold one when in action—with a half-bent elbow that brought the gun slightly in front of his body at about, or slightly above, the level of the waist.

In a shooting match at Cheyenne Hickok was defeated by Frank North, Johnny Owens, and a man named Talbot. While camped together at Deadwood during the summer of 1876, California Joe beat him almost every day at target shooting with a rifle. Joe used a .50-caliber Sharps rifle and Wild Bill a needle gun, but both used Colt revolvers of the frontier pattern. After firing several rounds Joe would always say: "Bill, I can beat you with your own gun." Then they would exchange, and the result was always the same. But Wild Bill was more at home with a six-shooter, and he was the only man who ever defeated California Joe with this weapon.

In Deadwood, in addition to being a gambler, Bill's reputation allowed him and his self-styled peace officers to enforce what they called law and order.

Harry Young, the barkeeper at Carl Mann's saloon and a long-time friend of Hickok, said of the gunman's arrival in Deadwood:

About the middle of June, there arrived in Deadwood my old friend Wild Bill. Accompanying him was Charlie Utter, commonly known as Colorado Charlie. They were mounted, and a more picturesque sight could not be imagined than Wild Bill on horseback. This character had never been north of Cheyenne before this. Many in Deadwood knew him; many knew him only by reputation, particularly those who came from Montana. Among these Montana people were a good many men of note. I mean by that, gunmen, and the arrival of this character in town caused quite a commotion.

They rode up to the saloon where I was working, both of them having known Carl Mann before. He being a great friend of Bill's, they naturally called on him first. They dismounted and walked into the saloon, great crowds following them, until the room was packed. Mann cordially received them, asking them to make his saloon their headquarters,

30

which they agreed to do. This meant money to Mann, as Bill would be a great drawing card. After the excitement of Bill's arrival had subsided, Bill looked at me a few minutes.

"Kid, here you are again, like the bad penny, but I am awfully glad to see you." And turning to Carl Mann, he remarked: "I first met this kid in Hays City, Kansas, and wherever I go he seems to precede me, but he is a good boy and you can trust him. Take my word for that."

Contrary to common belief, Hickok did have some interest in mining while at Deadwood. Hickok wrote several letters to his wife from South Dakota, the following being the first:

Deadwood, S.D., July 19, 1876

My Own Darling Wife Agnes:

I have but a few moments left before this letter starts. I never was as well in my life, but you would laugh to see me now—just got in from prospecting. Will go away again tomorrow. Will write in the morning, but God knows when the letter will start. My friend will take this to Cheyenne if he lives. I didn't expect to hear from you, but it is all the same I know my Agnes and only live to love her. Never mind, pet, we will have a home yet, then we will be so happy. I am almost sure I will do well here. The man is hurrying me. Good-bye, dear wife, Love to Emma.

J. B. HICKOK

This letter was last in the possession of G. Robinson, who married Emma Lake. Some of the English has been corrected to make it easier to read, but only the spelling and punctuation; the complete substance remains.

Hickok appeared to have a premonition of doom when he entered Deadwood Gulch that his end was near. He said to Colorado Charlie: "I have a hunch that I will never leave this camp alive."

"That's nonsense, quit dreaming," laughed Charlie.

A letter written by Hickok to his wife on the evening of August 1, 1876, lends reality to his concern:

Deadwood, S.D., Aug. 1, 1876

Agnes Darling

If such should be we never meet again, while firing my last shot, I will gently breathe the name of my wife—Agnes—

and with wishes even for my enemies I will make the plunge
and try to swim to the other shore.

J. B. HICKOK

The plot to kill Hickok was hatched by Tim Brady and
Johnny Varnes, two of the toughs of Deadwood who feared
him and who did not want him appointed official marshal of
the town. They suggested to Jack McCall, an unsavory character, that he kill Hickok to avenge the death of his brother.

On August 1, Hickok sat down in a draw-poker game with
Jack "Buffalo Curly" McCall, not recognizing him as the
Jack McCall of Rock Creek Station. Ordinarily McCall
wouldn't have had enough money to take part in the average
game of poker that went on almost continuously in Saloon
No. 66 (where Harry Young was bartender) owned by Carl
Mann and Jerry Lewis. (Some writers have stated the saloon
was called No. 10 or No. 6.) But on this occasion the game
was for small stakes. Bill played more to pass away the time
than with a thought of winning much.

Some claim that Wild Bill won five hundred dollars from
McCall, but that does not seem to compare with Jack's reputation of always being broke, unless the money had been provided him by Brady and Varnes as part of the murder plot.
At the time he killed Hickok, McCall was a typical saloon
bum and "moocher" of free drinks and lunches, living a more
or less hand-to-mouth existence. He worked as a part-time
saloon swamper, and his duties in the Lewis and Mann
Saloon consisted of sweeping the floor, mopping it, and doing
the menial work which is necessary in such an establishment.

On Wednesday, August 2, another game of draw poker
was in session at Saloon No. 66, a four-handed game. This
game was destined to be long remembered by those who seek
the favors of the goddess of chance. It produced the draw-poker hand that was to become famous as "The Dead Man's
Hand."

In that game, besides Hickok, there were Charles Rich,
Con Stapleton, Carl Mann, and Captain William Rodney
Massie, the latter a Missouri steamboat pilot. When he entered the saloon Hickok stopped to chat with bartender Harry
Young, and being the last to seat himself at the card table he
had to take a seat with his back to the door. So unusual was
this position to Bill, who always sat with his back to the wall,
that he requested Charles Rich to change places with him.
Rich jokingly accused Bill of being too superstitious, and
goodnaturedly declined to exchange places with him.

32

Close to four that afternoon Jack McCall entered by way of the back door. His manner was carefree, and he gave no indication of his murderous intention, but with calculating care he walked up to the bar and then over to the table where the four players were seated. With an anxious glance around, to see that no one was watching, he took a position directly behind the chair occupied by Wild Bill.

McCall had been standing behind the chair for only a short while (it was 4:10 p.m.) when he suddenly snatched a pistol from his pocket and, before anyone could stop him, placed the muzzle within three feet of his victim's head and squeezed the trigger. The bullet from the heavy .45-caliber Colt, serial no. 2079, crashed through Wild Bill's head, coming out through the center of the right cheek. But before it had spent its force it struck Captain Massie in the left wrist, passed between the bones of his forearm, and lodged in his elbow. Some reports state that a Dr. McGowan removed this bullet from Massie's arm, but such is not the case. This writer has a statement from Raymond Thorp, who was a close friend of Massie. At the trial of Jack McCall Massie testified:

> My left arm was resting on the table when the pistol was fired. I felt a shock and numbness in my left wrist.... The ball was not found on examining my arm. It is still there, I suppose.

It stayed there. This bullet, possibly the most controversial in American history, stayed with the greatest and most famous steamboat pilot who ever navigated the Missouri River. Eleven years later Massie stated:

> "Doctor" Hill, one of the "horse-doctors" at Deadwood, told me that he could extract the bullet, but since it was lodged in the muscles, it would be a difficult job with the tools at hand. I told him: "It doesn't bother me at all; I'll just leave it there. Just as soon as Bill is buried I must leave for Pierre."

A July, 1885, issue of the *Bismarck Tribune* carried the following item:

> The ball that killed Wild Bill arrived in the city yesterday. It is in the wrist of Captain Massie, an oldtime steamboat pilot, who arrived from below yesterday. Massie is well known to Bismarckers, and those who have read the history of Wild Bill are familiar with his name. He was playing cards in Deadwood when the latter was shot; the ball passed through Wild Bill's head, lodging in Massie's wrist where it now remains.

The bullet went to the grave with Captain Massie when he died on January 29, 1910, and was buried in Bellefontaine Cemetery in St. Louis, Missouri.

After being shot, Hickok sat stiffly for a second or so, then pitched headlong to the floor, dead. The five cards he held in his hand fluttered to the floor: the Ace of Diamonds with a heel mark on it, the Ace of Clubs, and the two black Eights, Clubs and Spades. The odd card? The Queen of Hearts with a small drop of Bill's blood on it.

Until several years ago the hand was simply referred to as "Aces and Eights," since the identity of the fifth card was unknown. This piece of information was obtained from Neil Christy (also known as Dan Simpson), whose father was a friend of Hickok and who was in the saloon when Bill was killed. Mr. Christy's story agrees substantially with what had already been related. He further stated that after the crowd had left the saloon and the door had been locked, Carl Mann asked Christy's father to help clean up the place after Doc E. T. Peirce had removed Bill's body. It was then that Mr. Christy saw all five cards that had fallen to the floor. He kept them for many years and passed them on to his son. But in the course of time they disappeared. So ends the story of the original Dead Man's Hand. Mr. Christy was also the man who provided the serial number of the revolver used to kill Hickok.

McCall, realizing the enormity of his deed and half crazy with fear, drove the crowd before him out of the saloon; then he ran out of the front door, snapping his pistol at the bartender. Deadwood was quickly ablaze with excitement, and the cry went up all over town: "Wild Bill has been killed!"

McCall backed away up Main Street, holding a pistol in each hand to keep at bay a large posse of excited citizens. Although McCall's revolver was fully loaded at the time he killed Hickok, the cartridge that killed Wild Bill was the only one that would fire. McCall crept into the butcher's shop and hid behind one of the meat-cutting blocks. It is claimed by some that Calamity Jane chased McCall around Jake Shoudy's shop with a meat cleaver, but there is no foundation to this story. Calamity Jane herself stated that it was not true. By no means was Calamity Jane a paramour of Bill Hickok, and she later denied that Bill had been her sweetheart, and we cannot blame her for that. On August 1, 1903, when Calamity Jane died, her last request was to be buried next to Wild Bill. The people carried out her request, burying her within twenty feet of Hickok's grave. This action alone would leave many to believe that "Jane had been close to Bill in life as she was in death."

Doc Peirce removed Bill's body to his tent home, where he had lived with Colorado Charlie, preparatory to burial. At one point he said: "When Bill was shot through the head, he bled out quickly; and when he was laid out he looked like a wax figure. I have seen many dead men on the field of battle and in civil life, but Wild Bill was the prettiest corpse I have ever seen. His long mustache was attractive—even in death; and his long tapering fingers looked like marble. We buried him in a rough coffin with his big Sharps rifle by his side, with his hand resting on his rifle."

Jack McCall was finally overpowered and captured, and brought back to the scene of the killing. He was held under heavy guard to await disposition of the case. Within an hour the whole of Deadwood was seething with excitement. Threats of lynching were freely and openly expressed.

After McCall's capture and a brief examination at the saloon where he was questioned, he was removed to a building at the lower part of town and a guard placed over him. A coroner's jury was empaneled, with G. H. Sheldon as foreman. After meeting, it rendered a verdict in accordance with the evidence: "That the deceased, Wild Bill Hickok, had come to his death at the hands of Jack McCall, the result of a shot fired from a pistol, through the back of Wild Bill's head."

Immediately upon receiving the coroner's verdict, preparations were made to bring McCall to trial. McDaniel's Theater was chosen as the place to hold the proceedings. The citizens of Deadwood held a mass meeting, at which Judge W. Y. Kuykendall was chosen to preside at McCall's trial. The jurors selected were: Charles Whitehead, Foreman; Ed Burke; J. J. Bump; L. D. Bookaw; J. F. Cooper; S. S. Hopkins; L. A. Judd; John Mann; Alex Thayer; J. H. Thompson; J. E. Thompson; and K. F. Towle.

The trial opened on Thursday, August 3, 1876, at two p.m. McCall took a seat to the right of Judge Kuykendall. He presented a most forbidding appearance. McCall was about twenty-seven years old, but dissipation made him appear ten years older. His brow was low and retreating, suggesting a lower order of intelligence. His sandy hair, small straggling mustache, and one crossed eye completed the suggestion of a villainous character.

After the jurors had been sworn, the taking of evidence began. It revealed the wantonness of the killing. There was no provocation and no motive, except possibly a love of notoriety to be gained, as McCall thought. At the conclusion of the evidence, McCall was asked if he had anything to say. He leaped to his feet and shouted: "Yes, you danged right I've got plenty to say. Years ago at Rock Creek that killer Hickok killed my younger brother Andy with a hoe. I swore then and there that I'd kill Wild Bill for it, and I have. I've been following him around for years just waiting for the right chance."

The *Cheyenne Daily Leader* in its August 31st issue published a statement given them by McCall in an interview at Deadwood. The item is lengthy and so full of inaccuracies that it is not worth mentioning here.

The trial was concluded about six o'clock, when the jury retired to deliberate on a verdict. After an hour and thirty minutes, under the foremanship of Charles Whitehead, they filed back into the improvised courtroom and took their seats. The crowded theater building was overflowing with spectators as the judge rapped for order.

"Gentlemen of the jury, have you reached a verdict?"

"We have, your honor," replied Foreman Whitehead.

"Will you please hand your verdict to the clerk, who will read it?" instructed Judge Kuykendall.

The clerk took the folded paper and read slowly as his eyes widened in surprise: "We, the jury, find the prisoner, Jack McCall, not guilty!"

There was a moment of intense silence; then gradually a low growling, like an angry bulldog's, was heard. The judge rapped for order.

"The bench wishes to warn the spectators there will be no demonstration. The verdict has been rendered by a jury of your own choosing, and whether right or wrong, it is not for me to say." He paused for a moment, and then said in a rather disgusted tone: "Prisoner dismissed."

Immediately Colonel May, who had been appointed prosecuting attorney in the case, flew into a paroxysm of wrath. He called the jurors all the unpleasant names his eloquent tongue could bring to mind. He accused them of selling out, and said he could prove that several thousand ounces of gold dust had been given them to render a "not guilty" verdict for the hired assassin, as he called McCall. He declared that he would follow McCall's trail until justice was done.

The following funeral notice was printed and distributed among the miners:

FUNERAL NOTICE

Died in Deadwood, Black Hills, August 2, 1876, from the effects of a pistol shot, J. B. Hickok (Wild Bill) formerly of Cheyenne, Wyoming. Funeral services will be held at Charlie Utter's camp on Thursday afternoon, August 3, 1876, at three o'clock P.M.

All are respectfully invited to attend.

The townspeople buried Wild Bill on the side of a hill now known as Ingleside. His pall bearers were Bill Hillman, John Oyster, Charles Rich, Jerry Lewis, Charles Young, and Tom Dosier. After the brief ceremonies his old friend, Colorado Charlie Utter, wrote on the slab that was placed on the head of his grave:

WILD BILL
J. B. HICKOK
KILLED BY THE ASSASSIN
JACK MCCALL
DEADWOOD CITY
BLACK HILLS
August 2, 1876
Pard, we will meet again in the happy
hunting grounds to part no more.
GOOD BYE
Colorado Charlie
C. H. Utter

Another crude marker was first used; it simply said, carved on a large tree stump at the head of the grave:

A brave man, the victim of an
assassin, J. B. Hickok (Wild
Bill) age 39 years; murdered by
Jack McCall, Aug. 2, 1876.

Hickok's body was first buried in a graveyard near where the Fourth Ward school building is now located. Three years later, on August 3, 1879, J. S. McClintock assisted Charlie Utter and Lewis Schoenfield, old friends of Bill, in the removal of Bill's remains to Mount Moriah Cemetery. They were astounded to find that by some natural enbalming process of the soil-permeated water which had percolated through the coffin, the body of Hickok had been so well preserved as to retain even the outlines of his features and the lines of the manifold pleatings in the dress shirt he had worn. This preservation of the body gave rise to the report that it had been petrified, but Mr. McClintock stated that from his examination he could call it an embalming rather than a petrification, by the disposition of minerals in the tissues of the body.

The admiring people of Deadwood did not forget Wild Bill quickly. For several years following his death wild flowers were placed daily on his grave. Could Calamity Jane have been responsible for this touching attention?

As in the case of other famous frontiersmen, the tombstone of Wild Bill was chipped away by morbid souvenir hunters until nothing was left of it. Even the new monument made by sculptor James H. Riordan of New York, erected in 1892, was so badly defaced in a few years that it had to be replaced in 1902. Finally a steel fence was erected around Bill's grave to save it from futher desecration.

As for Jack McCall, as soon as he was released from custody he left the Black Hills, knowing full well that the friends of Wild Bill would be seeking revenge. He went to Laramie City, Wyoming, and there, while drunk, bragged how he had killed the world's greatest gunman. He felt safe. He couldn't be tried twice for the same crime, so he thought. But he was in a locality where constituted law prevailed, and where the kind of verdict customary at that time in a Black Hills miners' court was not considered legal. He was taken at his own word about the killing of Wild Bill, and was arrested and sent to Yankton, the capital of the old Dakota Territory, to stand fresh trial.

Jack McCall was without friends, and so the court appointed General W. H. Beadle and Oliver Shannon as attorneys to defend him. They contended that the crime had been committed in a lawless region wholly outside the jurisdiction of the court. They were overruled.

McCall's trial in the United States District Court began on November 27, 1876, and continued for several days.

McCall gave high tribute to Hickok when he answered this question, "Why didn't you go around in front of Wild Bill and shoot him in the face like a man?"

"I didn't want to commit suicide," was his sober reply.

He was convicted and found guilty of murder in the first degree. An appeal was taken to the Supreme Court of the United States, but the finding of the lower court was affirmed, and on January 3, 1877, McCall was sentenced to be hanged on March 1.

On February 21 McCall sent the following note to the local Yankton newspapers:

Editors *Press* and *Dakotaian:*

Sirs: I intend to write an article which I wish your paper, after my death, would publish. If you will be here the day of the execution I will hand it to you. If you accept, or decline, to publish it, let me know.

He prepared the article, but on the evening before the execution tore it to bits. It was the consensus that it would have thrown some light on his motive for killing Hickok, and explained his irresponsibility.

Under the date of March 1, 1877, one Yankton newspaper carried the following:

At half-past nine, everything being in readiness, the condemned man bade farewell to his fellow prisoners, and left his prison house for the last time. The mournful train, bearing its living victim to the grave, was preceded and followed by a long line of vehicles of every description, with hundreds on horseback and on foot, all leading north, out through Broadway. Not a word was spoken during the ride of two miles to the school section north of the Catholic Cemetery [where the scaffold had been erected, and near where the South Dakota State Hospital for the Insane now stands]. McCall continued to bear up bravely, even after the gallows loomed in full view.

As soon as possible, after reaching the place, the prisoner mounted the platform of the gallows, accompanied by Deputy Marshal Ash. Here he evinced the same firmness and nerve that had always characterized him since his arrest and trial. He placed himself in the center of the platform, facing east, and gazed out over the throng, without even a quiver of the lip. U.S. Marshal Burdick, Deputy Ash, Father Daxacher and his assistant, Mr. Curry, were the only other parties upon the platform.

Immediately the limbs of the unfortunate culprit were pinioned, when he knelt with his spiritual adviser. Turning his face toward heaven, his lips were seen to move in prayer. Upon rising he kissed the crucifix; and after the black cap had been placed over his head, the U.S. Marshal placed the noose around his neck. He then said: "Wait one moment, Marshal, while I pray."

Marshal Burdick waited until he had uttered a prayer, and then adjusted the noose; when McCall said, "Draw it tighter, Marshal."

All was now in readiness, and the assemblage of nearly one thousand persons seemed to hold their breath. It was an awful moment—the single step between life and death. At precisely 10:15 a.m. the trap was sprung, and with the single choking expression, "Oh, God!" uttered while the drop fell,

39

the body of John McCall was dangling between heaven and earth.

On the day following the execution United States Marshal J. H. Burdick received the following letter:

Louisville, Ky., February 25, 1877

To The Marshal of Yankton:

Dear Sir: I saw in the morning papers a piece about the sentence of the murderer of Wild Bill, Jack McCall. There was a young man of the name of John McCall left here about six years ago, who has not been heard from for the last three years. He has a father, mother, and three sisters living here in Louisville, who are very uneasy about him since they heard about the murder of Wild Bill. If you can send us any information about him, we would be very thankful to you.

This John McCall is about twenty-five years old, has light hair, inclined to curl, and one eye crossed. I cannot say about his height, as he was not fully grown when he left here. Please write as soon as convenient, as we are very anxious to hear from you.

Very respectfully

Mary A. McCall

It seems to me that this letter could be disputed. Certainly a sister would have known her brother's age; also there is little possibility McCall would have grown any after reaching the age of twenty years. McCall was born in 1851 and died in 1877.

Many answers McCall took to the grave with him. Perhaps in years to come members of his family might be located and shed some light on his early life and what prompted his actions in the matter of Hickok's death.

As for Hickok's widow, she came to Deadwood with the intention of removing Bill's remains to Cheyenne. When she saw how much the grave meant to the people of the town, she changed her mind. She left Deadwood for Cheyenne and did not return. It is believed she remarried.

The last chapter is ended, and John McCall and James Butler Hickok crossed the Great Divide into eternity. Truly life is a dream filled with exciting shadows—sometimes ending suddenly in deeper shadows, like the frightful awakening from a horrible nightmare.

Dance .45-caliber 1863 model

2   Wild Bill Longley

WILLIAM PRESTON LONGLEY was nurtured in the South's blackest moment, lived hard, died young, and fought his own personal version of the Civil War right up to the day he walked to the gallows, thirteen years after Appomattox. He left behind a record of wanton, wholesale murder seldom equaled in the history of the West. During his brief but boisterous lifetime he put thirty-two men in their graves, counting Negroes and Mexicans.

At one time in his almost charmed life he rode reckless and wild through the State of Texas while every law officer was on his trail, and both the United States Government and the Governor put a price on his head. He once cheated a hangman's noose in a fashion so bizzare it would be laughed off if it appeared in a piece of fiction. For half of his twenty-seven years he seemed so invincible that when he did walk up to the noose for the last time more than four thousand people crowded around the gallows to see the sight. To this day there are those who earnestly believe that the ruthless killer framed his own hanging, and escaped to South America on that October day in 1878 when he supposedly met his Maker.

This was Wild Bill Longley. Cold-blooded, vicious, psychopathic. The only good thing that can be said of him is that he died young, and most of those who knew him thought that wasn't soon enough. He began life as a nineteenth-century juvenile delinquent, was a dead shot before he was fifteen,

41

and a killer before most lads his age were out of high school.

Longley was born October 16, 1851, in Austin County, Texas, along Mill Creek. He was the son of Campbell Longley, a devout, God-fearing, hard-working man. The Longley family moved to Evergreen in Lee County when Bill was two years old. At this time Evergreen was still a part of Washington County. It was a place familiar to the older Longley. Not more than a mile away was the San Antonio-Nacogdoches Road, the Camino Real, and the monument to the Valiant Texans who fought against Santa Anna in the Mexican War. Campbell Longley had been one of them. He had shown valor and courage above and beyond the call of duty at San Jacinto. He was a proud Texan and his son inherited that pride. Young Bill might never have embarked on his terrifying career of murder had it not been for the time and place he occupied in Texas history.

Longley was fourteen when the Civil War ended and when living in Texas became a nightmare existence. In the wake of the Confederate surrender Texas became a land of outrage and humiliation, overrun with scallywags, carpetbaggers, crooked politicians, and Negroes anxious to test their newly won freedom as "police officers" in a place which had once held them in slavery and servitude. Vandalism and viciousness became as common as the noonday sun. The Texas Rangers had been disbanded, and in their place ruled the State Police, controlled by ruthless opportunists with armed Negro soldiers at their backs.

However, it was not long before the corrupt police had to replace the firearms in the hands of the colored militants. They substituted a lead ball attached to a stout leather thong, the forerunner of the blackjack and a brutal weapon when used as a bludgeon. The rule of the state Police was a humiliating experience for men like Campbell Longley, and his young son was quick to feel the hatred which boiled up inside the broken Confederates.

At fourteen Longley was a boy large for his age, whose schooling had included little more than learning to read and write. What he learned outside the classroom, however, he learned well. By the time he reached his fourteenth birthday Bill was an accomplished marksman who could put six shots into an oak tree in an area the size of a dinner plate while riding past at breakneck speed. Such shooting was done with his father's antiquated percussion-cap revolver. For the calling Longley was eventually to follow, this was all the schooling he needed.

It was in such a climate of hate, fear, oppression, and degeneration that Longley quickly matured, a bitter, resentful youth with a volcanic temper. It was inevitable that he should put his pistol to use against the society he hated. The clash came in Houston, ironically at a time when Bill Longley had run off to the city to obtain a good Colt revolver, a prize he had yearned for since he first fired his father's outmoded pistol.

He hopped a Texas and Houston freight train and leaped off as it slid to a halt in Houston on a cold, rainy day in 1866. Friendless, he spent his first night huddled around a common camp fire blazing in the square, listening to the older men discussing the tragedy of the times. The next day he struck up a friendship with a youth several years his senior, and that night he experienced his first brush with violence. It came in a windswept alley while the two youths sought a place to spend the night. A burly Negro in the blue uniform of the Union Army, swinging a lead ball at his side, blocked their path and demanded to know their names and their business. Then the bully demanded that they undress in the street in the bitter cold. When they hesitated he charged at them, swinging his lead mace. Longley's companion pulled a Bowie knife from under his shirt and struck swiftly, burying the blade deep in the Negro's side.

Both boys knew the consequences of killing a Negro policeman. They parted company, and the next day Bill was back in Evergreen, sporting a Dance six-shooter, the gun made famous by the Confederacy during the recent war. He didn't bother to explain where he got it, and nobody asked. Now Billy Longley was happy—he had two pistols. Many writers have claimed that a two-gun gunman was a creature of legend, that using two pistols simultaneously to advantage was impossible. Young Longley proved an exception to this belief. He could use either hand or both at the same time with equal effect. Many of his friends reported he could empty both guns into a six-inch area at the same time.

It was shortly after his return from Houston that Longley had his first solo clash with the Negroes. A surly colored man carrying a rifle rode down the Camino Real cursing all white men. As he passed the Longley ranch he called to the older Longley, damning him. Young Bill was nearby. He walked into the front yard and ordered the Negro to throw down his gun. The sullen soldier swung the rifle up and fired a shot at Bill, then switched his horse into a gallop. Longley, firing from a crouch, sent his first shot through the Negro's head.

He tossed a rope around the dead man, dragged the body into a shallow ditch, and buried it. The crime was never reported and nobody knew this Negro was Longley's first victim until Bill confessed on the gallows, twelve years later.

One thing, however, can be said for young Longley. In those days of general discontent many armed men turned to outlawry. Longley, as far as is known, never used his guns in a hold-up, although later he was involved in some unsavory deals.

Bill joined in partnership with another local youth, Johnson McKowen, breaking wild horses for training. Shortly after Bill had killed his first victim, he said McKowen went to Lexington, Texas, to enter one of their horses in a race. They withdrew just before the race when several Negroes also signed up for the run. The two young men well knew that, even if their horse won, their chances of collecting the purse were slim. That night Longley took his revenge against the colored people. The Negroes were having a dance in the street when Johnson and Bill rode into town. The sixteen-year-old boy spurred his horse to a gallop and rode into the midst of the gathering, firing both guns. Two men were killed and several seriously wounded.

Bill Longley had embarked upon a career which was to earn him the nickname of "The Nigger Killer." His reputation quickly spread throughout the state. Once, while riding on a H. & T.C. Railroad car, Longley fell asleep with his feet in the aisle. A new Negro porter ordered him to pull in his legs, but Longley ignored him. The porter forcibly pushed Longley's feet back. Then he boastfully explained to the conductor that he had just "showed some white trash a thing or two." When the conductor told him the man was Wild Bill Longley the porter jumped off the train.

Early in his youth Longley seems to have developed a mean streak that was more than just a hatred for Negroes. In 1868 a circus made one of its rare appearances in Evergreen. It was a holiday for the town, since there was little recreation in the small village. Longley and one of his chums went to the main tent and demanded free admittance. When the owner refused, the arrogant Longley slugged him unconscious and entered the tent, where he forced two clowns to dance a fast jig while he fired shots at their feet. His performance started a near panic. The spectators left on the run, and the show quickly folded its tents and left town. That was the last time that particular circus ever appeared in Evergreen.

Before he was eighteen Longley had become a self-appointed champion of the white man's cause. One night three heavily armed Negroes rode into Evergreen and entered the bar. They demanded drinks and boasted they had heard Evergreen was unfavorable to men of their race, and they were there to see just how rough it really was. Nobody offered resistance, but someone quickly got word to Longley. Young Bill came into town on the run. His intention, he said, was merely to disarm the three, to show them who was boss. By the time Bill got to the bar the boasters were gone. Longley followed them into Burleson County, about ten miles from Evergreen, and rode into their camp. He had no time to utter a word before one of the Negroes pulled a gun and took a shot at the white youth. Before the Negro had a chance to get his second shot off Longley put a bullet squarely between the man's eyes. The other two Negroes threw down their guns and ran. This killing put the law on Longley's trail.

On Christmas Day, 1868, a few days after he shot the Negro in Burleson County, friends warned Bill that law officers were on their way to arrest him. The young killer knew he wouldn't stand much chance in a Yankee courtroom, so he left home on the run. He got a job working for John Reagan, a large stock owner in Karnes County, which was then the scene of a bitter cattle feud between the Taylor and Sutton families. Soldiers had been called in to settle the range war. Although Longley took no active part in the struggle, he was a close friend of the Taylor family. While riding through Yorktown one day, Longley was mistaken for Charles Taylor. The army had been ordered to arrest members of both families in an attempt to end the feud, and they went after Bill. Not realizing it was a case of mistaken identity when some soldiers approached him, Longley thought they were after him for the Burleson shooting. He made a run for it, outdistancing all but the sergeant, who raced his horse close in beside Longley and yelled to him to surrender. Longley pulled his pistol, jammed it into the sergeant's side and killed him with one shot—the last one he had in his pistol. Fortune had begun to ride with Bill Longley.

With the army now at his heels, Bill returned to Evergreen, but his father insisted that the youth would not be safe there. He persuaded Longley to join forces with Cullen Montgomery Baker, who led a band of renegades and outlaws which constantly harassed the Yankees.

Longley went to the headquarters of the daring guerilla in Bowie County, but learned that Baker was in Arkansas. While awaiting his return, Bill met and befriended a local youth named Tom Johnson. Unknown to Longley, Johnson was a wanted horse thief. Bill accompanied young Johnson to his home to spend the night, but before dawn a band of vigilantes surrounded the Johnson house and dragged both boys into the yard. Without ceremony they carried the youths to a nearby tree and lynched them. Wheeling their horses, the posse rode out of the yard. As they passed the two swaying bodies they fired several shots at them. Luck was still smiling at Longley. One bullet struck Bill's heavy belt buckle and glanced off without injuring him. A second snipped the rope from which he was hanging and frayed it. Then the rope snapped, and Longley fell unconscious to the ground. He might have strangled had not Johnson's younger brother quickly pulled the rope from around his neck. Nothing could be done for Johnson. He was dead.

Suffering from shock, Longley hid in the brush near the Johnson home to recuperate. The Johnsons provided him with clothing and food, and passed the word to Cullen Baker of the Johnson-Longley hanging. Baker returned to Texas shortly afterward and invited Bill to join his gang.

Little is known about Cullen Baker's renegades except that they never robbed people of Southern sympathies. They looted government trains and protected friends from carpetbaggers and grafting tax collectors, often turning over their loot to poor Southerners, much the same as did the Jameses and Youngers when they first began their outlaw careers. Baker's career was shortlived. He was hunted down and killed in 1869, a year after Bill Longley joined the gang. Bill returned to Evergreen after Baker's death. It has been estimated that while with Baker young Longley killed seven men, not counting several Negroes shot to death by members of the group collectively. In Evergreen, Longley struck terror in the hearts of the Negro residents. Carrying on his strange and frightening vendetta, he killed eight more colored men before leaving on a trip to visit kinsmen in Utah.

· By now Longley's unrelenting death rampage was beginning to tell on the youth's mind. Blood-letting came to him naturally, and he killed at the slightest provocation. On his way to Utah, he joined a trail herd owned by a cattleman named Rector, who was driving his cattle from Bee County, Texas, to Kansas. Rector was as mean in temperament as was Longley, and abused his hands viciously. Bill was quick to criticize Rector's actions, and the cowman, believing he had an easy mark in a seventeen-year-old boy, invited Longley to step out and settle things with revolvers. Bill quickly accepted

46

the challenge. Man and boy walked out onto the prairie, but before Rector could clear leather he was dead. Bill shot him six times before the man hit the ground.

After the death of Rector, Longley left the camp with a cowpoke named Davis, heading for Abilene. They stopped at a general store for a drink, and were told by the proprietor that a posse was nearby chasing two horse thieves. While Longley and Davis were still in the store, two men named McClelland and Shelly entered, ordered whiskey, and openly bragged they were riding stolen horses. Longley thought over their boast, and the next day rode into their trail camp and arrested them both at gunpoint. The bold young killer led both men back to Abilene and collected a reward.

However, Longley didn't remain long in the Kansas cattle town. Marshall Tom Smith had a standing order that no firearms could be worn in town. Longley, whose reputation was beginning to grow, knew if he took off his guns his life would be worthless. He left his friend Davis in Abilene and headed for Leavenworth. The gunfighter pattern was now beginning to weave itself inexplicably around Wild Bill Longley. He had chosen to make the six-gun his career, and it now became his role to prove his prowess with the pistol at every provocation. While drinking in a saloon in Leavenworth one night he overheard a soldier say: "Well, if I were from Texas I'd keep it to myself, and be too ashamed to admit it."

Longley is recorded as replying: "There are a lot of honest, fine people in Texas. You can't judge all people there by the likes of me and others of outlaw breed."

The young trooper fancied himself quite a gunman, and chose to make an issue of the comment. It was his last mistake. He remarked there wasn't an honest man in Texas and that the women were no good. Without further argument Longley drew and shot the trooper dead. He escaped, but instead of taking a horse and heading for the brush Bill hopped a freight for St. Louis. A telegraph message tripped him up. He was captured as the train went through St. Joseph and was returned to Leavenworth's military prison. Oddly enough, the army never realized the man they had in custody was wanted throughout half of Texas. Bill was charged only with the shooting of the soldier, and after he had been held for several weeks a prison guard informed him that he was to be shot within a few days. Longley offered the guard fifty dollars, which he had hidden in his shoes, in exchange for freedom. The guard quickly took him up on the proposition. Once again he escaped death by a hair.

With the dragnet for him widening like a puddle in the rain, Longley decided to go north, this time into Indian country. From Leavenworth he made Cheyenne and joined a party of miners who were going into the dread Big Horn Mountains, a dangerous and foolhardy mission—125 white men into a section alive with Sioux war parties, all of them ready to kill. The party had several brushes with old Spotted Tail, one of the Sioux chieftains, but managed to battle their way along the Wind River to Camp Brown. Several men were lost, but the mining party had with it several field pieces. Had it not been for the destructive power of the cannon, the entire party would probably have lost their scalps.

At Camp Brown they were ordered to abandon the expedition, since it was a violation of General Grant's treaty with Chief Red Cloud for white men to enter the Black Hills and Big Horn Mountain country. Ignoring the order, the group headed into the Black Hills, followed by five companies of soldiers with orders to bring them back peacefully or otherwise. The miners ran headlong into another skirmish with the Indians, and although they managed to fight off the attacking redskins, the army companies ran them down. At the threat of a court martial, they finally turned back to the fort.

Young Longley, although he hated the idea of working for the Yankees, realized he was safe at the army camp, and took a job as a teamster. It was during the following winter that luck once again smiled on Wild Bill Longley. While on a hunting trip in the mountains, Bill and several friends were trapped in a violent blizzard. Three of the men froze to death in the icy blasts, but Longley dragged himself back to the camp, more dead than alive. For three months he was unable to walk. When Bill regained his health he was given charge of the Government corrals. That brought him the responsibility of taking care of the pack horses and mules.

The unscrupulous Texan was approached shortly by Quartermaster Greggory, a crooked scoundrel who was fleecing the Government in the transaction of horses and supplies. The two were birds of a feather, and Longley unhesitatingly agreed to Greggory's scheme—that the two men would collaborate, out-count the army of its horseflesh and sell the animals they could come by illegally at a clear profit. Longley, however, had a wider streak of crookedness than Greggory. He sold the first two mules the men embezzled for five hundred dollars and told Greggory he received three hundred. The crooked quartermaster had contacts of his own.

He learned Longley was cheating him out of his agreed share and threatened to kill him.

Bill and Greggory seem to have reached a friendly understanding about the other two hundred dollars, but Greggory returned to his rooms and brooded about his partner's double-dealing. He went armed to the corral to give his young partner a lesson. Bill saw him coming. When Greggory walked into the corral Longley stepped from behind a post and shot him down before he could draw his gun. Greggory died the next day, but Longley didn't wait for his demise. He mounted a slow-moving mule and headed for the brush again. Three days later the army caught up with him and he was returned to the stockade.

Nine months passed before he was tried, during which time Longley escaped once and was recaptured. He was eventually tried and sentenced to death, but the sentence was commuted, and Bill received thirty years in the Iowa State Prison. Before he could be transferred from the post he again broke out of the stockade, and this time made for Indian country. The army authorities did not follow. Longley insured his escape by taking up residence with the Ute Indians for nearly a year. It was apparently an experience Longley enjoyed more than any other in his entire life. Although homesickness finally got the better of him and he left his Indian friends to return to Texas, Bill often spoke of his life with the Utes and described his experiences with them.

On the way from Iowa to Texas he got in a card game with a young man named Charles Stuart of Parkersville, Kansas. An argument started and the hot-headed Longley used his gun again, shooting Stuart to death at the card table. Stuart's father quickly posted a fifteen-hundred-dollar reward for the return of his son's slayer, known to Kansans as Tom Jones. Always the conniver, Longley contracted two local outlaws and agreed to allow them to turn him over to the sheriff for the reward if they would then break him out of jail. The outlaws agreed, Longley was turned over to the law, thrown into jail, and the reward money was paid to Longley's co-conspirators. Next day the two outlaws entered the unsuspecting sheriff's office on the pretext of wanting to speak to Longley, overpowered the lawman, and freed Bill. The three men split the fifteen hundred dollars, and Longley continued his journey south. As usual, the gunman's luck had held. The outlaws could just as easily have left him to his fate and split the reward two ways.

Bill Longley returned to his father's farm in Bell County,

and for several months kept out of trouble, doing farm chores and caring for the ranch. With a thousand-dollar price on his head, however, Longley couldn't keep out of sight of the law for very long. When a posse was formed in Lee County to go and arrest him, a friend raced to the ranch and warned Bill. Longley took a Colt revolver and a fast horse, and rode to Comanche County, to hide out with friends. While performing an errand one afternoon he learned that a Negro had insulted the wife of a man named W. Forsythe, and forced her to cook his dinner and feed his horse. Longley followed the man into town. There the Negro faced Longley, pushed his hat back on his head, and demanded: "Who the hell are you?"

Longley's answer was two .45 slugs through the arrogant colored man's brain. Riding west from the scene of the shooting, Bill was overtaken by a five-man posse as he entered the Santa Anna Mountain range. Racing into the mountain underbrush, Longley killed one of his pursuers and sent the rest hightailing back to where they had come from.

Despite the constant efforts of the law to run him down and bring him to justice, Longley continued to keep ahead of his would-be captors. In Madison County he actually befriended a sheriff. Although he was using the assumed name of William Henry, Sheriff Finley recognized Longley from descriptive "wanted" dodgers. He carefully planned to gain Bill's confidence, then trap him. Bill, however, was also alert and suspicious of Finley's friendship. On the night Finley planned to arrest the gunslinger a game of cards was arranged. The sheriff had two men staked out at the meeting place. Longly didn't show up. He had fled to Gillespie County, there to meet several friends in a bar and plan another card game. An informant in the group warned Finley. A second trap was planned. And for the second time Longley eluded the lawmen, this time riding toward Kerrville.

Finley was not to be denied, however. He followed the wily Texan and surprised Bill at his camp the next morning. Finley showed Longley a warrant for arrest, and promised him safe conduct back to Austin. Longley's fame as a killer was so widespread by this time that crowds gathered all along the route, trying to tear off pieces of his clothing, seeking a lock of his hair, or just bunching up along the road for a look at the youthful badman.

Longley's fabulous luck held again. In Austin, Governor E. J. Davis, who had offered the reward for Longley's capture, had lost the election to Richard Coke. The new governor refused to take Bill into custody. Finley, who was only interested in the reward money, had Longley on his hands and wasn't quite sure what to do with him. William Patterson, a cousin of Longley, solved the dilemma. He offered Finley $563 for Bill's release. It was the best offer Finley got, and he took it. Longley went scot-free.

Bill wasn't loose long before a Mexican from Frio County fell victim to his fast draw and unerring aim. The Mexican had made the mistake of selling Longley a stolen horse. Traveling to Bandera County, Bill secured a job on the Wadkins Ranch and settled to hard, honest work. But his fame caught up with him before he became too firmly enamored of law and order. He had struck up a friendship with a man named Will Scrier from a neighboring ranch. Scrier turned out to be as unscrupulous and cold-blooded as Bill. Before long both men were suspicious of each other. Longley learned that Scrier, whose real name was Lew Sawyer, planned to turn him over to the sheriff for a new reward Bill's capture carried. He beat Scrier to the punch. Longley told the local justice of the peace that Scrier was a desperate and savage man wanted by the law and offered to capture him. The justice deputized Longley, and with a young man named Hayes the crafty gunfighter went after Scrier.

They arrived at Scrier's quarters at night and Longley realized that the victim would be suspicious if he was summoned from his home after dark without good reason, so he called out and told his prey that he had a side of beef down the road. He offered Scrier a share. The unsuspecting man came out and joined the two riders. As they rode down the path from Scrier's home, Longley fell back and drew, ordering Scrier to surrender.

The other gunman proved more of an opponent than Bill had bargained for. Pulling his pistol, he fired a shot over his shoulder and tried to make a break. Bill shot him under the right shoulder. Scrier kept going, firing behind him as he dashed down the glade. Hayes' horse shied and darted off into the brush, but Bill was determined to complete the fight, one way or another. He followed hard on Scrier's trail, putting four more bullets into his adversary's back. Scrier finally wheeled his horse in a tight turn, pulled his shotgun, and fired a blast at the oncoming Longley, Bill's horse plunged to the ground dead. The two men opened fire at close range, and Scrier was hit several more times. Still he kept up the bitter fight. Finally Longley swung into an advantageous position and caught Scrier squarely between the eyes.

The man rolled over dead. When Longley checked, there were thirteen bullets in Scrier's body. He later said that Scrier was the hardest man to kill he had ever met. Mounting Scrier's horse, Bill rode back into Uvalde, told the justice that Scrier was dead and resigned his commission. It was one of the shortest deputy commissions on record, and in his own peculiar way Longley had actually performed a service for the law.

During this period Bill continued to hold his terrifying grudge against the Negroes. Once in Logansport he heard a Negro had insulted an elderly white man. He simply rode up to the Negro's house, called him out, and shot him to death. In Angelina County he was riding along and came on a Negro and a white man fighting in the middle of the road. Bill ended the fight by killing the Negro.

In April, 1875, Longley committed the crime which was to bring about his demise. Bill had been working on the farm of William Baker on Walnut Creek, in Bastrop County. His brother was working on the same ranch, and Bill managed to keep in contact with the rest of his family for the first time in years. Soon after coming to the Baker ranch he learned that a cousin, Cale Longley, was dead. There were two stories concerning Cale's death. Some said he had been killed by Wilson Anderson, a boyhood friend of Bill's. Anderson, however, claimed that Cale had fallen off his horse and died as a result of injuries suffered in the fall. In most quarters Cale's death was accepted as an accident, but the dead man's father stubbornly stuck to the claim that Anderson had killed his son.

One Saturday morning Bill's brother told him that Sheriff Jim Brown of Lee County was on his way to the Baker place to arrest him. Longley revealed to the Baker family his true identity, and left, riding straight to his cousin's ranch. Cale Longley's father repeated the story that Wilson Anderson was responsible for Cale's death, knowing full well that Bill would wreak swift vengeance for the death of his relative. He was right. Longley rode to the farm of Wilson Anderson the morning of April 1, 1875. Anderson, ploughing a field, looked up to see Bill Longley riding toward him, a shotgun cradled in his arm. Before Anderson could say a word, Longley cut him down with the vicious weapon.

Mortally wounded, Anderson gasped: "Oh, God, what did you shoot me for, Bill?"

"Just for luck," Longley replied.

The death of Anderson might have gone unsolved had it

not been for Longley's penchant for bragging. There were no witnesses, but Bill later described the killing to Wash Harris at his father's ranch. Three years later Longley heard his words repeated, this time at the trial which was to result in his hanging.

A few months after the Anderson murder Longley secured a job under the name of Jim Patterson at the farm of Captain Sedbury. Apparently happy with his job as a farmhand, Bill put in over ten hours a day working the cotton machinery and other implements on the farm. Following a foxhunt and race at the Sedbury farm, however, Longley got into a trivial argument with George Thomas, a local bully and braggart. A fist fight followed, and there probably would have been a shooting had not Sedbury disarmed the two men. When Thomas finally left for the night Sedbury returned Longley's gun to him, thinking the matter was over. But Bill Longley's temper was far from soothed. He followed Thomas into town, waited while he awoke a storekeeper, Frank Jones, and bought a bottle of whisky, and then, while the two men stood on the porch of the store, Bill rode by. Thomas saw him coming and went for his gun, but Longley was much too fast. Only one shot was fired, and Thomas was lying dead on the doorstep. Once again Longley was on the run.

On February 12, 1876, while working as a woodcutter near Crockett, Texas, Bill stopped at a bleak farmhouse near the town of Ben Franklin, in Delta County. There he met and fell in love with Louvenia Jacks. Contemporary newspapers gave this as the statement Bill made after he met the Texas beauty:

> It was there I met the first girl I ever loved, and never on earth will forget the feeling of my heart the moment I laid eyes on her, and I never will be ashamed to acknowledge that I did love her with all my heart. It was on the 12th day of February in 1876 that I met her. I introduced myself as William Black of Missouri and had lived in Texas for three years, I said. We sat up late that night and I related many of my adventures, all of which the beautiful girl listened to with great interest. The family was composed of old man Jacks, his wife, and two grown daughters, Jennie and Louvenia, the last named the younger, and it was her with whom I fell madly in love.

Bill immediately made arrangements to work for a preacher named Roland Lay on a sharing basis. The Lay farm was only a mile from the Jacks place, and the girl's family seemed to like Bill. Shortly afterward Longley learned that Louvenia had another suitor, a man who had the reputation of being a badman. He was Roland Lay's cousin. Naturally the Lay family wanted their kinsman to win Lou's hand, and did everything possible to discourage Longley's courtship. When the local townsfolk heard about the "Mister Black" who was also courting the pretty girl, they assumed that the hired man was marked for a quick grave.

Longley received several threatening notes and traced them back to Preacher Lay. He accused the reverend gentleman of trying to beat him out of his share of the crops. Lay immediately paid off Bill's share and Longley left. Instead of moving on, however, he hired out to a farmer near Paris, in nearby Lamar County, and continued his courtship with Louvenia. The embittered Lay swore out a warrant against Longley, charging that Bill had threatened his life. Bill, as William Black, was arrested at once and lodged in the Cooper jail. Since he had no one to pay his bond he visualized months, perhaps years, as a prisoner. In desperation he set fire to the jail and escaped.

Astride his own horse, Bill rode to the Jacks farm, secured a shotgun, and made his way to the Lay farm. Lay was in the cowpen, his shotgun standing against the fence. Longley later described what happened:

> I walked into the cowpen and stood between him and his gun. He looked up and saw me and turned white as a sheet. He seemed to know that his time had come and that he would get no mercy at my hands. When he saw me I told him it was the last of "pea time" with him, and if he had anything to say he had better be at it. He said he hated to die and leave his wife and family. Then I asked him why he did not let me alone when I was at peace with him and all his kinsfolk. To this he gave no answer and I dropped my gun to level with his body and fired. The gun was heavily loaded with turkey shot. He fell backward and I left him.

On June 23, 1876, Gov. Richard Coke of Texas offered a reward of five hundred dollars for the arrest and delivery inside the jail doors of Delta County, Texas, of one William Black, alias William Longley, for the murder of Roland Lay, a minister. Things had changed in Texas. The newly elected governor had disbanded the Negro police and thrown out the State Police. The Texas Rangers had replaced them, and law and order in the state was returning. Thousands of "Joe Doe" warrants had been issued, and the Rangers were rounding up suspects by the hundreds. Many arrested on suspicion of one crime were indicted and convicted for other crimes they had committed. The governor doubled the reward for Longley, whose description was telegraphed throughout the state. Longley knew now that Texas was no longer a safe place for him. With the Rangers on his trail it would only be a matter of time before he was arrested. He fled across the border into Louisiana and rented land near Keatchie, in De Soto Parish.

Longley was no fool. He rented the land from the sheriff, who later said that Bill showed great signs of making money and becoming a prosperous farmer. In the months that followed Longley courted and became engaged to the lawman's daughter, settled down, and appeared to be a law-abiding, hard-working citizen. He also befriended a young constable named Courtney and they became good friends.

Longley, in his apparently earnest desire to change his life, offered to help Courtney in his official duties and in so doing inadvertently tipped his hand. Courtney began wondering how this stranger knew so many angles in the law business; slowly he began to suspect that Bill was not just a farmer. He discussed the matter with the sheriff. At first the sheriff refused to believe there was anything suspicious about the young man engaged to his daughter. Then for some unknown reason Longley revealed his true identity to the girl. Courtney and the girl's father contacted Sheriff Milton Mast of Nacogdoches, who rushed to the sheriff's home with Deputy Sheriff W. M. Burroughs. Bill was working in the fields with a revolver in his pocket. Mast and Burroughs hid in the shadows of the house, and when Longley came in from the fields the officers stepped out with cocked shotguns and ordered him to surrender. Longley stated later he could do nothing but give up in the face of the wicked-looking shotguns. Sheriff Mast never bothered to take our extradition papers, he was only ten miles from the Texas border. He hurried his prisoner across the border to Henderson and the next day took Longley into Biddings, Texas.

Longley was taken into custody on May 13, 1877, and a report of his arrest appeared on June 27, in the Panola, Texas, *Watchman:*

> On yesterday evening Captain Milt Mast of Nacogdoches County and W. M. Burroughs of the same county, arrived in Henderson, having under arrest one William Longley, a notorious murderer of Lee County, Texas. Captain Mast was corresponding with friends in Lee County and by this means got

on the track of the desperado. He and Mr. Burroughs captured the prisoner last Wednesday near Keatchie (De Soto Parish), Louisiana, at a point about ten miles from the Texas line and about twenty miles east of Logansport, La. They will take the train today for Lee County where they intend to deliver him to the proper authorities. A 1,050 dollar reward has been offered for his arrest by different counties. He says he has killed thirty-two men. Captain Mast requests all those counties that have offered rewards for William Longley to come and settle up. Captain Mast was furnished with the following letter from the district clerk of Lee County, which suits the description in every particular.

Giddings, Lee County, Texas
May 18, 1877

M. Mast, Esq.,
Nacogdoches, Texas
Dear Sir,

Your esteemed favor of April 24th was received today. Allow me to thank you for your interest in the arrest of criminals. Longley is today the worst man in Texas—he has committed many murders in this vicinity—he has even murdered a woman. He is about six feet high; weighs 150 pounds, tolerably spare build; black hair, eyes, and whiskers; slightly stooped in shoulders. I have been told by those who know him that he can be recognized in a crowd of 100 men by keenness and blackness of his eyes. There are several large rewards offered for him by citizens, one from this county for $250. He has assumed names. You will have to take advantage of him—he will fight and is a good shot. Please keep me posted—we want him. Our sheriff once followed him to the Louisiana line. Thanking you and tending you all official courtesy that I may be able to render, I am

Very respectfully yours,
W. A. KNOX

Lodged in the Giddings jail, Longley wrote many letters to the Texas newspapers, most of which were published. They give perhaps some insight into this cold-blooded killer's character. In some cases the writings are almost pathetic. Bill was not permitted to write to his relatives, nor were they allowed to visit him. The following letter was written to a Texas newspaper during Longley's incarceration:

Well, the blow is over; the die is cast and I am condemned to die without the sympathy of a single human being that I can recall. You are all eager and hope to see me brought to the scaffold. Then I hope your vengeance will be fully glutted, and that you will all be fully satisfied when you see the last footing from under me and my soul hurled into eternity. Then, folks, for God's sake I hope that prejudice will cease when I pay this dreadful debt which is exacted of me by the law. I am willing to pay this debt for the good of the rising generation, and I hope now, that the law will triumph over all lawless characters, for of course you know my reasoning faculties are good enough to know that the world would run back into barbarism if the laws of the land were not enforced. Certainly, life is sweet; yet I cannot expect to escape the penalty of the law. For, should I escape, either by pardon or by breaking jail, it would be encouraging to all boys who are now growing up and who are disposed to be outlaws. I have two dear brothers who are now in their boyhood, and are disposed to be wilder than I was, and I hope this will be a warning to them, for I would freely die, rather than see them live the life that I have been living, and yet I believe I have been the most successful outlaw that ever lived in Texas, as far back as I can remember.

But look at me now. After all the victories that I have gained over my enemies, the past ten or twelve years, I now sit through the dragging and weary hours of the days and nights, gazing out upon the beautiful earth over which I have roamed free as a bird many a day and hour. Here I sit, now in the felon's cell awaiting the death that I know is certain, and yet out of it all, I am thankful to Almighty God, that I have the opportunity to repent of my sins and fit my soul for the last step that will take my soul into the realms of an·unknown future, and also to advise the rising generation and tell them of the evils and dangers of a reckless life. There are many who may not take my advice. If I can be the means of saving only one soul from eternal ruin, it will pay me for all the writing I have done, since I have been in jail. Not for any good that it could do me, nor to boast of my exploits, but only to show the rising generation the great danger and folly of such life, and that those who persist in following such a career overlook the fact that they are liable to be cut down any moment without preparation for the future. I am one of the fortunate ones, who has been blessed with a little time in which to make this preparation, and I think I should devote every moment of time now, to doing good, after having thrown away so much precious time, that I could have put to profitable use. But now it is too late for me, but it is not too late for all young boys who may read this, and who are now blessed with being in possession of a happy home, and have the daily advice of Christian parents, as I once had, but never availed my self of the opportunity.

And now, boys, remember the road Bill Longley had traveled, in disobeying his parents, and when you start to do wrong remember that a very small wrong always leads to still greater ones, and so on until finally, nothing will seem wrong to you if you follow the wrong road. My first step was disobedience; next whiskey drinking; next carrying pistols; next gambling, and then murder, and I suppose the next will be the gallows. I hope my father and mother will never be blamed for what I have done for they tried to raise me right.

Signed,
BILL LONGLEY

Bill Longley was tried before Judge E. B. Turner in Giddings on September 3, 1877. The main witness for the state was Wash Harris, who swore that Longley admitted the murder of Wilson Anderson. The trial moved swiftly. The following day the case was argued and given to the jury. It took them an hour and a half to find Bill guilty, and he was sentenced to hang.

Longley apparently never gave up hope of rescue or escape until a few days before the scheduled hanging. The State Supreme Court upheld the decision in an appeal, during which Longley was moved to Galveston, and he was sentenced to die on October 11, 1878. While in Galveston he embraced the Catholic religion and was christened by the Reverend Chambodut. The Reverend Father Spillard of Austin was with Bill the night before and the morning of the hanging.

The day of the execution dawned murky and hot, with rain threatening in a leaden sky. A crowd gathered early and by one-thirty p.m. more than four thousand persons were assembled about the gallows, many of them Negroes.

It looked bad, but the authorities had foreseen such a crowd, and had assembled a company of infantry under Capt. W. G. McLennan and forty mounted deputies under Capt. S. P. Riggleton. Carpenters worked all morning building the gallows, and it was not finished until shortly before one o'clock. All the time hundreds of anxious spectators sat or stood around, waiting for "the curtain to raise." As one old-timer put it: "By golly, you'd think President Hayes himself was visiting Giddings. Effen he was, don't think any more folks could get in than come to see Longley die."

At one-thirty Sheriff Jim Brown and his army went for Longley at the jail. A deep feeling of friendship had developed between Brown and Longley, something akin to a father-and-son understanding. Brown opened the cell door and found Bill sitting on the bunk. The latter smiled up at the sheriff and greeted him with a wave of his hand.

"Howdy, Jim."

The sheriff took a deep breath and said: "Well, Bill, it's time to saddle up." His voice trailed off to a whisper and he avoided Longley's searching eyes.

"I've been listening to them building that contraption," said Longley, after a moment, "and I'm curious to see what it looks like. Never saw a real gallows in my life." He laughed at his joke as he lit a large black cigar.

"Sorry to do this," mumbled the sheriff, as he fiddled with the chains on Longley's wrists. "These blamed things are more trouble than anything I ever saw. Sorry I have to use 'em."

"That's all right, Jim. Come on. I'm anxious to get out of this cage."

They led Bill outside between the two lines of infantry and guards to a covered wagon. Four guards holding double-barreled shotguns were seated in the wagon, and Longley took his place in the middle—two guards on each side of him. A fifth guard sat on the seat with the driver. Mounted deputies rode in front and rear, and the infantry flanked the vehicle.

Driving through the throng, the wagon was drawn up at the foot of the gallows. Without a moment's hesitation Longley stapped lightly from the wagon to the ground and paused on the bottom step to survey the structure with a critical eye. Then for the first time he seemed to take notice of the heavy guard and the tremendous crowd.

"Expecting a king or something, Sheriff? Anyway, you got a good audience and a regular army too." With that Bill turned and gazed upon the rope as it dangled from the gibbet.

"The darn thing looks strong enough, all right." He took a couple of steps up and tested the steps by shaking his weight on it.

"Look out, the steps are falling. I don't want to get crippled." Then Bill laughed.

On the back of the platform was a short bench, and Longley walked to this and sat down, calling for a drink of water. Someone handed him a dipperful and he drank it with relish, returned the cigar to his mouth, and resumed his inspection of the gallows.

Sheriff Brown immediately took charge of things, and, stepping forward to the front of the platform, addressed the crowd.

"This is the first legal hanging in Lee County, and I hope it will never be necessary to have another. Our object here is a solemn one and the duty a disagreeable one, but one that must be done."

The sheriff's voice failed him as he searched in his pocket and drew out a folded paper. He rattled the paper nervously as he smoothed it out.

"At this time I must read the death warrant," and this he proceeded to do, but before he had finished his voice was nothing more than a whisper.

Longley, still occupying his seat directly behind the swinging hemp, appeared the least concerned man in the entire crowd. As the sheriff concluded his reading, he motioned Longley to come forward.

"Speak now, Bill, say anything you want to say. It'll be your last chance."

Longley patted the sheriff on the arm as if to encourage him against his blundering and took a step forward. Removing the cigar from his mouth, and in a clear voice which could be heard far back in the crowd, Bill spoke.

"I haven't much to say, but I hate to die surrounded by so many enemies and so few friends. I hope you will all forgive me for anything I have done. I have already forgiven all that did anything to me. God has forgiven me and I owe Him more than any of you. I know I have to die, and I hate it, for we all hate to die when the time comes, for I have killed many men who hated to die as bad as I do. If I have any friends about here who think of revenge, I hope they will forget it, as it is wrong. I hear my brother, Jim, is in the crowd. I hope not, but if he is I hope he will let revenge alone and pray for me, as I ask all others to do. I have taken enough revenge myself and must be punished for it. It is a debt I owe for my wild, reckless life. When it is paid, it will be over. I have nothing more to say."

He put the cigar back in the corner of his mouth, then took it out quickly as a prayer was being offered by the priest.

Longley kissed Sheriff Brown and Father Spillard, then he put the black cigar back in his mouth, raised his manacled hands to the crowd, and in a strong, full voice shouted: "Goodbye, all, goodbye!"

The black cap was drawn over Bill's head and the cigar fell from under it to lie smoking on the pine planks at his feet. The roped were adjusted, his arms and legs bound, and the word given.

The trapdoor fell with a loud clatter and the body of Wild Bill Longley shot downward twelve feet, and came to a sudden jerk at the end of the rope. There was an iron rail underneath which held the trapdoor in place, and this swung against Bill's legs, knocking him sideways as he fell. As the body shot down, the rope slipped on the extended arm beam above the platform and the knees of Longley dragged the ground. Sheriff Brown and two deputies had to pull the body partly up again and hurriedly readjust the rope. Eleven minutes later Drs. Johnson, Fields, and Gasley pronounced the gunman dead. After the body was cut down Sheriff Brown took Bill's head in his hands and turned it completely through 180 degrees. Brown placed the body in a covered hack, and the remains were taken to the cemetery and buried in a plain pine box on the outside of the iron fence.

There was nothing to mark the grave of Bill Longley except rude rocks which outlined it. Some twenty-five years later friends of the family erected over it a headstone made of a hollow petrified log.

Thus Lady Luck, who had been Longley's constant mistress for so many years, finally deserted him.

Or did she?

There were still the whispers. Still the unfounded stories and legends coming from just enough different places and people to make one wonder. Perhaps Longley had cheated the law and death so many times that no one believed he could die at the rope's end that afternoon in Giddings. Some said when the rope slipped and Bill's feet hit the ground his neck was not broken and he managed to stave off strangulation. Others said he had been fitted with a special harness which prevented any serious injury. As the stories go, Longley's "dead body" eventually found its way to Central and South America. Where did these fantastic tales start?

In San Saba, Texas, several years ago a man who had been a close friend and neighbor to the Longleys told this story: Three days after the hanging his mother saw a covered wagon pull up to the back porch of the Longley ranch. The driver got out, untied the ropes at the back, and got in. A few minutes later two men got out. Prior to that morning Longley's mother had been grief-stricken over her son's death. After the coming of the wagon she became more cheerful, almost happy, and went out of mourning. Was the second man Longley? And if so, how did he cheat the noose?

As late as 1892 Longley's father told an intimate friend that Bill was not hanged that day in Giddings. Old man Longley claimed that a rich uncle in California had put up forty thousand dollars to bribe the sheriff and doctors to rig the hanging so Longley could escape. A personal investigation shows that two of Bill's uncles did go to California prospecting for gold. One of them was injured in a mining accident; the other really struck it rich, retired from mining, built a fine hotel, refused to charge his friends, and didn't have any enemies, of course, under that arrangement, and soon went broke. It is believed that this uncle went broke *before* Bill was hanged.

In 1912 a young cousin of Bill then attending college in Russellville, Arkansas, was invited to the home of a fellow student. The student's father was a farmer of good standing in the community, with a fine wife and family. While there, the student's father told Longley's cousin a strange story. The farmer had once been a companion of Longley and had ridden with him on many occasions. They had parted company after the farmer killed a man in McLennan County, Texas, and fled to Arkansas to escape the law. There he had met and married a fine young woman, been converted to religion, and had confessed his crime. On the advice of his wife and pastor he had returned to Texas to stand trial and was acquitted.

"Is Bill Longley still alive?" the elderly man asked Bill's cousin.

"No, he was hanged in Giddings, Texas, many years before I was born," came the reply.

"Yes, I know he was hanged, but he did not die. He may be alive today," the farmer answered. Then he told Longley's cousin that he had received several letters from Longley, who had escaped to South America and was a rancher. At Longley's request he had burned the correspondence.

As late as 1934 an old gentleman, Capt. John Talley, who knew both Longley and Wes Hardin, stated he did not believe Bill Longley was ever hanged. However, Mr. W. J. McClelland, who was one of Bill's guards, and who put the noose around Bill's neck, is absolutely positive that Longley died on the gallows in Giddings. As he termed it: "Bill was deader'n a mackerel."

Many people believe that had Longley escaped the hangman's knot that day he would eventually have come home to claim his dubious fame; that was like Bill. Some years ago a sexton at the cemetery where Bill's grave is located told of a visitor who came to the place—a tall gray-haired man who asked: "Can you tell me where they say Bill Longley is buried?"

The sexton pointed to the piece of stone about two and a

half feet high—the petrified wood—that stands at the head of the grave. The old man leaned on his cane, looked at the mound, then at the stone, and chuckling said: "So that's where they say he's buried." Then thanking the caretaker he turned and walked away. The old sexton to his dying day believed that Longley had come back to look at his own grave!

Oddly enough, when the *Lusitania* was torpedoed and sunk by the Germans on May 7, 1915, the passenger list of the doomed liner bore the name of W. P. Longley, South American cattleman!

The grave is still marked to this day. But what of the stories? Are they legend, like the legends that grew around so many of those Western figures, to cloud and distort the truth? Or did Longley's luck hold that grim morning in 1878 and help him cheat his executioners? Nobody ever bothered to open the grave when the stories began. Nobody checked. It would seem almost certain that Wild Bill did go to his just deserts that day in Giddings, but the doubts still prevail.

Only the grave knows the answer to the secret!

Colt's 1848 model, .44-caliber 6-shot

3   Cullen Baker

ALTHOUGH LITTLE HAS been written concerning the history of Cullen Baker, no doubt the shadow he cast across the great Republic of Texas eclipsed those cast by daring outlaws and gunmen who followed him. Baker's cunning nearly touched the sphere of insanity at times, and the best talents of the United States Army could not cope with him.

Cullen Montgomery Baker was born on June 22, 1835, in Weekly County, Tennessee, the son of a God-fearing young couple.

In 1839 his father, John Baker, emigrated to the Red River country in Texas, arriving in Spanish Bluffs, Bowie County, late in December after a hardy trek in a small wagon with his family and their meager possessions. The Battle of San Jacinto had been fought and won by the Texans under Sam Houston only three years prior to that, and the only government in Texas was in the hands of two rival gangs, who indulged regularly in murder and marauding. The territory of the New Republic of Texas was so great that it took a number of years to bring a semblance of law and order into being.

Perhaps in the hope of finding peace, John Baker moved his family forty miles away, to the south bank of the Sulphur Fork of the Red River, and began farming just west of the Arkansas state line. This region was in Cass County, which during the Civil War was renamed Davis County, in honor of the Confederate President Jefferson Davis.

As a ten-year-old boy Cullen was sallow-faced and slender, the butt of boys who were amused at his bare feet and homespun trousers. One day he sprang with fury upon the biggest of his tormentors and bested him. This first victory led him to dream of conquering imaginary monsters, and he spent a great deal of time wandering alone in the forest with a rifle, pretending to be stalking dangerous beasts. He practiced continuously with the rifle as well as with an old six-gun he had managed to borrow. He became an expert marksman because he had plenty of time to practice throwing down with the rifle at a swift pace and drawing his revolver from his waistband with uncanny speed.

Because he liked to boast of his courage, it was a great disappointment to find himself without an opportunity for personal heroism. He made up for this by bragging of his aptness with the rifle and revolver; as a consequence, by the time he was sixteen every boy who knew him made a point of keeping out of his way. This, he told himself, was proof that he really was dangerous, and his bravado increased. In 1851 he started to drink whiskey, and when he was "high" he took pleasure in challenging any bystander to meet him in mortal combat. But his record as a crack shot was well known, and the townsfolk were careful not to give him any reason to draw his gun.

In his eighteenth year Cullen was still wearing homespun trousers with a single brace support held by pegs instead of buttons and a strap around his waist to hold his pistol. From under a slouch hat he squinted belligerently at anyone approaching him. He developed a quarrelsome disposition, and felt gratified when people backed away from him. On one occasion he displayed his menacing power before a crowd by forcing an old man to trot at the point of his gun. The sight of the old man's fear inspired him to continue the game beyond his original intention. He drove the old man out of town.

On another occasion Cullen gathered together some young men and started a battle against another group, all of them using knives and pistols, and the air rang with cries of mock-hatred. Cullen was felled by a blow from a tomahawk, and had to be kept in bed for several weeks.

During this period of suffering he seemed to look himself in the face, and it was confidently believed that he had reformed. Cullen told himself that the life of a gunfighter was not the thing; that some day another would come along and best him at his own game. In January, 1854, while his head was still bandaged, he married Jane Petty, a seventeen-year-old who had faith in his good intentions. For nearly a year he lived like a respectable citizen, and people were inclined to think of his past mistakes as the wild oats sown by youth.

The era of the gunfighter as we know him (between 1870 and 1900) had not yet arrived, and Cullen Baker had no challengers as yet to his claim of being one. Instead, he found glory in forcing men and boys to carry him on their shoulders through the streets, while he pecked them on the head with a knife or beat them with a pistol butt, to be sure they would obey his commands. Strangely enough, a large number of people succumbed to his bragging demands.

In August, 1854, he used a leather whip to torment an orphan named Stallcup, and neighbors urged the boy to take the matter to court. At the trial a Mr. Baily, the well-respected head of a large family, testified against Cullen. He had been present during the beating. An hour after the trial Cullen appeared at Mr. Baily's home and yelled for him to come out. Baily stepped on to his porch, an old pistol in his hand.

"So you'd talk against me, eh, Baily?" sneered Baker. "Well, you got a gun. Use it while you got the chance."

Baily was no gunman, but he thought he might have a chance since his weapon already was in his hand. The pistol in Baily's hand bellowed and the slug whizzed past Baker's ear. Baily was in the process of trying a second shot when Baker's right hand snaked down and came up working his deadly pistol. The porch rocked with its roar, and blood spurted from the dumbfounded Baily's mouth as the first slug slammed him backward. The second bullet caught its victim smack in the forehead, and Mr. Baily fell dead.

Through the smoke haze the horrified family saw the father collapse. Mr. Baily's son, armed with his own rifle, tried to follow Cullen on foot, but Baker, being mounted, outdistanced him.

It was two years before young Baker was seen there again, and all members of his family, including his wife, had been without any news of him. When he reappeared in 1856, he learned that the authorities were still searching for him, and he left once more, for another two years. In 1858 he arranged to take his wife and baby daughter to Perry County, Arkansas, where they made their home until Jane died on July 2, 1860.

Cullen carried the child back to the Sulphur country and

left her with her grandfather, Hubbard Petty, who was living near Line Ferry. This apparently released him of all his parental and other responsibilities, and he made no further effort to discipline himself in any way.

Back to Perry County, while under the influence of alcohol, Baker got into a fight with a Mr. Wartham and killed him with a dagger.

The authorities made every effort to bring Baker to justice after this murder, but he eluded them and skipped out of Perry County, returning to Cass County in Texas, where he had been raised. Years had elapsed since his killing of Mr. Baily, and nobody was prepared to press the old charge against him. Cullen seemed to settle down. He made it clear that he wanted to become a new man.

As a result of this seeming reformation he won the love of Martha Foster, and they were married on July 1, 1862, apparently with the consent of her parents, William and Elizabeth Foster.

About this time he was conscripted into the Confederate army and was ordered to Little Rock, Arkansas, with his company. He did not show any great loyalty to the service, but frequently went absent without leave to visit his wife. The gravity of the developing war situation must account for his officers' neglect in calling him to answer for these lapses.

While in the army, Baker saw so much cruelty and death that his desire to be a gunfighter returned. Again he slipped from his barracks and made his way to the Sulphur country. He decided to remain at home and raise corn for the troops. Since food was in constant demand throughout the war years, a farmer was considered to be doing patriotic work. Although Baker was a deserter, he thought he was doing the right thing.

Negroes seemed to have a special way of offending Baker for no explainable reason. In the spring of 1864 Baker was in Spanish Bluffs when a contingent of Negro troops under the command of Capt. F. S. Dodge entered the town. These were Union soldiers looking for deserters from the Federal troops stationed in Missouri. Captain Dodge instructed the big sergeant to billet down at the end of town, but he had other ideas. The sergeant told the corporal to carry out the captain's orders while he and three Negro soldiers entered the one broken-down saloon the town boasted. At the bar stood a lone customer—Cullen Baker. The soldiers stopped short. It was not the vicious six-gun the man carried that stopped them, but the battered gray hat the stranger wore. It was Confederate issue!

But the sergeant's hesitation was only momentary.

"What's your name and where are you from?" he asked Baker.

Baker's hand darted down and came up filled with a blazing six-gun. The sergeant fell dead before he could raise a hand. The second bullet Baker fired killed a private as he darted for the door. The remaining pair died where they stood, their mouths gaping.

Cullen had killed the Union soldiers without thinking first. Now he was in trouble with both sides, but characteristically he left town hurriedly and joined the Federal troops at Little Rock. After he took the oath of allegiance he was placed in charge of a contingent of freedmen. But Baker still hated Negroes, and decided to return to the home of his uncle, Thomas Young. His uncle, afraid to cross Cullen, made him welcome.

One day Baker was out riding when some Jayhawkers overtook him and accused him of being a Federal. It took all his powers of persuasion to make them believe they were mistaken, and in a final effort to convince them he joined their ranks. In spite of their first suspicions and their constant watch over him, they soon discovered that he was their most talented member—for he showed great aptitude in handling weapons and got them out of several tight spots.

In October, 1864, Baker heard that several citizens were trying to move out of the region which had been devastated by the Jayhawkers, so he waylaid them at the Saline River as they were embarking to cross.

"Hands up! Surrender!" Baker yelled.

"Who are you?" the emigrant leader retorted.

"We're outlaws and we want your goods."

This incident caused Baker's promotion to leadership among the Freebooters, and after that he exercised his power upon every man who owned anything he wanted. His speed with the six-gun always convinced those who opposed him that he was no man to tangle with.

After one raid Baker found they were being closely pursued by a strong posse, so they abandoned their loot and scattered wildly. Baker with three of his companions rode into Davis County, where he had been raised, but when news of his new activities arrived he left suddenly. He attempted to enlist some new followers for another bandit company, but did not succeed until February, 1865.

In the meantime Baker's wife was still living with her father near Line Ferry. She heard a rumor that her husband had been captured at Little Rock and was being court-martialed. Fearing that he would be sentenced to death, and desperately wanting to be with him until the last, she deceived her family by pretending to visit a nearby neighbor. Then through a violent winter storm, without adequate clothing and with no supplies, she rode two hundred miles. When she discovered that the rumor was mistaken and that her husband was merely in the hills organizing a new command for himself, she rode another thirty-six hours through a snow-storm to the home of Thomas Young, hoping that this uncle would have news of her husband.

Indeed, Baker did visit his uncle while his wife was there, and he was angry that she had followed him.

He said: "I wish you had been sick enough so as not to be able to move a hand or foot, so then you would have stayed home where you belong."

But she remained in the household of Mr. Young until the spring. Then, after Baker had made a number of raids upon scouting parties and army posts, he took his wife back over the two hundred miles to their home in the Sulphur country. The army of the Trans-Mississippi Department had now surrendered, and the war was reaching its end.

In July Baker met some of his former cronies on their way back to Davis County, and he congratulated them on the number of cattle and horses they had commandeered. While they were riding together he made a stop at the farm of Mrs. Drew, near Jefferson. Tearfully she told him of the raid on her ranch, and Baker made a great show of being horrified at this outrage perpetrated upon her. He even offered to try to get her cattle back. In gratitude Mrs. Drew offered a reward if he was successful.

Baker rode away, caught up with his companions, and selected Mrs. Drew's cattle from their haul. Then he returned the beasts to Mrs. Drew and accepted the bonus as well as her heartfelt thanks. In fact, Mrs. Drew gave this deed of Baker's such wide publicity that many people began to doubt he could be the unscrupulous individual they had heard he was.

Late that autumn Baker thought of settling down at Musk Island, ten miles north of Line Ferry, and starting a competing ferry as his own enterprise. But he was taken sick and had to abandon that project. He and his wife continued to live with her parents, the Fosters, until January 10, 1866. On that date they moved to Line Ferry, and Baker began to operate the boat from there.

On March 1 his wife died, and he seems to have been truly grief-stricken. At any rate, he made an effigy of her in clothes which she had worn, and he kept it standing in a life-like pose for all the neighbors to see. It was several weeks before he was prevailed upon to remove it.

But two months after his wife's burial he called on the Fosters again and proposed marriage to his sister-in-law, Bell, who was then sixteen. This proposal was declined by both Bell and her parents. Baker left them with a new bitterness in his heart.

Probably he sensed that the young school teacher, Thomas Orr, who was boarding with the Fosters at the time, had won the fancy of young Bell. Earlier, in January, Baker had been one of the sponsors of this school teacher, and had shown him considerable friendship. But on June 2, a month after Bell had refused to marry him, Baker forced a fight upon Orr.

Orr was just crossing the ferry during Baker's temporary absence at the grocer's. Baker reached the north bank with a jug of whiskey, and waited until the boat landed. He insisted that Orr drink with him. When Orr explained that he never touched alcohol, Baker took personal affront and started a fight.

Not only was Orr a studious man and far from muscular, but his right hand was deformed from rheumatism. Naturally Baker was getting the best of the fight, as John Herring, the operator of the boat during Baker's absence, later explained, for he stood by during the fracas, not daring to interfere. Baker made short work of the battle by hitting Orr on the head with a pine bough. When Orr fell to the ground Baker jumped into the boat and rowed off.

Orr was bleeding copiously when he regained consciousness. Herring helped him to mount the little roan which belonged to Mr. Foster. It was the same horse that Baker's wife had ridden on her wild ride through the storm to see her husband before his supposed execution. As quickly as he could, Orr rode to the home of Dr. Oats and had his wounds dressed. Until that day he had never suspected this violent side of Baker's character. In January he had arrived as a stranger. He could only explain Baker's violence by saying: "No doubt the whiskey went to Cullen's head."

However, when he was told of Baker's past wild life and his swiftness with the revolver, he expressed surprise that the authorities should countenance such actions. He procured a pistol and meant to have it out with Baker on his return trip. But friends persuaded him to go home by a different route.

It was a month later when Baker arrived at the schoolhouse while Orr was teaching and angrily demanded the ferry fare which Orr had forgotten to pay in the excitement of the fight. Orr paid it readily. Then, right before the class, Baker treated the school teacher to a tirade of abusive language.

"I'll shoot your head off smooth with your shoulders if I hear you telling any lies about me," Baker threatened.

After this scene one of the pupils, George Couch, walked out of the schoolhouse and attached himself to Baker as an enthusiastic admirer. Later George Couch delivered a letter to the school teacher:

> *Line Ferry, Arkansas*
> July 20, 1866

> THOAS ORR SIR If you wish to Teach your School you had bitter bea at it every day I here of you Beeing fishing. My Lad you Don't No that my Gizzard is Grinding on Dam lies that you told over the River Don't let me here of you beaing absent from that School Any more fir It is all that I Can do to keep from giving you another & good call & if I find one thing to Bee so You may Look for me I am Sir yours as Mad as Hell till Death.

> CULLEN M. BAKER

> Thoas Orr at Home I don't Want the friendship Any one that you Can turn Against me.
> Govner Orr at Home.

Though the missive has been described as an example of handsome penmanship, it can hardly be claimed that it is couched in the language of the scholar some people later pretended Cullen Baker had been.

After delivery of the letter some civic-minded residents of the region consulted the Justice of the Peace, but were informed that nothing could be done to stop Baker's progress farther into crime. It was evident that everyone was afraid of that swift gun hand of his. The patrons of the school held a mass meeting and discussed the possibility of capturing Baker in order to put a stop to his career, but one elderly gentleman urged them to take a more humane step toward correcting the difficulty. This member of the meeting suggested sending a delegation to deal with the outlaw, and, as it later turned out, he himself was the first member of that particular crowd to be killed by Baker. He was William Foster, not to be confused, however, with Baker's father-in-law of the same name.

The delegation did wait on Baker, intimating that the populace wanted to know his intentions for the future, and Baker made some heavy threats about what he would do if anybody attempted to interfere with his freedom. Nevertheless, he was finally prevailed upon to offer this much of an appeasement:

> *Line Ferry, Arkansas*
> July 27, 1866

I hereby sertify to the Neighbors of Hiett's Bind that I will in No Manner Interrupt Nor Bother one Thos Orr further more I Consider my word as good as any Body's or as good as the word of Jesus Christ I witness my hand.

C. M. BAKER

Two days later Baker wrote another letter and had it delivered to his father-in-law by Samuel Couch:

> *Line Ferry, Arkansas*
> July 29, 1866

MR. FOSTER Dear Sir Dear Father as I should say for you have bin a father to me So has Mrs. Foster Bin a Mother but I Recken you Both have Resind to Bee any more therefore I think It In vain to Ever Look for Either of you here any more and Whereas I have Bin Requested to Inform you of a Matter Concerning some Pills that the Old Man Bevel Requested you to take In Charge some years ago that he had left with some one Near Bright Star he Wanted you to send the Money for them here to me So he Could get it or Leave Word What you Done about them as he will be here Soon again.

Mr. Foster It is very hard for me to Bear and how it is that One Can throw away an old friend for a New one Mrs. Foster has surely here tofore held Me as a friend But she is now laboring under a wide mistake or Wanting me to put that that Don't fit me and wear It In Behald of that Damd Orr She Cannot think that I am mistake in a matter of that kind that has such an impression on my Mind as that Did If I had Killed Jesus Christ It would not Raised half the excitement this matter has I hope and Pray to live the ten months out and keep my Same mind for I am not a Negro Neither am I bound In this country I No that I am a Liar and a Drunkard and a Devil But I never tell lies on my Friends.

The matter Raised Between us the other Day has give me

72

no Little Trouble But as I sayd In a Note to Orr I dont want the friendship of any One that

he In any manner Can turn against Me I commenced in trouble and End in the same Hoping to see the 15th day of December.

C. M. BAKER

Wm. Foster Hyettes Bend, Arks

The date, December 15, is mentioned in this letter because Baker assumed that the school would close on that date and that Thomas Orr would probably thereupon leave the locality. However, the school closed on November 2, ten scholastic months after January 28, when Orr had first begun his duties.

Of course when November 2 arrived Baker knew very well that the school was closed. On November 3 he went to the home of the Fosters, hoping that Orr had left—perhaps even hoping that, in the absence of Orr, Bell Foster might look more favorably upon himself. Out of bravado he rode up to the house surrounded by five large mastiffs and searched the premises for Orr. After a while he blew a horn to call off the dogs and rode away. Doubtless he thought he was cutting a heroic figure for Bell's benefit.

It is true that Orr had left immediately after closing the school the previous day. But on hearing about Baker's dramatic circling of the Fosters' home, he tried to file a complaint with the Justice of the Peace and the County Sheriff. They both assured him they could do nothing in the matter. He then decided to waylay Baker on December 30 at Day's Creek, and there he waited most of the afternoon. But when some of Baker's associates passed by he supposed they would warn him, so he gave up the idea and went home. Nevertheless, Baker had not been advised of Orr's presence at Day's Creek, and about fifteen minutes after Orr gave up he crossed the bridge on his way to spend the night at the home of a Mr. Mayes.

Baker fancied himself as courting Mr. Mayes's daughter, and he told her she might expect him to pay another call on Wednesday evening. This promise reached Orr, who himself arrived on Wednesday evening. But Baker in the meantime had returned to Line Ferry.

When he was unable to outbid others for the Line Ferry concession, Baker threatened to run it anyhow. He went to Linden, Texas, to procure a license, defying any man to compete with him and emphasizing that his fast gun would back him up. But he gave up his plan shortly and instead chose a spot seven miles beyond the Texas state line, where he started a ferry of his own.

Orr, eager to avoid any further meeting with the desperado, took another school three miles farther into the state of Arkansas, hoping that there he would be left in peace. However, he continued to keep a double-barreled gun and a six-shooter handy.

Baker now became so embittered that he turned his spite on anyone whom he thought had insulted him. He also continued to send threatening notes to Thomas Orr, who believed that there must be some misunderstanding to have caused this rupture between them. He made one more effort to heal the breach. On April 27, 1867, he wrote:

MR. CULLEN BAKER, Sir: I have written to you before but have not received any answer. It may be possible that you did not receive the note. I, therefore, embrace the present opportunity of writing again. I suppose, or at least have heard, that you say you have nothing against me. I would be glad to know that it was a fact. I have also heard that you said you had understood that I had threatened your life. As to your having heard it, of course, I cannot deny, as I am not accountable for lies told by others. All that I can ask is for a man to be produced who ever heard me make any such assertion.

It would be a great pleasure to me if our difficulty could be settled, and we were, or could become, as we once were. If I had, or could be convinced, that I have any acknowledgments to make, I would do it with pleasure; but I don't consider that I ever gave you any reason for treating me as you have, and I am not aware of giving you any cause for even being mad at me; besides I am not appraised of what you got mad about. I want to go over the river occasionally and I have been compelled to put myself to much trouble and inconvenience, and have been deprived of the pleasures and comforts of life to keep out of your presence, and to prevent the execution of what I have feared to be your intentions. I hope to hear from you soon.

Yours respectfully,
THOMAS ORR

This civilized gesture meant nothing to Baker, for his hatred of his rival for Bell Foster's attentions continued to make him want to plot revenge. Orr had no realization that this was the root of the trouble between him and Baker.

About June 1 Baker went to Rowden's grocer's store on the road between Jefferson and Line Ferry and found it closed and the storekeeper absent. He demanded the keys from Mrs. Rowden and entered the store and took what he wanted. When Mr. Rowden heard of this, he went to call on Baker and asked for payment. He also took along a shotgun loaded with slugs.

"Oh, sure," said Baker. "I'll pay you in a few days."

Some nights later Baker appeared at the Rowden gate, shouting for Mr. Rowden to come down at once. Recognizing Baker's voice, Mrs. Rowden and her daughter begged Mr. Rowden not to reply, but Mr. Rowden saw no reason to be alarmed. He picked up his shotgun and stepped out.

"What do you mean by speaking disrespectfully to me?" Baker demanded.

"I'm sure I never meant to do such a thing," Mr. Rowden began.

He never had a chance to use the scattergun, for like a striking rattlesnake Baker's six-gun snapped up. Four times it barked, and four slugs slammed into Rowden's body. Hurled forward, dead on his feet, he pitched headlong to the ground.

When he heard that citizens were organizing in order to capture him, Baker issued a proclamation that he would gun down any man who dared to accuse him of killing Mr. Rowden except in a fair fight. The Federal commander at Jefferson, Texas, now sent a squad with instructions to bring Baker in, but before they could surround him he had left the state again.

As a matter of fact, he returned within a few days well armed and rode about the district, loudly defying the Federal authorities. But mostly he stayed in the byways of Sulphur Bottom, where he had camped during the latter part of the Civil War while avoiding the conscript agents. Now he made his home among the pines and oaks or in the swamps. Gradually he became bolder, helped himself to the best horseflesh he could find, and kept himself in ammunition by daring forages.

The troops were still supposed to be scouting for him, but nobody dared to give information about his whereabouts. Unlike Jesse and Frank James and the Youngers, who were to follow, he remained immune because people were afraid to talk. In the case of the Jameses and the Youngers, folks were proud to hide them.

After scouting in Bowie County Baker turned to Davis County. At Pett's Ferry, on the Sulphur, he was overtaken by the advance guard of a company trying to locate him. He had just crossed the river on the ferry when the guard rode up and engaged him in conversation.

"What's your name?" asked the sergeant.

"It's Johnson," lied Baker, "but what in hell makes you so particular?"

"We thought you might be Cullen Baker, the man we are searching for," replied the sergeant. "From your arms and the way your're dressed I'm inclined to believe you are Baker."

As the sergeant started to draw his revolver Baker's hand snapped up, and his own revolver belched flame. Three bullets spun the soldier from his saddle, and he was dead before he struck the ground. The frightened private who accompanied the ill-fated sergeant raced his mount back to warn the detachment.

Baker pushed deeper into the swamp and wound along the southern bank of the Sulphur for several miles. At a shallow place which was well known to him he forded the river, returning to Bowie County. The troops also crossed the river again and rode toward Boston, not realizing that they were drawing near to their quarry.

Baker heard them approaching his hiding place and, indeed, watched them as they drew nearer. At a crossroads he shouted from the bushes in a loud command: "Charge them, boys! Charge them!"

Evidently the troops believed that the woods were full of Baker's men, for they galloped off in panic. Coming out of hiding, Baker picked up an officer's hat which had fallen during the hasty retreat.

At another time when he felt particularly daring Baker exposed himself before a score of well-disciplined soldiers. They immediately fired on him. He discharged both barrels of his shotgun before resorting to his fast-firing six-shooters. The Federals were driven away in disorder, leaving one of their comrades on the ground dead. Though Baker was wounded in the right arm, he was able to mount his mule and ride off. The pain made it necessary for him to stop after covering two miles, but he was not followed.

The Federal officers were determined to get him, and they dispatched a courier for reinforcements. As soon as they had enough soldiers, they spread throughout the region on the lookout. But there were still a number of Southern sympathizers who considered Baker a Yankee-killer, and refused to help the Federals round him up. His fame as a dare-devil spread, and fresh troops were ordered to eastern Texas from every state in the Union with the express command to get Cullen Baker. Still he ranged through the familiar swamps and dense forests of Sulphur, keeping comfortably hidden unless he needed provender for his mount. He helped himself to whatever he wanted, the farmers always remaining carefully out of sight when he appeared. After a few weeks the Federals reported the chase fruitless and returned to Jefferson.

On October 10 Baker was riding along the road between Linden and Boston when he passed a government wagon without thinking much about it. However, on reflection he decided to capture its cargo. He turned his horse and rode past it again, getting far enough ahead to be able to secrete himself in the bushes. When the wagon approached he stepped into the road and ordered the driver to halt. The driver made a heroic effort to draw his service revolver, but Baker killed him before the gun had cleared leather. The four soldiers who were supposed to guard the supplies fired on Baker and then fled, leaving him in possession of the stores. He carried the stock into Sulphur Bottom and stacked it away for future use.

When the guard returned to Jefferson with the news of this latest attack a large force was sent in pursuit, but returned unsuccessful. The military commander then offered a reward of a thousand dollars for the capture of Cullen Baker.

During that autumn Baker remained in Arkansas unmolested. On Christmas Day he bought several gallons of whiskey at Bright Star and invited a group of men to drink as much as they wanted. After they had become intoxicated he led them to Howell Smith's farm in Sulphur, arriving after dark. Looking through the windows, he saw several freedmen sitting about the fire, where they were waiting for their own quarters to be prepared for them. Baker and his jolly colleagues fired through the windows, in the melee one of his own men shot him in the right thigh.

The shooting over, Baker found himself deserted as he lay on the ground wounded. Even his horse had been taken by one of his boon companions. Though he found a mule, he was not strong enough to mount. But he saw Mr. Smith's two daughters in the dark, and he ordered them to assist him in mounting the mule.

He rode to Mr. Foster's house, about a mile away, and urged Mr. Foster to see if the Smiths needed assistance.

A courier was dispatched to Jefferson, Texas, where captains Scott and Allen raised a volunteer company of citizens to go in pursuit of Baker. But the culprit remained safely at Mr. Foster's house for about sixty hours before he returned to the woods. General McGloffin arrived with his command of regulars to join the volunteers. Both the troops and the citizens met at Mr. Smith's house late in the afternoon to discuss tactics. They felt there was no use doing anything until the following morning.

Of course, by the time they found signs of Baker's night camp he had evacuated to a safer place. Though scouts trailed him into the Sulphur bottomlands, the main contingent was delayed by its very size. But they hurried on.

When the advance patrol caught sight of Baker's new camp they shouted the alert to the entire command. The troops and citizens all rushed forward, firing from every direction. At the first sound of the attack Baker calmly mounted a horse he had ready saddled for such an emergency, and became lost in the dense forest.

By January 1, 1868, more than three hundred men, both soldiers and civilians, were traveling under arms in search of the gunman-desperado, while twice that number remained at home well armed in case he should appear unexpectedly. But no trace of Baker was found again until the following October, when he appeared in Boston, Texas. There he walked boldly up to Captain Kirkham, the bureau agent, and said: "I'm Cullen Baker. You looking for me?"

The astonished agent made a frantic effort to grab a nearby pistol, but to no avail. Baker's six-gun leaped up and spit fire, sending a lethal slug into the captain's head. Governor Clayton then posted a reward of a thousand dollars for the outlaw's arrest.

By November 1 Baker had accumulated a score of followers, and with them he crossed Red River and raided several farms in Sevier and Little River counties, Arkansas. In this foray two government officers, Andrews and Willis, were killed.

Governor Clayton now called out the State Militia under the command of General Catterson. Warned of this, Baker crossed the Red River and called at Dr. Jones's farm, explaining that he was a militia officer in search of Cullen Baker. The farmer gave him supplies, and for a time was none the wiser that he had outfitted the dreaded fugitive.

Later Baker took his small force to the home of James Salmon shortly before daylight, calling Mr. Salmon to come down, since the Federals wanted to talk with him. As soon as the door opened, the outlaw rushed in, seized Salmon and

78

tied a rope around his neck and secured his hands behind his back. Then his men plundered the house.

It was already daylight when Baker and his gang arrived at the home of Mr. Scarborough. They called him to come out, but Mr. Scarborough refused to surrender until Baker had assured him for a third time that he would not be harmed. Later Baker persuaded Mr. Scarborough to promise that he would talk to Captain Scott and others to inquire if a compromise could be arranged.

From there Baker led his men to Parson Jesse Dobbs's house and held him captive all day until he, too, agreed to try to effect a compromise.

Scarborough and Dobbs did make the attempt, and a meeting of citizens finally came to the conclusion that a compromise was the best they could effect. A day was designated for a meeting at which all people interested should forgather at Scott's Mill, Davis County, Texas. Baker offered to give a bond in the amount of two hundred thousand dollars on his good behavior from then on, with the best security Bowie County could afford. Everybody seemed to consider this good news, and plans were made for the general amnesty.

Baker did not appear, however. And even while the compromise was being discussed at the mass meeting Baker shot and killed another Federal soldier in a duel.

The next move made by the citizenry was to send a committee to meet Baker and inquire his intentions. As a result of the good offices of three citizens, R. P. Crump, F. M. Henry, and R. M. Stewart, he permitted a friend to write the following letter, which appeared in the *Weekly Austin Republican* under the date of December 2, 1868, as well as in the *Jefferson Times* and the *Jimplecute:*

> *Bowie County, Texas*
> November 14, 1868
>
> Editors of the *Times:*
> Permit me to publish a statement in your paper in order to place myself right before the Government and the people of the country. Various rumors have obtained circulation through the country in regard to my course of conduct; and many persons are now committing offences against law and good order, on my credit. And hence, I deem it necessary to declare my sentiments and intentions for the future. It is rumored that I have said that no civil officers should perform the duties of their offices in the counties where I stay. To which report I have to say, that I am strictly in favor of the enforcement of the civil laws of the country by the legitimate

authorities. And I now declare that it shall be my steady purpose to *protect the quiet* citizen and his laborers, either white or black, in the pursuit of their avocations. And I request all good citizens to *inform me* of all depredations committed by other persons, charged to have been committed by me. This is my native country, and my interests are identical with those of other citizens of the country; and I hope to remain in the counties of Davis, Bowie, Marion, and the adjoining counties in Eastern Texas. And I further declare, that it will not be *my purpose to make war* upon the good and peaceable citizens or laborers of this or any other section. Nor do I intend to interfere in any way with the powers that be. The white man and the black man will be perfectly safe in my hands so long as he lets me alone and pursues his peaceful and lawful business.

By accident, I happened to detect a party of five men on Col. Hook's farm, on Red River, robbing and plundering the Negroes, taking from them guns, ammunition, needles, soap, and every other small article of value, calling themselves Cul Baker, Bickerstaff and company. I arrested the parties, and found their names to be J. Sharp, J. Poterfield, George Robertson, George Franks and Tom Franks— all of whom I denounce as being beneath contempt. I disarmed said party, relieved them of their plunder, which I returned to the proper owners, and sent the scoundrels to their homes. I would have carried them to Boston and had them committed to jail by the civil authorities, but heard there were no officers in the county in whose charge I could place them. When the said parties were discharged I notified them that if I ever caught them under like circumstances, they would not again be dealt with. In conclusion, I have to say that I am not the great manslayer that scandal has made me—killing white and black wherever found, and I am determined in the future to do all the good I can for the peaceable and quiet citizens in the country where I stay. I shall in future publish the causes that led me into my present difficulties, and feel satisfied that I shall not be deemed by a just community, wholly to blame for my action in the past. I am now, and have ever been, willing to submit the whole of my conduct to a decision of unbiased men of my country, and abide by their just verdict.

> Your obedient servant,
> CULLEN M. BAKER

Whoever acted as Baker's ghost writer on this occasion was adept at making an impression of power and virtue. Certainly Baker believed himself to be able to control other plunderers and to be willing to champion the innocent, for his whole view was distorted in his own benefit.

The citizens who had effected this much of an agreement

were required to back it up, undoubtedly under duress, and they appended these words to the above letter:

Jefferson
November 16, 1868

We, the undersigned, have to state that at the request of a number of citizens of Davis County, we went out in search of Cullen M. Baker, to see him and ascertain from him what his course in the future would be. We found him, and the result of the interview with him, was as above set forth in his card, which we believe he will abide by.

R. P. CRUMP
F. M. HENRY
R. M. STEWART

The Weekly Austin Republican made a sarcastic comment:

So Cullen M. Baker has assumed the protection of quiet citizens. As the chicks shelter under the wings of the parent bird, so may all apprehensive souls rest under the aegis of this thief and murderer! Let all good citizens report to him; he will see their wrongs righted. They, black and white, will be "safe" in his hands! And R. P. Crump, F. M. Henry, and R. M. Stewart go bail for him!—We miss the name of W. P. Saufley on the back of this paper. It naturally belongs there; and for the want of it we send the document to the nearest notary for protest.

Seldom have we seen a more melancholy instance of moral perversion than this manifesto. Long success in outrage has so inflamed the vanity of Cullen M. Baker that he imagines himself a power in the State, and condescends to be gracious. ... We cannot imagine what Messrs. Crump and Co. think of Cullen M. Baker or of themselves. Other honest men "in search" of him, if as fortunate as they were in finding him, would have bound him hand and foot, and would have left him at the nearest military post to answer for his manifold atrocities. But they, after a cordial interview with this outlawed felon, return by themselves and endorse his word of honor!

Thomas Orr had by this time been married to Bell Foster for about a year. He was teaching school in Lafayette County, eight miles northwest of Line Ferry. But he and his wife were spending the winter at Mr. Foster's house four miles southeast of Line Ferry. He and Baker had not met for more than two years. Naturally Orr had no confidence in Baker's promise to kill no more, and he still went armed.

On November 20 Baker had accumulated a small army on the grounds that he wanted to cross the Red River in pursuit of the Militia, in order to recapture property they had unjustly confiscated and to redress wrongs inflicted by them upon various citizens. He paraded all the men he could muster and started a march toward Little Rock, enlisting recruits as he went. But when he had gathered together as many young men as believed his claims, he recrossed Red River, explaining that he had to go into Lafayette, Bowie, and Davis counties to meet the balance of his contingent.

The Militia had set out for Little Rock to meet him, but after hearing of his raid into Sevier County they faced about and proceeded to Red River.

On December 7 Baker and his men appeared before Mr. Foster's home. It was then ten o'clock and the family had gone to bed. The outlaws surrounded the house and demanded Mr. Foster come forth.

Mr. Foster went to the door and with some dignity demanded: "What is the cause of this untimely visit?" taking it for granted that his long years of kindness to this former son-in-law entitled him to courtesy.

"We want Thomas Orr," cried Baker, giving way once again to his long-dissembled purpose to punish the man who had won Bell's love.

Orr agreed to surrender after Baker assured him that he would not be harmed, for this seemed to be the only way he could save his young wife from molestation. Baker kept the prisoner under close watch all night, glorying in this opportunity to prove to Bell that he was master of her husband.

About sun-up the whole band started off in a westerly direction, Thomas Orr being forced to ride behind a boy, still tied, while Baker held one end of the rope about Orr's neck as they rode. Half a mile off Baker tied his end of the rope to a dogwood branch and commanded the boy to ride his horse forward. That left Orr suspended by the neck, his feet dangling in air.

Later when Baker needed rope with which to hang another victim, he cried: "Cut down that wretch and drag him away! And bring me that rope."

When the marauders rode off to Bright Star for a fresh supply of whiskey, they left Orr lying on the frozen ground.

The following day Baker rode on his way to Rondo. At Rondo two companies of citizens had organized under orders from General Catterson. Several thousand troops had also been ordered to capture the desperado. Baker himself had only a score of followers.

On December 10 Baker crossed into Texas, going westward as far as Mount Pleasant. On December 20 he returned to Davis County and was very nearly captured before he retreated across the Sulphur. About January 1, 1869, the Federal troops once again abandoned the chase and returned to Jefferson.

On January 4 Baker recrossed the Sulphur at Musk Island, and the next day returned to the place where he had killed Mr. Baily. He took Mr. Haynes into custody and held him in his camp overnight.

"What do you know about Thomas Orr?" Baker asked him.

"I suppose he's dead," said Mr. Haynes. "I heard that you hung him about a month ago."

"I hung him, but he's not dead," said Baker. "I have heard from him since. But one of us has got to die, and that before long."

"I guess you mean before tomorrow's setting sun," said Mr. Haynes grimly.

On January 6 Baker started for Arkansas, a two-and-a-half-hour ride. After crossing the state line he and his companion proceeded directly to Mr. Foster's house.

Thomas Orr was in the house and saw them approaching, but when they passed by he concluded that they must be on their way to Mr. Lamar's place, where several men had assembled to butcher hogs. He slipped out, and by a circuitous route through the woods reached that place. He found Baker had already been there.

Thomas Orr called upon the men at Lamar's to help him track down and kill Baker. Only three of the men offered to go with him.

A mile away Baker had stopped for a bite of lunch, thinking he was perfectly safe. His pursuers came quickly and discharged half a dozen guns at him, killing him and his companion instantly. It would have been suicide for Orr to try capturing Baker or to call him into a fair fight. A direct attack was what he thought best. Indeed, it was the only way for a novice gunman like him. Future outlaws and gunmen met the same fate—a bullet in the back: Jesse James, Wild Bill Hickok, John Wesley Hardin, Ben Thompson, and King Fisher, to mention but a few.

The attackers found on Baker's corpse a double-barreled

shotgun, four six-shooters, three derringers, several silver dollars, twenty-seven assorted keys, six pocket knives. He had also been carrying a copy of the *Louisville Courier Journal* of December 16, 1868. In vanity Baker had marked this item:

> Cullen Montgomery Baker, the Arkansas brigand, and his band, have left the State to join the Cuban expedition. If Clayton's militia could be induced to go to Cuba, Halifax or any place else, the State would enjoy peace and prosperity.

In spite of the years through which many official attempts had been made to capture Cullen M. Baker, it was the studious schoolteacher with the withered right hand who finally closed his notorious career.

Those with a penchant for painting vicious, swaggering gunmen and usually neurotic killers as frontier Robin Hoods have not overlooked Cullen Baker, although very little research has been done on him in the past. The few who have written about him have shown him as a brave, soft-spoken, courteous Southerner ever respectful to women, a man of high ethics, who was forced to live by the gun. And in all fairness, Baker did have guts . . . but there his virtue ended.

.45-caliber Colt's Peacemaker (1873)

4   Bat Masterson

WILLIAM BARCLAY MASTERSON, far better known as Bat Masterson, whose life has been so authentically portrayed and publicized by Gene Barry on the television screen, said he was born in Iroquois County, Illinois. His parents, Thomas and Catherine McGurk Masterson, ran a farm near Lawrenceville, New York, close to the Canadian border. Shortly after their marriage the Mastersons moved to Henryville, County Rouville, Quebec Province, Canada, about a hundred miles from Lawrenceville.

On September 22, 1852, their first child, Edward J. Masterson, was born. The next child would become the most famous, and for years the place of his birth was debated back and forth. His baptismal record reads: "On November 27, 1853, Bartholomew born yesterday of Thomas Masterson and Catherine McGurk, was was baptized at this parish, County Rouville, Parish of St. George."

The County Rouville records indicate that the Masterson family lived there between the years of 1851–1855, with Ed Masterson also being born there; the other children were born in Illinois. For reasons known only to himself, Bat Masterson changed his name to William Barclay and also stated he had been born in Iroquois County, Illinois. Edward's obituary states that he was born September 22, 1852, in Henryville, Canada, East.

Five more children followed Bat: James P. (1855–1895),

Nellie (1857–1925), Tom (1858–1941), George (1860–1892), and Emma (1862–1884). Ed was the oldest and most cherished, not only by Bat but all the others, particularly his mother. In most large families there seems to be one member with a noticeable grace and gentleness. Among the Mastersons this paragon was Ed, the peacemaker, the pale dreamer, who always seemed a little too good for the rough world into which he had been born. According to the rules of psychology, Bat and Ed should have been rivals and enemies, especially since Mrs. Masterson never made any secret of her preference for Ed, but it was simply impossible to hate or envy the older boy. Instead of being possessed by a Cain-like hatred, Bat felt protective toward his older brother, an attitude that was to endure into manhood, until the tragic evening when even that staunch loyalty was not sufficient.

Bat was Ed's opposite, lively, aggressive, full of pranks, always in trouble, or on the edge of trouble, or looking for trouble. He was the eternal Huck Finn, and the scant education provided for families in the sod huts of the Kansas homesteaders did not dismay him in the least. Self-education and a resourceful mind later supplied much that should have been instilled by a prairie schoolmarm, but spelling always remained something of a mystery to him. This weakness was illustrated by a letter he wrote to the Colt firearm factory at the age of thirty-one, beginning: "Gents, Please send me one of your nickle-plated .45 calibor revolvers. It is for my own use and for that reason I would like to have a little extra paines with it. . . ."

The sort of education that Bat wanted was not to be found in any classroom. It was provided eventually by a pre-Civil War musket acquired by his father in a swapping session with a townsman. The elder Masterson proposed to trade it off for something more useful on the farm, but Bat persuaded his father to keep it. The gun wasn't worth much. It was an old Springfield that had probably seen service in the Mexican War, and was jerked from its rack in the St. Louis arsenal to help arm one of the amateur regiments that saved the Border States for the Union during the early years of the Civil War.

But it meant a lot to Bat. A boy growing up on the frontier considered himself practically naked without a firearm of some kind. His powers of persuasion must have been considerable even then, in his early teens. He took the smooth-bore musket to a blacksmith with whom he had struck up a warm friendship, and talked the old fellow into rifling the barrel of his gun so that it would shoot farther and straighter.

Top: Wild Bill Hickok; only known photo in existence with signature

Bottom: Wild Bill Hickok's gun—.45 cal. Deane-Adams English 5-shot (Kansas State Historical Society, Topeka)

TOP: Wild Bill Longley, after capture

BOTTOM: Dance .44 cal. 1863 revolver used by Wild Bill Longley to kill his first man

Top: Bat Masterson, around 1886 (Kansas State Historical Society, Topeka)

Bottom: .45 cal. Colt's, used by McCall to kill Hickok

TOP: Henry Starr as a boy

BOTTOM: .38 cal. Colt's, once property of Henry Starr, outlaw. Starr also used a 1909 Colt's Army .45 cal.

TOP: Henry Brown as a marshall

BOTTOM: Ben Wheeler's .44 SA Colt's revolver (Harry Leah, Todmorden, Lancs., England)

Top: Ben Thompson as marshal of Austin, Texas

Bottom: Ben Thompson's famous revolver, Colt's .45 cal. 1871

TOP: Clay Allison from painting by Lon Pyrtle
BOTTOM: Clay Allison's Colt's .45 cal. revolver

TOP: Frank Leslie

BOTTOM: Frank Leslie's Colt's .45 cal. Peacemaker

Bat became a crack shot, practicing behind the barn with the old musket.

Another essential of his education was provided by occasional trips in the spring wagon to Wichita. That dusty trail town was a place of evil splendor to Bat, with its saloons, gambling houses, dance halls, variety theaters, horse traders' corrals, stores, and hotels, ramshackle as this cow town would have appeared to the infrequent visitor from the East.

Even more fascinating were the men who swaggered along its streets, all of them with a great pride of occupation. You could tell at a glance what a man did for a living—the tall-hatted Texas cowpunchers, the merchants with their boiled shirts and string ties, the scrofulous and blood-smeared buffalo hunters, the gamblers immaculate in broadcloth and silk hats. Of the whole passing scene, the boy gaping from his perch on the hitching rack was especially fascinated by the gamblers. They exuded such a worldly air with their pomaded hair, carefully tended moustaches, diamond rings and heavy gold watch chains, and their measured geniality. But his eyes bugged out even more at the men he heard talked about only in whispers—the gunfighters. Quiet, self-contained men to whom others gave respectful berth along the crowded boardwalks. Lonely men set apart from their fellows by their godlike tendency to dispatch lesser men to another world. And there were the females. They came in two classes, as Bat knew, good and bad. There were the bedizened women of the town, the girls who worked in dance halls, the actresses who played in the variety theaters, and there were women like his mother and sisters. But all these people represented the adventure he knew he would never find following the plough on his father's farm.

He was seventeen when he managed to persuade Ed, who was a year older, that it was time for them to venture forth on their own. Ed agreed that the farm did not produce enough as yet to keep them all in abundance, and that the younger brothers were hefty enough to help their father. The two brothers decided to head for western Kansas, which was enjoying a boom in the buffalo-hide market.

The first place they stopped was Dodge City, the wildest town on the frontier. The Atchison, Topeka, and Santa Fe Railroad was then stretching west through Kansas toward Colorado.

The rail company provided Bat and Ed with their first jobs. They obtained a subcontract from a contractor named Ritter to grade the right of way a mile west from Fort Dodge. It was along that stretch that Front Street sprang up in all its crapulous glory.

When they finished the back-breaking job they found that Mr. Ritter, taking advantage of their innocence, had skipped out and neglected to pay them the three hundred dollars promised for the grading. Heartbroken and purse-broken, they considered their next move.

"I think I'll go home and see Ma and the kids," Ed said. "I've been mighty homesick, Billy, and I can't hide it anymore. You better come with me, as it's better than starving and being cheated out here."

"I'll be damned if I will!" Bat said. "I'm going to stay here and lay for Ritter. He owes us three hundred dollars and he's going to pay up or I'll put a slug in him. I'll just wait here for a while, Ed. Ritter's going to be passing through here one of these days. The railroad will be pushing on for Granada across the Colorado line, and he's got contracts to fill up ahead."

So Ed went home and Bat went to work driving a team for a local tycoon named Tom Nixon, no longer an independent subcontractor, but a mere hireling like the swarm of Orientals and Irish working on the railtracks. Not long afterward, however, a friend came to Bat with the news that Ritter was "coming through on tomorrow's train and has a roll of three thousand dollars on his hip."

Bat, who had bought a six-shooter with his wages as a teamster, was waiting when the westbound train rolled in the next day. He boarded it and found Ritter sitting in one of the cars. He forced his debtor out on the platform at gunpoint. A crowd of loafers had gathered to watch the fun.

"You owe me three hundred dollars," Bat told the spluttering Ritter, "and, damn it all, if you don't pay up you won't get back in that car alive."

"This is robbery, you young whelp." Ritter appealed to the crowd. "Somebody run and get the marshal. I'm being robbed in broad daylight."

Bat jammed the gun in Ritter's ribs. "I'm only collecting what you owe me, and everybody here knows it for a fact. You tried to run out on me and Ed, but you're going to pay off on the barrelhead."

Ritter shrugged, pulled out a roll of bills tied with a buckskin thong, and peeled off three hundred dollars.

The loafers cheered, the elated Bat jumped off the train, and they all headed for the nearest saloon. The drinks, of course, were on Bat. Anyone big enough to see over the bar was served in those days, especially if he clutched three hundred dollars in his fist.

This episode marked Bat Masterson's first gunplay. His vigorous method of collecting his debt also earned a certain amount of respect for him when he joined the buffalo hunt of 1872, a stripling among a hard-bitten and ruthless group of men. The great slaughter of buffalo was just then approaching its gory climax, covertly encouraged by the government, which correctly and coldly foresaw that the day the buffalo herds were killed off would be the day those Indians who were still warlike would be forced to seek food and shelter in the reservations.

Bat managed to buy a Sharps rifle with his hundred-dollars-a-day earnings as a buffalo hunter, but he was not allowed to keep it for long. One day, alone on the prairie, he was approached by five braves of Bear Shield's tribe. They looked peaceable enough, and it had been agreed among the hunters that they should avoid trouble with the Indians, never fire unless fired upon. The braves approached in all amiability, but once they were close the smiles vanished. One of the bucks held Bat at bay with a lance while the others stripped him of rifle and revolver. It was bad enough to be disarmed without putting up a fight, but one of the braves added injury to insult by inflicting a smashing blow on his forehead with the rifle barrel. The braves rode off, leaving Bat with blood dripping in his eyes. He stumbled back to the hunters' camp and proposed that they help him hunt down the Cheyennes.

"The hell with that," the leader of the outfit said. "I'm in favor of high-tailing it for Dodge. There might be war parties out all over the plains."

The hunters and their wagons pulled out that night for Dodge, sixty miles to the north.

Bat, nursing his lacerated scalp and his sorely bruised pride, rode along with them for a few miles and then slipped away on his own. Bear Shield owed him something—like Ritter—and he planned to collect it.

Before dawn he located Bear Shield's pony herd, and an hour later he was headed for Dodge with a fine bunch of stolen horseflesh. The ponies, almost forty of them, brought him twelve hundred dollars in Dodge. Bat felt that was fair recompense for a rifle, a revolver, and a gash on his forehead.

He returned to the buffalo range, joining the hunters on the Salt Fork of the Arkansas, and there he met Wyatt Earp for the first time. Years later all that Earp could remember of that first meeting was that Bat was homesick. Bat, however, would never forget the kindliness with which Earp treated him, nor the impression made on him by the tall, blue-eyed, and steadfast man six years his senior. Bat was particularly impressed by the fact that Earp did not brag and bluster, like the other hunters.

Naturally an exuberant fellow, Bat made a conscious effort to pattern himself after Earp, cultivating a quietly confident manner and learning to hold his tongue. Men like Earp, who were widely respected, he observed, were not given to much pointless conversation.

This admiration of Earp, however, did not extend to being a teetotaller. In that winter encampment Bat learned how to drink in a hardy school indeed.

In the spring of 1874, although barely twenty years old, Bat Masterson was accounted a veteran plainsman and hunter. That spring, in Dodge City, he joined up with an expedition organized by several merchants to strike deep into Indian territory in pursuit of the southward-receding buffalo herds decimated by three years of all-out slaughter above and below the Arkansas.

This further encroachment on the Indians' sacred hunting grounds promised a lot more trouble than any previous forays. According to the Medicine Lodge treaty between the government and the Indians, the Arkansas was to be the "deadline," with the buffalo country to the south reserved to the Indians. Now, prodded along by profit-hungry merchants, the hunters planned to plunge far south of that deadline, through the Indian nations, across the Cimarron, down to the Canadian River, in the Panhandle of Texas.

Bat Masterson, at twenty, was the youngest member of the party. The next youngest and his particular friend was Billy Dixon, who later said he "never knew anyone that loved practical joking" more than Bat.

Bat looked as harum-scarum as he behaved. He had a mop of black hair with oddly contrasting light-gray eyes that danced with deviltry and merriment. He was of medium height, slender but wiry, strong, and resilient. In store clothes and with his hair slicked down, he was described as one of the handsomest young men on the frontier. But it was his slate-gray eyes that attracted attention. Gunfighters came in all shapes, sizes, and temperaments, but almost invariably they had blue eyes. Billy Dixon further noted that for all his fun-loving tendencies Bat was "a chunk of steel," and anybody who struck him in those days drew fire.

Much of Bat Masterson's life makes him appear like the

hero of a picturesque novel. Some of his best friends were murderers and ruffians of the gaudiest hue, and the atmosphere in which he lived for many years was compounded of violence, chicanery, greed, and ruthless devotion to the laws of survival. He never apologized for his friends, and the murky moral climate suited him, but he often seemed to be keeping one foot in heaven.

On the night of June 26, 1874, the buffalo hunters were attacked by Cheyennes and Billy Tyler was killed. It was a terrible battle but Bat escaped without a scratch. In time the battle itself became a rather dim memory to Bat—there was so much other and more personal violence in his life—but he never forgot the dying face of Billy Tyler.

Bat and his companions rode northward through a countryside stiff with terror over the worst Indian outbreak since the Civil War. They reached Dodge without even catching sight of a hostile face, but most of the ranchers, hunters, and traders had cleared out for the nearest post of the United States Cavalry. Dodge was in a state of alarm over the border war. The merchants wore long faces and the buffalo-slaughtering trade was at a standstill.

Although several of Bat's fellow adventurers bought tickets on the first train for the East, Bat thought he should stick around for a while. Pride wouldn't let him go home broke, and staring at the rump of a plough horse seemed as unattractive as ever. So he found himself among the unemployed. He had plenty of company that summer, following the depression of 1873. Buffalo-hunting was suspended until the Indians returned to their reservations.

Bat did not fancy a town job such as counter-jumping in one of the stores—too tame for a fellow who had seen the Indians charging out of the dawn, and had been acclaimed as a hero of that battle. But one could not eat congratulations.

The only occupation that offered employment of his unique talents now was scouting for the army, which was preparing large-scale punitive operations against the tribes. At the invitation of Col. Nelson A. Miles, Bat signed on as a civilian scout at Fort Dodge, and was sent to the Texas Panhandle.

After many months of meritorious service as a scout, Bat Masterson limped back to Dodge City in the summer of 1876. In his Texas Panhandle encounters he had acquired some smashed bones in his pelvis that would always give him trouble and cause him to limp slightly, but there was still pride in the way he walked and held himself.

He was a gaudy figure when he stepped along Front Street

wearing gold-mounted spurs, a crimson Mexican sash, a red silk neckerchief, a gray sombrero with a rattlesnake band, silver-plated and ivory-handled revolvers, silver-studded belt and holster. Out of earshot the wisecrackers along Front Street said any prospective adversary would be blinded by a mere glimpse of the frontier dandy.

Soon after his arrival he was offered a job as a peace officer. The city marshal was Larry Deger, a political type with little taste for the rigors of keeping order in a wild trail town, but the operating head of Dodge City's law enforcement was Wyatt Earp, the assistant marshal. Earp, remembering Bat as a cool-headed youngster among the buffalo hunters a few years before, put him on the force as assistant marshal.

From the start, Bat was an easy-going enforcer of law and order, refusing to take a man in unless he was definitely out of hand—invariably from the effects of "forked lightning" sold as whiskey—and a menace to himself and others.

Tact was a mighty useful and inordinately rare quality in Dodge City in the roaring seventies. There were more hot tempers, touchy dispositions, and ancient grievances rubbing up against each other in that trail town, once the Santa Fe Railroad hooked up with the intersection of cattle trails and the Arkansas River near Dodge, than in any other known district. Everybody had a grudge and an acute sense of pride. It was a hardcase town in a hardcase country.

Bat Masterson was one of the few peace officers in Western history who entered a sheriff's election through the jailhouse door.

Early in 1877 he plied his trade as a gambler in Dodge and elsewhere, joining briefly in a stampede toward the scene of South Dakota gold strikes, halting in Cheyenne instead, and enjoying a fine run of luck at the tables. He lingered so long in Cheyenne that he decided the best claims around Deadwood would already be staked. Besides, he had already absorbed a lesson most gold-rushers learned only through brutal experience: the best pickings were to be found not in the ephemeral veins of ore in the earth, but in other men's pockets.

While returning from Cheyenne to Dodge that spring, Bat ran into Wyatt Earp in a Nebraska crossroads settlement. Earp remarked that he had just been offered the marshal's post in Dodge, since Larry Deger was being eased out of office. The saloon keepers of Dodge wanted a hard-boiled marshal to crack down on lawlessness that summer, when two hundred thousand head of cattle would be coming up the trail from Texas, and with them more than two thousand rumbustious cowhands. Earp suggested that Bat run for sheriff of Ford County, of which Dodge City was the county seat, that autumn, but Bat shook his head at the idea. The prospect of taking the Texans over the gaming tables was much more pleasing than protecting the Dodge City saloons and citizens on a sheriff's pay.

But a street brawl, in which Bat intruded himself in a way that clearly showed he held the majesty of the law in no great esteem, was paradoxically the means of changing Bat's mind.

He was strolling along Main Street shortly after his return to Dodge when he noticed a commotion in which Marshal Larry Deger, whom he regarded as an overblown slob, and a little fellow known as Bobby Gill were the principal figures. Gill, who was slightly wobble-headed, was capering about and jeering at the 300-pound marshal. Deger announced he was taking Gill in on a charge of disturbing the peace. Gill declared this a violation of the right of free speech. The marshall began kicking Gill in the direction of the lock-up.

Bat, quite forgetting his background and training as a lawman, rushed to the prisoner's aid. He clamped an armlock on Deger, who outweighed him by more than 140 pounds, and allowed Gill to scamper away to temporary freedom. Deger then began grappling with his ex-deputy. The marshal, unable to cope with the wiry and infuriated—and possibly half-intoxicated—Bat Masterson, yelled for help. Deputy Marshal Joe Mason snatched Bat's revolver out of its holster. Seeing Bat without his gun gave half a dozen bystanders courage to help subdue him. They held Bat while Deger pistol-whipped him until blood spurted. Even so, it took Deger, Mason, and all their helpers to drag Bat to the jail. Next day he was hauled into court before his old friend Judge Frost and fined twenty-five dollars for fracturing the "peace" of Dodge City's uproarious saloon and red-light district. Bobby Gill was arrested during the night, and made a remorseful plea before the judge: "Jesus Christ died for sinners just as me!" Judge Frost was so touched he let Gill off with a five dollar fine.

A few days later the Dodge City Council showed its sympathy for Bat Masterson by ordering that the fine be remitted.

Somehow this incident convinced the Republicans of Ford County that Bat was the man for the sheriff's office, particularly since Larry Deger, being detached from his marshal's star, was running for sheriff as the nominee of the Democrats.

There were two schools of thought in Dodge regarding how severely the laws should be enforced. The saloon keepers and smaller merchants wanted their property protected and the wilder visitors segregated south of the Santa Fe. They naturally favored stern treatment of Texans who felt the urge to hurrah the town. On the other hand, the big store owners, who handled the large transactions with cattle barons and trail bosses and had become their personal friends, felt the men who brought prosperity to Dodge should be treated more hospitably.

Enough of both factions believed Bat was the man to wear the sheriff's badge. They knew he could be tough, but preferred not to be. Bat agreed to run for sheriff, if for no other reason than to beat Deger out of the job. At the same time he bought a piece of the Lone Star Dance Hall with his winnings at Cheyenne, so he would not suffer financially from assuming public office.

It was a close election. The town was pretty well divided on the subject of Masterson *versus* Deger. Deger had more political influence, Masterson more general popularity. Bat was elected by a margin of three votes in November, 1877, for a two-year term.

Bat would have been entirely happy that autumn of 1877 but for the presence of his brother Ed, who had returned to Dodge during the summer and signed on as a deputy marshal. Bat liked having Ed around—he probably loved his brother more than anyone else in the world—but not as a peace officer. Ed just wasn't cut out for it. He was gentle, easy-going, liked everyone, and was liked by everyone who knew him longer than a minute.

Despite Bat's warnings to him that he was no gunfighter, Ed had a run-in with a gunslinger on the night of April 9, 1878, and was fatally wounded. He died in Bat's arms as the latter wept like a child.

Life never looked quite so good to Bat Masterson after that April night his brother was killed. Nothing ever hit him so hard as his brother's death, and nothing ever would.

Bat never did have any time for politics, and he couldn't keep it out of the sheriff's office, hard as he tried. Near the end of his term he came to the conclusion that it was time to move on, especially as his fellow citizens in Dodge City had shown a disappointing preference for beer and bartenders over all-out law enforcement. Bat took his leave of Dodge City with a certain amount of regret—it was the place where he achieved youthful fame—but he would be back soon enough and his guns would be speaking for him in another defense of the family honor.

Tombstone seemed the place to go. That little hellhole in Arizona was reported to be bursting with easy money, violence, and opportunity for the quick-witted.

Tombstone was in its uproarious heydey when Bat appeared there in 1881. Wyatt Earp, Earp's brothers Virgil and Morgan, and Doc Holliday were already established there.

Tombstone attracted the high-rollers, not only because of the proximity of fabulous silver mines in the vicinity, but because it had natural advantages for men who lived outside the law.

Bat's stay in Tombstone was comparatively short—he decided that Trinidad, Colorado, offered greater opportunities to a man of his talents. The day after his arrival there he pinned on the badge of a deputy sheriff of Las Animas County, and later served as city marshal of Trinidad.

Not nearly so lively as Dodge City, Trinidad was determined to keep the lawless elements under control, which probably explains the thousand-dollars-per-month salary paid to Bat Masterson as the chief law-enforcement officer.

When Bat left Trinidad in the mid-eighties for livelier scenes and more lucrative opportunities he made his home base in Denver, but wandered through the Western Border towns and mining camps for several years as a free-lance gambler. Occasionally he would take on an assignment to restore or preserve the peace. In the meantime, of course, he was always ready to rescue a friend or take a hand in straightening out the civic affairs of Dodge City. In appreciation, the citizens of Dodge during the Fourth of July celebration in 1885, voted Bat "the most popular man in Dodge City," and awarded him a gold-headed cane, which he carried for many years. Many duplicates of this cane were made, which Bat presented to friends, even to an Indian chief with whom he palavered, and to governors and United States senators—unto this day it is his symbol, his trademark. He became an adept in using the cane as a secondary weapon—it bruised, but it did not kill.

For several years Bat continued his stern supervision over Dodge City, and was practically a commuter between there and Colorado. In 1884 he decided to start his own newspaper in Dodge, which he called *Vox Populi*. It did not survive its first edition, but Bat did, which was more than some people expected, considering the things he printed about some of the citizens.

Then the temperance movement hit Dodge, and Bat Masterson jumped into the controversy with both feet and became involved on both sides before it was over. The following spring Bat did a complete and unexplained flipflop. He became a convert to the prohibition cause, and fought just as hard to close Dodge's saloons as he had campaigned less than a year earlier to keep them open. Perhaps he had gone on the wagon himself—he occasionally forswore hard liquor and apparently became as insufferable as most drinkers while on the sarsaparilla—and like all converts wanted to carry others with him.

A legendary figure like Bat Masterson inspires an amazing assortment of untrue or distorted stories from hero-worshipping would-be historians and mouth-to-mouth gossips. Bat was widely credited with killing twenty and thirty men in gunfights. The actual number, to his eternal credit, was only three. Unable to dissuade the legend-makers, he actually handed out guns with twenty-odd notches to souvenir-hunters who wanted to buy "the gun you killed all those men with," and took his friends out to buy a drink with the proceeds.

Bat Masterson was no superman who believed that his sixshooter placed him above natural and human law. It can be said that he never killed anyone except in defense of himself or a friend.

Since he and his associates lived by the gun, it might be well to examine the qualities which made Bat shoot better than the next man when it came to a showdown with a Colt .45. For young and inexperienced gunfighters, he had a masterly standard discourse on the subject:

> The main thing is to shoot first and never miss.
> Never try to run a bluff with a six-gun. Many a man has been buried with his boots on because he foolishly tried to scare someone by reaching for his hardware. Always remember that a six-shooter is made to kill the other fellow with and for no other reason on earth. So always have your gun loaded and ready, and never reach for it unless you are in dead earnest and intend to kill the other fellow.
> A lot of inexperienced fellows try to aim a six-shooter by sighting along the barrel, and they try to shoot the other man in the head. Never do that. If you have to stop a man with a gun, grab the stock of your six-shooter with a deathgrip that won't let it wobble, and try to hit him just where the belt buckle would be. That's the broadest target from head to foot.
> If you point at something, you don't raise your finger to level of the eye and sight along it; you simply point, by in-

96

stinct, and your finger will always point straight. So you must learn to point the barrel of your six-shooter by instinct. If you haven't that direction instinct born in you, you will never become an expert with the six-gun.

The qualities a man needed to qualify as a man-killing expert with the revolver, Bat Masterson believed, were courage, skill at handling his weapon, and, not the least, steadiness, the ability and coolness to make the first shot.

Like most professionals, Bat had little respect for trick shooting when it came to a showdown. It was all right for exhibitions and friendly contests, but not when facing an opponent.

In 1890 Bat became associated with Ed Chase's elaborate Palace gambling hall on Blake Street, in Denver. He managed the burlesque troupe housed in the Palace Theater, a sort of dream job, considering the fact that some of the most beautiful women west of Chicago were cavorting there.

Bat Masterson selected his own wife from among the ladies of the Palace ensemble. She was a blonde song-and-dance girl named Emma Walters, a native of Philadelphia, and a comparative veteran of show business. Bat was thirty-seven and his bride thirty-four when they were married on November 21, 1891. Emma realized she was marrying a sporting man, who slept days and was out on the town from sunset to dawn. She was content to stay in the background while Bat lived in the limelight. Since the marriage lasted until the day he died, two months short of their thirtieth wedding anniversary, it may be presumed that she was able to adjust herself to Bat's night-roaming proclivities. The marriage was childless.

A few months after they were married Bat gave up the job of managing the Palace burlesque troupe. He went to Creede as manager of a gambling house and saloon. Emma had given up her career and was pleased with the change. Bat was riding the water wagon with a bridegroom's good intentions, and devoted most of his time to business.

During a period of discontent Bat decided to enter boxing promotion. Prizefighting had been his favorite sport for a long time. Perhaps it came closest to the hand-to-hand combats of his youth. All other sports seemed effete by comparison.

Never having been a boxer, and having preferred to use his cane instead of his fists when dealing with unruly drunks as a peace officer, Bat acquired a considerable knowledge of boxing as a second and a referee. He was in Jake Kilrain's corner when Kilrain lost the heavyweight championship to John L. Sullivan in New Orleans. But he was far from infallible in picking winners. He dropped a large bet on Kilrain against John L. He went broke backing Charlie Mitchell in the latter's fight against James J. Corbett. And he was anything but prophetic in predicting the outcome of the fight in Carson City, Nevada, between the graceful and spectacular Gentleman Jim Corbett and the small, angular Bob Fitzsimmons.

Bat was discomfited in pride and pocketbook by the spectacle of Corbett, the old dancing master, going down under the sharpshooting fists of the bald Australian.

What may have impelled Bat to enter fight promotion was the threat that Soapy Smith, one of the old West's most notorious crooks, would take over and make a travesty of a sport that Bat regarded with a certain primitive reverence. Soapy, in fact, did take a fling at matchmaking, and the result was almost disastrous enough to ruin the fight game forever in Denver.

As an aftermath, the Colorado Athletic Association was organized on April 9, 1899. Less than a month later Otto Floto, the sports editor of the *Denver Post*, used the influence he had acquired in that position, and his closeness to the two powerful political men who published the *Post*, to freeze out competition to himself as promoter.

Bat found that being a fight promoter was a great deal more complicated than merely signing up pugs and counting the box-office receipts. In the first place, prizefighting was illegal in Colorado, and the promoter had to go through the motion of obtaining an injunction to prevent the Denver Fire and Police Commission from interfering with the fight. The commissioners, mostly staunch sporting men themselves, never opposed the injunction.

Floto, by making every use of the powerful influence of his employers, F. G. Bonfils and Harry Tammen, took every unfair advantage of Bat he could in his effort to control the business. The feud produced legislation which resulted in breaking both Floto and Masterson.

At the turn of the century Bat was forty-six years old, broke, ill-fitted for the pursuit of any career outside gambling and the sporting life.

Theodore Roosevelt, then President of the United States, had met Bat on one of his Western tours. Hearing through mutual friends that Bat needed a job, he offered him the post of United States Marshal for the state of Oklahoma. Bat's refusal was one of the sadder verbal mementoes of the old West:

> I am not the man for the job. Oklahoma is still woolly, and if I were marshal some youngster would want to try to put me out because of my reputation. I would be a bait for grown-up kids who had fed on dime novels. I would have to kill or be killed. No sense to that. I have taken my guns off, and I don't ever want to put them on again.

Bat brooded over the way Otto Floto had taken advantage of him. One evening in July he trailed the oversized Floto to a café at Sixteenth and Champa streets, near the *Denver Post* building. When Floto emerged there was a tangle, Bat using the gold-headed cane he carried to good advantage. Floto thought it best to run, and, big as he was, outdistanced Bat. However, Bat had managed to give him a good beating with his cane.

As a result of this escapade Bat was forced to leave Denver, due to the pressure exerted by Bonfils and Tammen. He went home to pack, and told his wife he was going East and would send for her. Nobody went to the depot with him except two detectives who had been detailed to see that he got on the first train out of town.

Bat Masterson arrived in New York City early in June 1902, disillusioned with the West and eager to test the truth of the claim that no metropolis in the world knows better how to treat a celebrity, no matter what his leasehold to fame. He liked the looks of the big town.

Three days after his arrival he stood on the corner of West 69th Street and Columbus Avenue talking to two card sharks he had known in Dodge City, and whom he had met again by chance. The long arm of the law reached and grabbed the three of them. They were charged with fleecing an elder of the Mormon Church on a train which had arrived in New York that day. It was a bum rap for Bat, as he hadn't even been on the train, and had just run into the two crooks.

He was quickly released when his New York friends heard of his arrest. But the New York Police were not quite through with him. They had little affection for Westerners who felt naked without their personal armament. On June 15 Bat was picked up again, and charged with carrying a concealed weapon. This time he complained to a reporter of the *New York World*.

"Why, there's thousands of jokers running wild in New York carrying guns bigger than mine, and not a word said about it. Why did I carry it? Well, I'm accustomed to carrying bunches of money in the night, when good people are asleep."

The reporter made a good story out of it, and again Bat was turned loose. This time he decided to hang up his gun belt for good.

President Theodore Roosevelt, in Washington, read the story in the papers and decided Bat needed a job to keep him out of mischief.

The President telegraphed Bat, offered him the post of United States Marshal for the southern district of New York. This time Bat accepted it. It was a political sinecure, a desk job, and there was no chance of running into trigger-happy youngsters such as abounded in the West. The marshal's job made Emma Masterson happy too, for it had the solid virtues of a government salary and daytime hours. Bat lost no time in bringing her to New York and finding a suitable apartment.

In exchange for providing him with a place on the federal payroll, President Roosevelt insisted on Bat's coming down to Washington occasionally and talking with him on two of his favorite subjects—the old West and prizefighting.

The visits continued even after Bat resigned as Federal Marshal to enter journalism.

Bat had known the Lewis brothers, New York newspaper and magazine writers from New York, when they ventured to Dodge City to write Western stories. In New York he renewed the acquaintance. W. E. Lewis provided Bat with a job as sports editor on the *Morning Telegraph*, and the other Lewis brother, Alfred Henry, became Bat's constant companion, chief admirer, and propagandist.

Bat made the transition from Federal Marshal to sports editor of the *Morning Telegraph* with more grace and ease than might be expected. He had long been inclined in that direction, and the job combined his love of sports, particularly boxing, with his flair for expressing himself with the vividness demanded of a sports writer. It is not easy to take up a new profession when a man is past fifty, but Bat had just written a series on gunfighters for *Human Life* magazine that was well received and gave him a certain amount of confidence.

As the years went by Bat was more than satisfied with his life in New York. He no longer felt any overwhelming nostalgia for the West. He had gained a wide reputation for his fearless writing. Four-square to all the winds that blew, he despised hypocrisy and dishonesty, and he had a forceful way of expressing his feelings.

By the time the 1920s rolled around, Bat and the men of his generation were trying to adjust themselves to a strange new world. Prohibition had come, and Bat could not give his approval to the speakeasy, the blind tiger, and the beer flat which had succeeded the saloons. The tommy-gun had taken the place of the six-shooter. Well-organized gangsters had supplanted the badmen, the horse thieves, the cattle rustlers, and stage robbers of the old days. It was a different world to Bat Masterson.

In 1921 Bat was sixty-seven years old, a gentle old fellow, mellow and good-natured, except when he wrote of the frauds and pretenders of the prize ring.

On October 25, 1921, shortly before noon, Bat strolled up Eighth Avenue from his apartment to the *Morning Telegraph* office and wrote his column for the next day. Fifteen minutes after he finished it he died alone in his office, slumped over his rolltop desk. A more prosaic death scene for a less prosaic man could hardly be imagined. When his body was found, his last column was clutched in his hand.

Bat's death was reported on the front pages of the afternoon editions of the New York papers, one of which said: "He died at his desk gripping his pen with the tenacity with which he formerly clung to his six-shooter."

Emma Masterson lived another eleven years, faithful unto eternity. As her obituary in the *New York Herald-Tribune* said: "She remained an obscure figure behind the bright flare of her husband's fame."

Colt's Army .45-caliber (New Service Model of 1909)

5   Henry Starr

HENRY STARR has been called, by those who should know, the most spectacular outlaw who ever operated in the Southwest, with the possible exception of Jesse James. Not that Jesse's exploits were more spectacular than Starr's, but he was able to remain out of prison all the years of his bandit career, whereas Henry Starr spent three-fourths of his time behind prison walls.

An uncanny marksman and a man with a strange sense of honor, Henry was known as "The Bearcat" because of his cunning and his forthright courage. Yet a large share of the notoriety which surrounded this gunman was probably due to the fact that he bore the same name as Bella Starr. Indeed, there were stories that he was her son and some said he was her brother-in-law. Actually Henry was no blood relation to Bella Starr at all. He was Sam Starr's cousin, and as such a cousin-in-law to the infamous Bella.

Henry's career as probably America's most spectacular bank robber didn't actually begin until four years after Bella was shot in the back in 1889. He was the only man who ever successfully carried off two robberies in the same town on the same day. That feat had been tried unsuccessfully, and with dire results, by the Daltons at Coffeyville, Kansas, years before Starr did it in 1915. And if ever a man died with his boots on, in the popular phrase, Starr did. He was mortally wounded trying to carry out a bank robbery in the grand

102

tradition of the Western frontier as late as 1921, three years after the end of World War I. It was the last of the outlaw-breed bank robberies, and Starr was probably the last of the breed.

Henry was a man of vast personal incongruities. Although he made no excuse for his devastating career as an outlaw, other than to blame a mistake by the law when he was a youth, in his personal habits Starr was a man of strong moral convictions. He was not addicted to liquor, tobacco, coffee, or tea, and was the son of well-to-do parents. Although he stole thousands of dollars during his long career, he died a pauper. His only assets were his burial expenses, paid years before to a Tulsa, Oklahoma, undertaker. At the time he said that he was certain he would die while performing some robbery, and he did not wish to bring unnecessary hardship to those he left behind.

Henry Starr first saw the light of day on December 2, 1873, at Fort Gibson, Indian Territory. He was the son of George (Hop) Starr, a half-breed Cherokee, and Mary Scott, a quarter-blood. He attended the Cherokee Indian Mission until his eleventh birthday, when he left school following the death of his father. At first Henry attempted to shoulder the responsibility of taking care of his mother and two brothers. Two years later his mother remarried, and Henry, after trying in vain to get along with his stepfather, finally left home and became a cowboy on one of the large cattle ranches then scattered over the Cherokee Nation.

Although it is known that Henry Starr and Bella Starr had a brief alliance in the late eighties, Henry did not run foul of the law until 1892, when he was arrested on a charge of horse-stealing. According to Starr's own story the arrest was an unfair one and embittered him to the point where he turned completely to a life of crime. Starr, then a youngster, claimed that the horse in question was a stray and wandered into the pasture of the ranch, where he was working. He watched it for several days and when nobody claimed the animal he mounted it and rode into Nowata. The owner of the animal saw him, recognized the horse, and had Henry arrested as a thief. Starr spent several months in jail before the trial, at which he was acquitted.

"When they let me out I was bitter against the world," Starr said. "I decided that if they sent people to jail when they had violated no law they couldn't do more to a real criminal. Having been branded a criminal, I thought I might as well be one in fact.

103

"I was only a kid, and father and mother had brought me up to think it was an awful disgrace to be in jail. They chained me to a bed that time. That was a bad thing to do to a kid. I was innocent. When I was released I felt that I might as well be dead as disgraced. I came out of that jail with blood in my eye."

Henry Starr was nineteen at the time, and from that day on he was an outlaw. An incurable gambler, Starr had disastrous luck at cards. He regularly turned over every penny he made or stole to those with whom he gambled, and yet he never held up a gambling table—another example of his strange sense of honor. Henry robbed his first bank at Caney, Kansas, in 1893, and after that kept his purse full from the proceeds of attacks on small country banks.

"Guess Henry just figured that the banks owed him what he could take from them, is the way I look at it," remarked an old-time friend of the outlaw. "I don't believe he thought it was wrong. I know he thoroughly enjoyed raiding. He's told me of how he laughed inwardly until he could hardly control himself at the enormous fright some victim banker would show when Starr and his men would step in and take charge of all the loose currency with the 'Hands up and hands steady' that Starr always sung out."

That was Henry, a recklessly bold practical joker at heart; but a gunman at hand. His complete underestimation of the dangers involved in his illegal occupation accounted for Henry's somewhat surprising record as a highwayman. He was wounded on several occasions and was captured several times. These misfortunes didn't seem to provide any serious deterrent to his choice of career. He kept right on holding up banks—even after he was paroled from prison sentences on two occasions, once when Teddy Roosevelt was President of the United States.

During the early part of his career Henry was implicated in cattle and horse thefts, the robbery of the Carter store in Nowata, the Schufeldt store in Lenapah, the stick-up of the depot at Nowata and of the M.K.T. train at Adair. In 1812 the express office at Nowata was robbed by masked men who made their getaway on horseback. One of the robbers' mounts bolted into a wire fence and its rider was thrown. The horse ran away and was found later wearing a saddle Henry Starr had borrowed from a friend.

A few days later Henry rode into Lenapah, in Nowata County, and was recognized by Floyd Wilson, a deputy marshal and special officer for the Iron Mountain Railroad. The men rode up to each other on horseback, Wilson pulling his Winchester in a gesture for Henry to surrender. The rifle jammed and Henry pulled out his six-gun, calling to the officer to give up, that he didn't want to shoot him. Wilson was game, and believed he could get his man. He pulled his revolver. Starr's strange sense of fair play prevailed. Even though his pistol was already drawn Henry allowed Wilson to get in the first shot. The bullet whizzed past him and Starr answered with a bullet through Wilson's heart.

It was two years before the law caught up with Henry, and during that time he fashioned a career which was fairly remarkable for the times. In January, 1893, he and several others shot up the town of Choteau, Indian Territory, and robbed two general stores and the depot. A few days later they robbed the general store and depot at Inola, Indian Territory. On March 25 Henry tried his first bank robbery. With a friend, Frank Chaney, he stuck up the Caney Valley National Bank and got away with $4,900. His notoriety spread, and by April dozens of lesser-known bandits were offering him their services.

Starr's escapades were not without their romantic overtones, either. On March 5, 1893, his gang held up the Katy passenger train at Pryor Creek, Oklahoma. They seized a $6,000-consignment of diamonds. During the robbery, a young girl named Mary Morrison, of Joplin, Missouri, rushed past Starr and leaped off the train. Starr was standing on the platform of the first coach in order to direct the operations of his men. The work of robbing the train took about half an hour, after which Starr and his men rode off through the woods. Half a mile from the scene the desperadoes found the young girl cowering in the weeds, half crazy with fright. Starr carried the near-petrified young woman to the outlaw camp and sat up consoling her all night. In the morning he sent her with one of his men as an escort to catch the train from Nowata to Joplin. But he had been smitten. Two weeks later Henry rode into Joplin and visited Mary Morrison. A brief courtship followed, and then Henry Starr, under his alias of Jackson, married Miss Morrison.

Riding into Arkansas on June 6, 1893, Henry and his men held up and robbed the bank at Bentonville of nearly $12,-000. With the law in close pursuit, the band broke up, and Henry met his wife in the Osage Hills and they started for Emporia, Kansas. It was their intention to go to California, where they could start a new life. With them was Kid Wilson, another desperado whom Henry had come to know since the start of his wild and lawless escapades.

In Colorado Springs, Colorado, Henry Starr was recognized by a man named William Feuerstine, a resident of Fort Smith, Arkansas, who was in Colorado on business. On July 3, the local police found that John Wilson, and Frank and Mary Jackson, had registered at the Spaulding House. On July 4th, the trio returned from a sight-seeing tour at Manitou Springs, and Henry and his wife remained at the hotel. Wilson rode on to a bawdy house, where he was later arrested. Henry had left his wife at the hotel and gone to get some supper. At the restaurant he was arrested without a struggle and taken to the city jail. Mrs. Starr was arrested at her hotel room, but was later released. Under her pillow the police found $500 in gold coin and $1,460 in currency.

The prisoners were taken back to Fort Smith by Deputy Marshal William Smith, who had been dispatched there by "Hanging Judge" Parker's Court. Henry was indicted for the killing of Deputy Marshal Wilson, as well as being jointly indicted with Kid Wilson for the holdup and robbery of the Bentonville, Arkansas, bank. Starr was convicted of murder and sentenced to be hanged. His attorney appealed to the United States Supreme Court and he was awarded a second trial. This happened twice. In March of 1898 he pleaded guilty to manslaughter and was sentenced to five years in the Columbus, Ohio, prison. Kid Wilson was convicted on several counts of robbery and was sentenced to serve twenty-four years in the penitentiary at Brooklyn, New York. While he was waiting to be taken to Columbus a strange incident took place in the Fort Smith jail, one which indicates yet again that Henry Starr had an uncanny sense of justice. It also shows that if luck sometimes looked the other way on Henry Starr, he did at times manufacture a little of his own.

Occupying a nearby cell in the jail was Crawford Goldsby, better known as "Cherokee Bill," one of America's most vicious murderers. Cherokee Bill was born at Fort Concho, Texas, February 8, 1876, of mixed Negro, Indian, and white blood. His father was a member of the famous Tenth Cavalry, colored, of the United States Army, and was of Mexican extraction with white and Indian blood mixed in. His mother, Ellen Beck, was half Negro, a fourth Cherokee, and a fourth white. Cherokee Bill was educated at Cherokee, Kansas, and at the Catholic Indian School at Carlisle, Pennsylvania, until he was twelve. His parents separated soon after his birth. By the time he was eighteen Goldsby was a burly, mean, undisciplined trouble-maker.

After shooting a Negro named Jack Lewis, Goldsby, and two other tough customers, Jim and Bill Cook, escaped into Indian Territory and in the spring of 1894 got a woman named Crittenden to draw their share of money being paid by the Federal Government to the Indians of the Cherokee Strip. Soon after receiving the money they went on a monumental bender. Two nights later a sheriff's posse finally trapped them in a house, and in the ensuing fracas Sequoyah Houston, who had a Cherokee warrant to arrest Cook on a larceny charge, was killed. Following the battle, in which Goldsby escaped, one of the members of his makeshift gang referred to him as "Cherokee Bill" and the name stuck.

Soon afterward the famous Cook Gang was organized. Its members were Bill Cook, Henry Munson, Curtis "Chicken" Gordon, Sam Williams, known as the "Verdigras Kid," and Cherokee Bill Goldsby. In 1894 the gang robbed the Schufeldt store in Lenapah, and Bill shot an onlooker at a window across the street from the scene because the man "was annoying him."

Goldsby was finally captured by two deputies, Isaac Rogers and Clint Scales, after they first attempted to drug him with morphine-loaded whiskey, and then knocked him cold with their pistols. A huge crowd attended the trial, which opened in February, 1895, before Hanging Judge Parker. Goldsby was accused of killing thirteen men.

Cherokee Bill was awaiting his trip to the gallows when Henry Starr was confined in a nearby cell. On July 26, 1895, a gun was smuggled into the jail. The weapon was tied at the end of a long pole and thrust through the window of Bill's cell during the night. Bill later said the gun was supplied by Ben Howell, believed to have been a confederate of the Doolin and Dalton gangs.

On the afternoon of July 26 a guard named Lawrence Keating came in to lock the cells following a free period in the jail and found Cherokee Bill's foot blocking his cell door. As he leaned to move the badman out of the way Bill shot him dead. Then the loco Indian went on a rampage, exchanging shots with the guards and gobbling like a turkey every time he fired. He finally backed into his own cell, from where he could fire without exposing himself. The guards retired to discuss the situation. That was when Henry Starr volunteered to disarm the wild man. Without a word he walked down the runway, swung open the door to Cherokee Bill's cage, and

107

entered. The officers, safe around the corner, heard only a faint whispering. A few minutes later Starr stepped out, locked the cell, and delivered the badman's gun to the astonished officers. Henry never explained how he had unarmed the vicious Cherokee Bill.

After another trial for the killing of Keating, followed by numerous appeals, Cherokee Bill was finally hanged on March 17, 1896. When he stepped on to the gallows and was asked if he had any last comment to make, Bill's reply was the classic: "I came here to die, not to make a speech."

Superstitious persons might be interested in one facet of Cherokee Bill's life. The number 13 appeared with almost supernatural regularity throughout his days. It took Judge Parker 13 minutes to instruct the jury. There were 13 witnesses against Bill, the jury and baliff numbered 13, and the trial lasted 13 hours. Bill was first sentenced to die April 13, and the gaurd was killed on March 26—twice 13. Bill is said to have fired 13 shots during his escape attempt, and there were 13 steps up the gallows the day he was hanged. There were 13 knots in the hangman's noose and the trap was sprung at exactly 2:13 p.m. Also Bill is said to have murdered 13 men.

Starr's heroic act in disarming Cherokee Bill eventually led to his pardon, but he served eight of his thirteen years before that act was brought to the attention of Teddy Roosevelt. During those eight years Henry devoted himself to reading, particularly law books. Upon leaving prison he announced his intention of settling down on his farm near Tulsa and trying to obtain a law degree. During his prison stay Henry had made the acquaintance of Al Jennings, an Oklahoma outlaw, who was also intending to go straight when he was released. Later Starr said his intentions were honest.

"I meant it. That's why I named my son after Roosevelt— Roosevelt Starr."

In 1907, after he and his wife had lived in Tulsa for a while and successfully operated a real estate business, the monotony of his everyday existence began to pall on Henry Starr. He moved to Skiatook. Meanwhile Oklahoma became a state, and the Starrs were among the notables at the inauguration of Charles N. Haskell, its first governor. But Arkansas had not forgotten the Bentonville bank holdup. When Oklahoma became a state, Arkansas authorities asked that Starr be returned on an indictment. Starr was uneasy while awaiting Haskell's decision. Finally he had a friend call the governor's office to find out what that decision was. The friend misunderstood the answer. He thought the secretary had said "He's granted it" instead of "He hasn't granted it."

Starr fled west and joined his old pal Kid Wilson, who also had been released from prison. On Friday, March 13, 1908, the two men robbed the bank in Tyro, Kansas, and escaped. Starr had carried out his operations in his usual daring manner. The bandits fled into the Osage Indian country with a posse in hot pursuit. Women even took part in the chase, telephoning the whereabouts of the outlaws, who had made off with $2,500. Throughout the day messages poured into the sheriffs' offices.

"The outlaws have just stopped on a hill above our house."

"The bank robbers just stopped here and asked for a drink of water."

One posse blundered by accident into the outlaws when they stopped at an oil camp and ordered the cook to prepare dinner. The posse had taken a pack of trail hounds with them, and a hunting horn was dangling from the saddlehorn of one posseman.

"What the hell you fellows want?" Starr asked.

"Why, we're wolf-hunting and we're looking for a bob-tailed hound of mine. Have you seen him?" came the reply.

"Damn you and your bob-tailed hound," Starr snapped. "You're after me and you know it. Get their guns, boys."

Starr's usual good humor and sense of sportsmanship prevailed. After emptying the posse's guns and restoring them to the owners, he recognized one man in the group, A. P. Tullock. This man had been a member of a posse which had captured Starr on a previous occasion. He had sworn to kill Tullock at the time.

"I have a notion to kill you," Starr said to Tullock as he walked over to him.

"Don't do that without giving him a chance, Henry," said one of the outlaws who had assisted in the Tyro robbery.

"I guess you're right. Give him a gun and I'll fight it out with him."

Tullock knew Starr's reputation as a gunman, and begged not to be killed. The genial outlaw finally conceded. In the distance he saw two other riders galloping as though a prairie fire was chasing them.

"Who are those fellows, and what's their hurry?" Starr asked one of the lawmen.

"I don't know anything about them."

"Better tell me the truth or I'll kill you," Starr snapped.

The posseman told him one of the riders was a man named

Cunningham, and the pair were probably racing to warn the other lawmen scouring the countryside.

Almost smiling, Starr remarked: "I'm gonna have to kill that Cunningham one of these fine days."

Before Starr and his men made their getaway the entire area was in an uproar. Posses shot at each other; one account put it this way:

> It was reported that natives all along the road were out with corn knives and shotguns and it would be dangerous for a stranger to pass along the highway after the sun had set. Behind every fence post and in every clump of weeds lingered one man or a dozen, ready to shoot down a bank robber or a peaceable citizen without the last provocation.

Henry Starr, however, made a clean getaway. It was remarkable that nobody was killed. But Starr had that reputation. He once claimed he never had killed a man with the exception of Deputy Marshal Wilson, and that is generally conceded to be the truth, with the possible exception of Kid Wilson.

An acquaintance once described Henry's ability with a gun as almost unbelievable. This man was taken to meet Starr in a thicket hideout where Starr was relaxing following a stick-up. They were taking in the sunshine on the bank of a stream, and the heads of turtles bobbed up through the shining surface of the water. The man remarked that he had heard of Starr's ability with a pistol. Without further word Henry stood up, and pulling both guns fired twelve shots, hitting a turtle with every one.

He never seemed to lose his sense of humor either. Once, after robbing a bank and making off with a great deal of paper material by mistake, he commented to a friend: "These things are of no value to us, but I'd hate to see the farmers have to pay."

The papers were all mortgages and loan records. Starr went through all the papers and delivered each one personally to the names therein. Tears of gratitude and words of thanks flowed in the wake of Henry's many visits, and as he left each place he remarked: "Be sure to burn those papers, and if the loan sharks try to get you to sign another, tell them to go to hell."

On one occasion after robbing a bank in Caney, Kansas, Starr and his band shot craps in a barn all night; then when the sheriff rode into the yard Starr called a temporary truce and walked out, shaking hands warmly, as though they were old pals.

"I'm going to leave here at three o'clock. There are three of us. If you don't want your men hurt you better get them out of the way. When we start we're going through the lines. You tell your men that for me."

The sheriff told his men, and within five minutes there wasn't a man within rifle range of Henry. At three o'clock he and his men rode away unmolested. On another occasion, when a sheriff's posse was on his trail, friends went to warn him. They found Henry calmly trailing the sheriff.

"If I keep him in front of me all the time I'll know exactly where he is," Henry commented at their surprise.

In the summer of 1908 Wilson and Starr robbed the Amity, Colorado, bank and escaped. Starr remained within ten miles of the town while the Colorado authorities were scouring the countryside for him. A few months later Starr and Kid Wilson parted company—Starr later telling friends he was afraid Wilson was going berserk and would kill him. Wilson was never seen or heard of again, but in later years Starr reported as having told a friend: "Wilson won't bother anyone else." Wilson's fate is still a matter of conjecture.

After splitting with Wilson, Starr went to Arizona, where he felt he would be safe from the Colorado authorities. Needing money, he wrote to a man he believed was a friend and asked him to dispose of an Indian allotment he had in Tulsa and to send him the money. The trust was misplaced. The real estate dealer promptly gave the Colorado police Starr's address and Arizona officers arrested Henry. The daring outlaw was captured and returned to Colorado, where in 1909 he was tried and sentenced to twenty-five years in the State Penitentiary.

Henry Starr conducted himself as a model inmate of the prison, finally convincing the warden and others that he was going to give up his outlaw career and live a respectable life. He was a smooth talker, and soon had most of the prison personnel on his side. Henry served only four years, and was pardoned by the governor in 1913 on the agreement that he would never again set foot in Oklahoma. Here once again is shown Starr's utter contempt for the authorities. He remained in Colorado only a few months and then returned to his home state. Taking the alias of "R. L. Williams," which was the name of a candidate for governor, Henry settled in a bungalow at 1534 East Second Street. Gas and light meters were registered to Laura Williams, Starr's wife, as was the telephone. Two doors away lived Jim Woolley, the sheriff of Tulsa County. Next door was the city's largest school and every day at recess children played in the backyard of the noted outlaw.

During this period Al Jennings, who had returned to Oklahoma and settled down after his release from prison, was running for the Democratic gubernatorial nomination against Robert L. Williams, J. B. A. Robertson, Charles West, and Robert Dunlop. Probably to muddle the situation as much as possible for Williams, the favorite candidate, Henry Starr had his alias of R. L. Williams placed on the ticket to help his pal Jennings. But Robert L. Williams won the election anyway. It was a typical stunt for Henry to pull, however, and many folks got a big laugh out of it in later years.

Many of Starr's close friends believed that during this phase of his career he also directed many of the numerous bank robberies in Oklahoma from his quiet little home in Tulsa. On March 27, 1915, Starr led his men in the most daring robbery of his entire career. The dual attack on the city of Stroud, Lincoln County, Oklahoma, was his masterpiece. Starr later said he planned the robbery for his son's sake.

"I wanted to make a stake for him. I wanted to make a big haul, fix the boy out, and go off somewhere and be forgotten."

The Stroud hold-ups were daringly planned. The robbers rode into town, tethered their horses to the stockyard fence, left one of their number in charge of the mounts, and then held up and robbed the town's two banks of more than five thousand dollars. As the robbers rushed to make good their escape Paul Curry, a fifteen-year-old boy, ran into a butcher's shop, grabbed a sawed-off rifle, and fired at the bandits. The bullet smacked into Starr's leg, shattering it. Louis Estes, another of the robbers, was shot in the neck and captured. As Starr fell the youth cried: "Throw away your gun or I'll kill you sure!" Starr complied.

"I am a bank robber and have been caught. That's all there is to say," Starr shrugged.

Convicted at Chandler, Starr was sentenced to twenty-five years. His life was saved before the trial by the veteran peace officer Bill Tilghman, who quickly quelled a threatened lynching. The remainder of the bandits escaped with the loot and were never caught.

In prison Starr's charm, good nature, and amazing knack of convincing penal authorities of his sincerity once again won him a parole. In 1919 Governor Robertson granted him a pardon. This time the parole petition had on it the signatures of the prosecuting attorney, the judge who presided at the trial, and most of the jurors who convicted him. Starr had convinced the whole group that he was going into the motion picture business.

"After all, there's more money in the motion picture business than there is in bank-robbing," pointed out the Lincoln County prosecutor.

He was right. Starr went into the motion picture business with great vigor. A company was quickly formed and the first film was a re-enactment of the infamous Stroud robbery complete to the last detail, with Starr playing himself. The picture even included the youth who had shot him. Starr made considerable money out of the picture and was the leading character in several others that followed. George Davis, a motion picture official in Tulsa, said that Starr received an offer from Hollywood to assist in staging a bank robbery, after which the possibility of engaging him in other Western films was to be considered.

Starr was mulling over the offer when he went to Harrison, Arkansas, to his death. It would seem strange that on the brink of what promised to be a surprising career as a motion picture actor, Starr would have suddenly turned back to his old habits. But the urge must have been in his blood, and he could not resist it. Davis said that he believed Starr had been engaged in bank-robbing almost from the time he was paroled. While making pictures, Starr visited Chandler and Davenport, Oklahoma. On both occasions the banks there were robbed, although Starr was never even suspected.

For Henry the end came in February of 1921, at Harrison, Arkansas. It was a crisp winter morning that February 18th when Henry Starr and his men strolled into the Peoples National Bank at ten o'clock.

"Hands up and hands steady!" The familiar command resounded through the bank building like the peal of doom.

Henry's three confederates began to rob the bank, hoping to get a good haul and to make their getaway in an automobile which they had driven up to the bank building.

Everyone in the bank threw his hands high except the president, William J. Myers. Myers was a shrewd banker with masterful coolness, courage, and foresight. His bank had never been robbed, even during a virtual epidemic of robberies a few months earlier. Yet he hadn't overlooked such a possibility, and twelve years before that February morning he had built a back door to the vault, opening into his office.

While his customers were being scared to death and the outlaws were busy rounding up all the loose cash in the place, Myers slipped into the vault. As an added precaution, he had stashed a loaded rifle inside.

In all previous accounts (including my own), the weapon used by Myers is referred to as a shotgun. However, recent research into the matter reveals this weapon was a Winchester 1873, .38 caliber rifle, and presently is the property of William J. Myers, son of the man whose shot killed the noted Henry Starr.

Stealthily Mr. Myers took up his rifle and crept to the front of the vault and slowly pushed open the door. Henry was busy stuffing money into a canvas bag. The bank president took careful aim at the outlaw and fired. The bullet ripped through Starr's spine, and he fell to the floor, writhing in agony. The rest of the outlaws went berserk. None of them could tell where the shot had come from. One of the bandits leveled his pistol at the head of the bank cashier, Cleve Coffman.

"Don't shoot him!" cried Starr. "Just get out of here, the lot of you!"

"I don't blame you at all," unlucky Henry told Myers. "I would have done the same thing if I had been in your place."

Henry Starr seemed in no way ashamed of his profession, but in a message to his son advised the boy to keep on the straight and narrow path; not to try to imitate his father.

The bandit had been shot in the spine, and was paralyzed. He asked to see the cashier, and when the youth came in he said: "You know I saved your life." Cleve Coffman nodded. He remained with Starr almost until the very end, and the robber gave the cashier his pistol as a souvenir. According to the man whose life Starr had spared, the outlaw stated that he had never killed a man in the course of his career as a bank robber, and had conducted his notorious affairs in the "whitest manner possible."

Four days later, on February 22, the amazing career of Henry Starr came to an end. He was buried on February 25, at Dewey, Oklahoma.

Throughout his entire life Starr seems to have been plagued more with the excitement and adventure involved in the robbery of a bank than in the actual riches gained from it. He was constantly entranced with new ideas and schemes for outwitting the law. He even tried camouflage, once painting his horse black and pasting white spots on it, then washing it clean later. He resorted to fake moustaches, shaggy brows and beards, but rarely wore a mask. His inherent sense of fair play is obvious throughout his career. He once wrote a friend:

> A man who commits a crime and then shoots an officer who tried to capture him is a fool. The officers never quit hunting you if you kill a man, but they don't pay too much attention if you just rob a bank or stick up a train. While I'm scouting I am going to take good care not to kill a man.

It is also apparent that he tried time and time again to throw off the cloak of outlaw. While in prison in Colorado he said: "I know I have been a bad man in my days; but I am innocent of a whole lot of these crimes. I believe I will be pardoned out of here in another ten years. Then I can look the whole world in the face and be a man among men."

But try as he might, it never quite worked out that way for Henry Starr. In all, he served seventeen years and eight months in prison, and he knew the tragedy of his ways. He gave a newspaperman just before his death what is perhaps a clue to his insatiable appetite for crime:

> Once a fellow falls it is hard to rise again. Never let any vice get a firm hold on you as you will not be able to shake it off. One thing leads to another and before you know it you are in too deep to back out. Gambling was my vice. I could never get enough of it and always had to have money, no matter whose it was, to satisfy that awful craving. All young men should know crime is a losing game, no matter who the players may be. I would not take 17,000,000 dollars to again face the agony I have endured.

Colt's single-action .45-caliber Peacemaker (1873)

6   Henry Brown

No ONE KNEW very much about a young fellow who called himself Henry Brown when he joined the buffalo-hunting party of A. C. Myers in the spring of 1874. Even his birthplace has been a bone of contention these many years. This writer firmly believes that Brown was a native of Rolla, in Phelps County, Missouri, and that he went into Kansas to become a whiskey peddler, then a buffalo hunter.

The Myers' wagon train crossed the Arkansas River at Dodge City, Kansas, and made Crooked Creek by sundown, and there went into camp. By the second night they had arrived at the Cimarron River. All the while lithe Henry Brown was doing his chores as one of the members of the band. With him were the noted frontier scouts, Billy Dixon, Dutch Henry Born, later to become a notorious rustler, and the youngest of the party was William Barclay (Bat) Masterson.

The scouts reported that a solid mass of shaggy buffalo was on the way north. Myers and some of the men continued until they reached a point about a mile and a half above the ruins of Bent's Fort. They settled down there and began constructing their buildings. Myers chose to build a picket house for his store. A picket house was built by digging a trench and setting upright poles in it. The logs were filled in with abode mud and grass, as in the log cabins of the pioneers, who chinked the space between the logs with mud.

Henry Brown assisted Jim Hanrahan, a saloon keeper, to

construct his building. They also built another sod house, which became Rath and Wright's store. Soon rumors drifted into camp that the Indians were on the warpath because the hunters had settled at the new Adobe Walls location. Chiefs Quanah Parker, Lone Wolf, White Shield, and Stone Calf called the party invaders of Texas territory and violators of the Medicine Lodge Treaty. Later two hunters named Dudley and Wallace were slain on Chicken Creek. Emanuel Dobbs and his party were attacked near the Salt Ford of the Red Canadian River, southeast of Adobe Walls. Three of them were killed.

On June 27 there were still twenty-eight men and one woman at the Adobe Walls camp. These men had decided to remain and hunt the buffalo. By midnight they had all retired to their bunks, or were sprawled on the ground, for it was a hot sultry night. Suddenly a sharp cracking sound rent the still air. Inside Hanrahan's saloon Henry Brown jumped up.

"It's the ridge pole. Too much earth on the roof. The weight has cracked the ridge pole. Got to prop it up or it will all topple in on us."

A light was hastily lit and shouts for help soon brought the men to Hanrahan's, and a stout prop was installed in place. Bat Masterson took a careful look at the ridge pole and then looked at Mike Welch, who also was in the saloon when Henry jumped up.

"Henry, you must have been dreaming. That pole is as solid as your own head."

No sound reason has ever been given regarding this phenomenon, one which saved the lives of all those present. No visible crack was ever found in the ridge pole.

Hanrahan then spoke up.

"Whether the pole was cracked or not, we are all awake, so we might as well get an early start for the hunt."

Calling Billy Ogg, Hanrahan told him to drive up the horses. Billy Dixon headed for his wagon, which was outside O'Keefe's shop. Henry walked out into the night for a breath of fresh air. He looked to the east, then to the south, where he could see Billy Ogg bringing in the horses. He looked again! Something was moving beyond the horses. Suddenly out of the night came the unmistakable sound of a bugle sounding the charge. This was followed by the shrill war-whoops of Plains Indians, as a war party rushed toward the building. Henry Brown, Billy Dixon, and Billy Ogg dashed back into Hanrahan's, shouting a warning as they ran.

Henry Brown hastily tossed up bags of grain to protect

the window openings. He then calmly reached for his famous rifle and sent lethal slugs into the Indian ranks. By now all of the hunters present were shooting at the attackers and the first charge of the redskins was blocked, but some of them managed to rush right up to the building and to fire through the windows. Although every pane of glass was broken not one of the hunters was wounded.

At a picket corral to the north two brothers named Shadler were killed and scalped.

Time after time the massed Indians charged, riding up to the buildings, where they hammered furiously against doors and window frames with their tomahawks. Like bees they swarmed around the thick sod walls, while the steady and devastating fire of the defenders toppled warrior after warrior from his pony. Henry Brown made every shot count, and once an enemy was struck by a heavy Sharps bullet he seldom got up to rejoin the fight.

In the ranks of the Indians was a renegade bugler, who summoned the braves to the attack. Ex-soldiers among the hunters interpreted the calls and warned the inmates, who then met every charge with deadly results.

Henry Brown and Bat Masterson stood shoulder to shoulder at a window, shooting until the space outside their window was so littered with corpses that fresh attackers could not draw near without trampling the bodies.

By noon the Indians had withdrawn and confined their tactics to circling the valley out of rifle range.

Morning of the second day still found the Indians keeping their distance. The hunters spent that day burying the dead Indians as well as the two white men who had been killed.

"Our ammunition is running mighty low," said Henry Brown. "If those devils find that out we're goners."

The third day arrived with the Indians still congregated on the high bluff to the east across the valley, a distance of almost a mile. It seemed to all present that they were well out of range of even the powerful Sharps rifles. Others maintained that the Sharps would send a lethal charge that far. One of the Indians could be seen fairly well, and he was making grotesque signs at the white hunters. Billy Dixon was conceded to be the best shot present, and then Henry Brown. It was finally decided that Dixon should "waste" a bullet on the taunting redskin.

Taking careful aim, Dixon dropped the hammer. The roar of the big .50-caliber rifle was immediately followed by the Indian's diving headlong from his pony's back. Later the dis-

118

tance was measured off and proved to be 1,538 yards. This was indeed a record shot, even among the dead-shot hunters.

This fantastic feat discouraged further attack, and Chief Quanah Parker and his allies withdrew their forces.

Any record of the movements of Henry Brown after the Adobe Walls fight until 1877 has been lost. In that year the young and daring rifleman arrived at old Fort Griffin, located on the Clear Fork of the Brazos River.

It was plain that the days of the buffalo hunter were over. The depleted herds offered little or no recompense for a man's labor. Henry decided to try his fortune in another direction. At Fort Griffin he learned of the trouble brewing in Lincoln County, New Mexico, and soon was to become embroiled in the bloody struggle between the paid gunhands of the McSween-Chisum gang and those of the Murphy-Dolan faction.

Henry listened closely. His wide-spreading ears twitched and his blue eyes sparked as he learned of the high wages being paid gunmen in Lincoln County. He quickly bid his friends adieu and hit the trail for New Mexico.

Lincoln, New Mexico, was an armed camp when he arrived. Riffraff and gunslingers from all over the Southwest had migrated into Lincoln County, seeking both excitement and the high wages being offered by both feuding sides.

John Simpson Chisum, Alexander McSween, his attorney, and an Englishman named Tunstall were at dagger's point with the Murphy-Dolan outfit, and the feud threatened to burst into flames at the slightest pretext. Both parties wanted control of the Pecos River ranges. Into this melting-pot of hatred and treachery rode the indomitable Henry Brown, who cared not a tinker's cuss for whom he fought, just as long as he was paid regularly and plenty of excitement was furnished.

Scarcely had Brown become acquainted with the lay of the land when an excited cowboy asked him to join the Chisum faction.

"If he's paying high wages, tell your boss he has another gunhand," Henry informed the man. Henry, an expert with the rifle, was reluctant to apply for such a job and use that type of weapon. He had left his Sharps back in Kansas, and was prepared to rely on his expert handling of his six-guns.

The smoldering fire burst into flames with the foul murder of J. H. Tunstall as he made his way to Lincoln. Dick Brewer, foreman of Tunstall's ranch, immediately contacted Tunstall's partner McSween, who went before Justice of the Peace John P. Wilson and had Brewer appointed a special constable. Now armed with legal authority, Brewer gathered a posse and set out to arrest the men responsible. In Brewer's party were Billy the Kid and Henry Brown. Morton and Baker, the two men they wanted, were located in a dugout and held the band at bay until their ammunition ran out. Constable Brewer told them they would not be harmed if they surrendered, but Billy the Kid, a close friend of Tunstall, killed both prisoners while on the way to Lincoln. McClosky, one of Brewer's men, attempted to save them, and was shot from his saddle by Henry Brown.

Henry Brown was also one of the posse which attempted to kill Buckshot Roberts. Roberts, however, killed Brewer and wounded another man in a fight at Blazer's Mill. Although Roberts was mortally wounded, the old Texan still managed to hold off his attackers and was left to die in peace.

Following the end of the Lincoln County war, Henry Brown and Billy the Kid refused to accept the amnesty offer of Territorial Governor Lew Wallace, both choosing to continue their lives of crime. All through the fight Henry Brown had worked hard to achieve notoriety, but his exploits were always overshadowed by those of Billy the Kid. Even though Henry had sided with the Kid in all his deviltry, and had killed just as many men as Billy, he was overlooked while the Kid became nationally known as the number-one badman of the wild and woolly West.

Henry Brown enjoyed being outside the law. He decided to break away from Billy the Kid and to make a name for himself. In many ways Brown and the Kid were similiar. Both were fair-headed, had blue eyes, and were endowed with the same diabolical dispositions—blood-thirsty, treacherous, and homicidal. Brown was also said to be equal to the Kid on the draw, and just as deadly. So while Billy the Kid chose to stay in New Mexico, Henry Brown decided to seek adventure elsewhere. Brown's last association with the Kid was late in 1878, when they drove some stolen horses into Tascosa, in the Texas Panhandle. Brown did not return to New Mexico with Billy the Kid, but remained in the town to become, of all things, its first constable.

It was common practice in the old West to hire killers to keep other killers in line. Henry Brown was a good constable, and his New Mexico reputation had preceded him to Tascosa. He was so feared that no gunslinger would tackle him. It was not long before Henry became bored with the job, and left Texas for Fort Griffin. There he learned that the Cherokee Strip was soon to be opened to white settlers seeking homesteads, and also that Stoner's store, adjacent to Indian Territory, had become the meeting place for all types of riff-raff and gunmen. Near Stoner's place a town had sprung up almost overnight, and it was named Caldwell. Gamblers, gunmen, and men and women of all creeds and professions flocked to the new Kansas town. They proceeded to make Caldwell the most evil, wild, and attractive town west of the mighty Mississippi.

Caldwell sounded just right to Henry Brown. He decided to make it his next stopping-place. Travelers whom he met upon the trail relayed to his eager ears the latest news of the town. He decided that Caldwell was the most lawless town then in the West. Killings were frequent, lawmen were helpless, and anyone having the nerve to wear a badge was committing suicide. Good wages were offered deputies—with no takers!

Deputy Sheriff George S. Brown was the first lawman to be killed. George W. Flapp, his assistant, was made town marshal, but the nervous strain forced him to seek refuge in the whiskey bottle. Before that he had tangled with a group of Texans, and in two days killed five men. Several days later he was riddled with buckshot from ambush.

Deputy Marshal Frank Hunt then took over. He lasted exactly one week, during which time he killed seven men. While attempting to make an arrest in the Texas House Saloon he was shot dead. Several more peace officers followed him. One was gunned down by the Jim Talbott gang, and another died on the floor of the Red Light Dance Hall on June 22, 1882.

When Henry Brown rode into Caldwell a certain B. O. (Bat) Carr was the marshal. Valuing his life, Carr had lined himself up with those who ruled the town, and had hired deputies to act as targets for those bent upon homicide.

On the trail Henry had made a decision. The excitement offered a peace officer in Caldwell appealed greatly to him, so he decided to seek out the marshal and apply for the vacancy of deputy marshal of Caldwell.

Brown rode up to the office of Mayor Hizzoner, halted his mount, and dropped stiffly from his saddle. Throwing off some of the trail dust, Henry walked up the steps leading to a wide rocking chair, nervously wringing his hands.

"Mayor Hizzoner?"

"Yes. What can I do for you, young man?"

"I hear you need a new deputy, and I'd like to have the job."

121

"You! Why, you're not more than a boy—or, at least, not much more." The mayor began to smile.

The deadly glint in Henry's cold blue eyes seemed to send him reeling back. Mayor Hizzoner then looked Henry over—closely. He had failed perhaps to see the two pearl-handled Colts draped on Brown's lean hips, or the .44 Winchester cradled in his arm, or the decided thrust of the young man's jaw. He failed to recognize that the applicant was a full-grown, expert gunman, one who had sent a number of men to their graves, and not a punk show-off hoping to make a name for himself.

Hizzoner handed Henry Brown a five-pointed deputy's badge.

"Here, pin this on. You are now a deputy marshal of Caldwell, Kansas. Report to Bat Carr, he's the marshal. I hope you live until morning, and good luck."

"Thanks," said Henry as he walked away.

Pinning on the badge, he made his way to the Texas House Saloon. The bartender grinned as the new deputy pushed his way through the batwing doors.

"Hello, Marshal," he said, "going to be with us long?"

"That all depends. Where is Marshal Carr?"

"That's him sitting to the rear of the room. You'll always find a whiskey bottle handy when he's around."

As Henry turned to meet his new boss an instant buzzing went around the room. In a few minutes everyone there knew that the visitor was the new deputy, and they were already giving odds as to how long he would last.

"Your name Carr?" inquired Henry.

"Yes, why?"

"I'm your new deputy, for better or for worse," Henry told him.

"Who in hell appointed you?"

"Mayor Hizzoner."

"Hell, he's always going over my head! Oh, well, all right by me. You start on the night shift, around six."

Henry executed a quick turnabout and left the saloon. He then obtained a quiet room and prepared for action. He cleaned and oiled his six-guns, got them ready for instant use by practicing his quick draw before the mirror in his room. He then placed fresh cartridges in his guns and spent the few remaining hours in quiet, observant maneuvers. He did not advertise his intentions by presenting himself in the streets to attract attention, but confined his quest to learning the locations of all entrances and exits of the various saloons, honky-tonks, and gambling halls.

While Henry was making his plans, so were others. Sandy Jim, boss gunman and gambler, called some of his cronies together in the Golden Wedding Saloon. As the three men talked, their notched gunbutts displayed grim evidence of their prowess.

"We'll take care of him tonight when he passes the Golden Wedding," grinned Sandy Jim.

As Deputy Marshal Henry Brown was a methodical person, it was exactly six o'clock when he stepped into the street. Down Main Street he walked, passing the red-light district, the blacksmith's shop, and Hubble's General Store. He glanced in at the Red Light Dance Hall and saw that all was peaceful, with no trouble brewing. It seemed as though everyone was waiting for something to happen.

"What have they got in mind for me?" Henry wondered. He would soon know.

As he passed the Golden Wedding Saloon several shots sounded from the barroom. Shouts that might have been those of a drunken Texas cowboy rent the night air, then three more shots sounded. Henry recognized an old trick—he was being baited as the other deputies had. They wanted him to rush in to quiet a fake drunk and then they would gun him down.

Assuring himself that no one was watching, Henry turned from the front door, where he knew he was expected, and ran through an alleyway leading to the rear entrance. Like an Apache Indian, he entered the barroom from the rear. Just as he had thought, all present were intently watching the front door, and none present became aware that the trick had backfired until they heard Henry command: "Deputy Brown speaking. Put up your hands!"

The crowd turned, gaping with amazement. The two "put-up" men went for their guns. They thought Henry must be crazy, for his six-guns were still in their holsters. Like streaks of lightning Henry's Colts leaped into his hands. When the firing stopped the two men lay dead on the floor. The fake drunk stood as though petrified. Henry walked up to the man and pistol-whipped him. Then turning to ringleader Sandy Jim, Brown said: "I'll still be around if you want another try."

Sandy Jim could hardly wait for the next day. He rushed to Marshal Carr's home and demanded that he get rid of Henry Brown at once.

"Who, me? you're crazy," said Carr. "He'd never stand for it, especially not now."

"You better do as I say, or you'll take the one-way trip to Boot Hill yourself."

"All right, I'll try," cringed the marshal.

Henry Brown was seated in the jail office, half asleep, when Marshal Carr stomped into the room. His courage bolstered with whiskey, Carr blurted out: "Brown, you're fired. Get your things and get out."

Henry Brown rose slowly. "You got it backward, Marshal. You're the one who's fired." He leaned over the desk and jerked off Carr's marshal's badge, at the same time placing his right hand on his pistolbutt. "Any objections?" he added.

"No, none! I was going to leave this town soon, anyway," stammered the ex-marshal.

Having ousted his superior, Henry Brown presented himself before the city fathers and announced that he was appointing himself to fill the vacancy in the marshal's office, created by the sudden resignation of Bat Carr. Discretion proving the better part of valor, the city council to a man gave its consent.

Shortly after Henry's self-appointment to the marshal's job a minstrel show arrived in Caldwell. It was learned that the performers were scheduled to parade down Main Street, wearing high silk hats. Sandy Jim got the idea to use the hats as targets, with a money pool going to the man who shot off the most.

Mayor Hizzoner was frantic. He rushed to Marshal Brown and demanded that the affair be called off.

"I can handle this, Mayor, to everyone's good," Brown assured him. "Just be patient."

The parade started the next morning. Drums boomed and several musical instruments in inexperienced hands made an attempt to play some national song. Marshal Brown managed to secure a position close to Sandy Jim. Sandy Jim fired at the first top hat that appeared and that piece of wearing apparel fell to the dusty street. Quick as a cat, Henry Brown drew his revolver and fired a slug close to Jim's new boots.

"What in hell's the idea, Brown?" demanded Sandy Jim.

"Dance!" cried Marshal Brown, and fired his gun again and again.

As Sandy Jim hopped about in the street Brown cried out: "Call that dancing? Try running." Again Brown's revolver roared, and Sandy Jim fell dead in the dust.

The dead man's astonished friends did not try to avenge

Sandy's murder. "He was resisting arrest," was what Brown said.

About this time Marshal Brown wired a former friend of the Lincoln County war days to join him. This character was Benjamin F. Wheeler, a tall, wavy-haired individual with a drooping moustache. His sad eyes and melancholy attitude masked his real homicidal nature. He was one of these gunmen who had no more compunction in shooting down a man than in brushing away a fly which annoyed him. He was as treacherous as a rattler, but never gave warning of attack.

Marshal Brown had put into force an anti-gun ordinance. All weapons were supposed to be checked while a man was in town. Wheeler, a pawn in the hands of the shrewd Brown, always enforced this ordinance and killed several men in the process. In one instance Wheeler arrested a man named Morton Boyce. The prisoner was rude and insulting, especially to Marshal Brown. Soon after Wheeler told Brown about it, Boyce was found dead in the street. The marshal explained that he had shot the prisoner when he attempted to escape.

Caldwell was quiet and tamed by October. Time hung heavily upon Henry Brown's shoulders. Now he became surly and troublesome, no longer caring to enforce the law when it was not done at the point of a fast and exploding pistol. With his split personality, he was ready to join the opposite side if it provided danger and an opportunity for more killings.

In April, 1884, Brown suggested to Ben Wheeler that they rob the bank at Medicine Lodge, Kansas.

"What for, Henry? We're sitting pretty good here."

Brown hit Wheeler in a soft spot and ignored his question.

"There's a lot of money there, Ben, and I know we can use it. We can be back here in safety before anyone knows what happened."

Henry Brown's jurisdiction ended at the town limits of Caldwell, but when word reached him that horse thieves were operating on the outskirts the marshal said he was going to look into the matter. It was the excuse he needed. Fully armed, he and Wheeler left Caldwell.

A few miles beyond Caldwell, either by appointment or by accident, Brown and Wheeler met Bill Smith and John Wesley.

The four gunmen rode into Medicine Lodge early on May 1. It was raining, and that seemed to please Henry. It would keep people indoors. In front of the bank Brown told Smith to hold the horses in readiness while he, Wheeler, and Wesley went inside. Brown drew his pearl-handled pistols and pushed through the bank door, closely followed by his two cronies, guns also drawn.

"Hello, Mr. Brown," greeted Mr. Wiley Payne, the bank president.

"This is a hold-up, Payne," replied Brown. "Put up your hands."

Wheeler covered the cashier, George Geppert, and kept an eye on the front door at the same time.

Payne was no coward. He tried to grab a pistol from the desk drawer. Brown fired, and the bullet dropped Payne to the floor. Ben Wheeler lost his head and fired at the cashier. Geppert, dying, staggered to the vault door and twisted the lock dial.

Just as Northfield, Minnesota, was the Waterloo of the James-Younger gang, so Medicine Lodge, Kansas, was the end of the trail for the Henry Brown bunch. Empty-handed, the three killers fled. Bill Smith still held the horses but a body of men, firing as they came, rushed toward the outlaws. Brown grabbed his Winchester and drove them back with five fast-fired shots.

Into the Gypsum Hills rode the four outlaws, closely pursued by a posse led by Marshal Barney O'Connor of Medicine Lodge. This was strange country to the outlaws. What looked like a canyon offering an avenue of escape ended in high cliffs, impassable to man or beast.

The four wanted men leaped from their mounts and fortified themselves behind large boulders. Wesley and Wheeler whimpered, but Brown and Smith were made of sterner stuff.

"We'll fight our way out," said Brown.

But it was a hopeless fight. By noon most of their ammunition had been used and the determined posse was closing in.

They all agreed to call it quits, so Brown tied a wet handkerchief to the barrel of his Winchester and waved it slowly in the air.

The prisoners were returned to Medicine Lodge and secured in a wooden shack which served as the jail. The bank president was still alive at the time the outlaws were captured.

A lynch mob circled the crude and weakly built jail. The county attorney wanted statements from the prisoners, so he was allowed to enter the building and talk with them.

"Payne still lives," he said, "but if he dies I'm afraid no one will be able to stop that mob."

The mob grew larger as the night lengthened. Sometime during the first hours of darkness Payne passed away. Four hangman's nooses were tied as the crowd converged upon the jail. The county sheriff and his men gathered before the door, but their resistance would be weak at best. The prisoners managed to get their shackles off about the same time two huge men crashed in the jail door.

"Fight, Ben!" cried Henry Brown.

Ben Wheeler knocked aside the first of the men who tried to enter the jail. Brown rushed through the opening and dashed into the street. He had gone about a block when he fell dead with two loads of buckshot in his back.

Wheeler was wounded from the blast of a .45 and managed to run several hundred yards before he was recaptured. Wesley and Smith made little effort to escape.

The mob dragged the prisoners to the bottomlands near Medicine Lodge. Three ropes were thrown over a limb of an oak tree. Wesley and Wheeler pleaded for mercy. The plucky Smith merely said: "Let's get it over with."

For the record, the coroner held a hearing the next day. He declared that Henry Brown, Benjamin Wheeler, William Smith, and John Wesley had met their deaths at the hands of persons unknown.

As in the case of other noted gunmen, the word got out that Henry Brown was not killed that day in 1884; that someone else was responsible for the attempted bank robbery and the murders at Medicine Lodge.

Lucius Dills, long-time resident in Roswell, stated that Henry Brown went to Tascosa, Texas, after that date, where he served as a deputy sheriff under Sheriff C. B. Willingham. Later, he claimed, Brown served as a deputy sheriff under Sheriff Higgins of Chaves County, New Mexico. After his service with Sheriff Higgins this particular Brown faded into obscurity and was never heard of again. But no doubt this was another Henry Brown. Had it been *the* Henry Brown he never would have gone willingly into obscurity.

On the other side of the ledger we have an item which appeared on May 17, 1884, in the Lincoln County *Leader*:

> Readers of the daily papers are familiar with the facts of the attempted bank robbery at Medicine Lodge, Kansas, and the killing of the president and cashier of the institution by four men whose names were Henry N. Brown, Marshal of Caldwell, Kansas, Ben Wheeler, his assistant, W. Smith, and a man by the name of Wesley, both cowboys. The citizens gave pursuit, and the quartette of robbers were caught and lynched. The man Brown had been married but six weeks, and was a member of Billy the Kid's gang in the Lincoln County war. Better for the world that he has gone.

Colt's single-action .45-caliber (Frontier model, 1871)

7 Ben Thompson

IN THE FRONTIER TOWN of Austin, Texas, in the year 1856, a thirteen-year-old printer's apprentice was brought to trial for shooting mustard seed into the buttocks of a playmate. His English parents engaged a capable attorney, who presented the defense that the boy had shot on a dare, and that he showed sympathy with the victim's pain while the seed-shot was being removed from the flesh. The jury recommended clemency, the judge delayed sentence, and Governor H. R. Runnels issued a pardon.

This is the first recorded incident in the life of Ben Thompson, whose career from then on gurgles like a blood bath. There was almost no extensive period during his forty-one years on earth when he was not guilty of shooting some man, and almost always he was under a charge of murder. But outwardly he showed such deference to the letter of the law and to enforcement officers that he almost always won acquittal. His faith in his own righteousness gave him a plausibility which smoothed the way for him on many occasions.

Various sources list Ben's birthplace as anywhere from Nova Scotia to Texas; this author finally was able to locate his exact birthplce after years of research. Ben was born in England. The Parish Register of St. Botulph's Church, Knottingley, Yorkshire, England, records the following: Benjamin, son of William and Mary Ann Thompson of Knottingley. Father's occupation, Mariner. Baptized November 13, 1843, by George Steward, Curate.

Ben was a stout five foot nine. He had a swarthy complexion, black hair, and blue eyes. He possessed indomitable energy and was quick in all his motions. His mother and his wife and his son and daughter—possibly also his father, who was either lost at sea or else deserted the family on a trip to England—thought of him as the champion of underdogs and revered him for his generosity, though even they probably deplored his addiction to gambling.

Thompson as a youth went to New Orleans for adventure. But there he encountered such difficulty in making his way that he decided to book passage for San Francisco. After paying all the money he had for a berth, he reached the dock only to learn that the ship had sailed earlier than scheduled, leaving him penniless.

He thought he might be able to get a job in a printer's if he went back to the town. On a bus he saw a Frenchman offering unwelcome attentions to a young woman, and he affected a sudden chivalry. By accosting the Frenchman he became involved in a duel, and later killed him. As a result, he had to hide out in the Sicilian quarter, where hot tempers and murder were condoned. While a reward was offered for his apprehension, his new friends, defiant of any civic law, helped him escape across the river. He stole a mule, and rode back home to Austin.

Thompson resumed setting type, but he had by now acquired expensive tastes. Therefore he supplemented his earnings by the new method he had learned in New Orleans. He played faro, monte, roulette, rouge et noir, Boston, seven-up, euchre, draw poker, or any other of the gambling games which were then the rage. Before long he took a job as a monte dealer, and from then on he always "relied upon his skill as applied to the laws of luck and chance."

At the outbreak of the Civil War Thompson enlisted in Col. John R. Taylor's regiment, and was on duty at Fort Clark, New Mexico. In a quarrel he shot and killed the mess sergeant and then attacked a lieutenant who had tried to interfere. The captain of the company put him under arrest, and in the guardhouse he was chained to the floor, flat on his back, for more than a month, without trial or court martial.

Inducing a friend to supply him with matches, Thompson contrived to set the guardhouse on fire because he preferred death to further suffering. He was on the verge of suffocation when rescuers arrived to loosen his chains and carry him to safety.

The friend who had brought him the matches was about

that time taken ill with what appeared to be smallpox, and Thompson was the only one who volunteered to nurse him. It turned out that the patient merely had a case of chickenpox, but Thompson and he made use of the camp scare to escape. They filled in the last twelve months of their enlistment at another army post two hundred miles away.

At the time of Thompson's discharge the war was still in progress. He re-enlisted with a company on the march to Galveston for active service. During a stop-over at San Antonio, the soldiers elected him to sneak out at night for a supply of whiskey. The sentry gave the alarm. In order to avoid pursuit Thompson had to turn along a paved section of road. His horse slipped and fell upon him, crushing his leg. He was caught and sent to the prison hospital for six weeks. In the meantime his regiment had moved on, so, without permission from the medical officers, he followed on crutches. He overtook the regiment in camp on the St. Bernard, and found that his best friend, Phil Coe, was under arrest but not under guard because he had given his parole. Phil was a civilian who had been acting as an officer without authority, and he had refused to enlist as a private.

Thompson and Coe slipped off one night to get some whiskey and were carried back drunk. Because Thompson was still using crutches he was kept to the rear, among the sick. Coe was ordered to be conscripted, but he fled to Mexico and stayed there until the close of the war. Thompson afterward claimed that, although he had to move on crutches, he had participated in the capture of the *Harriet Lane* and the destruction of other Union vessels at Galveston.

However that may be, he quarreled with another sergeant, beating him with his crutch. There might have been another murder on his record if the crutch had not broken after the first few blows. He was placed in the guardhouse, but two days later the whole command was ordered to Louisiana, and his refraction of rules was forgotten.

The regiment routed Pyron's opposition at La Fourche— and Thompson and his younger brother Billy found themselves to be the only living men on a battlefield strewn with corpses.

Ben was in great pain because of his unhealed leg injury, and when he and Billy finally located the remainder of their company he was furloughed indefinitely. After a period of convalescence he obtained for both himself and Billy a transfer to the regiment of Col. John S. Ford, Old Rip of Comanche battle fame. They joined him at Eagle Pass, for patrol duty along the eastern bank of the Rio Grande.

Billy had seventy dollars, which he allowed his older brother to use as a start in a monte game. Ben lost all the money, as well as his spurs and his hat, but he retained his six-shooter. As he said later: "When that hatless, barefooted, one-gallus thing called luck frowns, a man sins against good gambling if he don't quit."

In disgust over his hard luck, Thompson quarreled with both soldiers and officers who had won, and finally he decided to go to a little Mexican village across the Border from Laredo, for a really good game. During the first night his winnings at monte were over twelve hundred dollars. This increased his daring, and, against his better judgment, he opened his game to Mexicans who, he knew, were crafty and experienced gamblers. After playing for many hours, and suspecting that the losers would soon be in a fighting mood, he signaled Billy to go and get his pistol. But the trouble broke out before Billy had returned, because it became apparent that Thompson meant to close the game while he was in possession of all the money as well as all the six-shooters of the other players.

There was considerable shooting when the two candles were extinguished, but Thompson and Billy were safe outside as the smoke cleared. They eluded the troops that galloped up to investigate the noise. It was, however, important that Thompson should not be seen in the neighborhood. With great difficulty he managed to float himself across the river on an improvised raft. On his way to the home of a Mr. Riddle he had to pass along streets where Mexicans slept in the open. Watchdogs attacked him, one after another, and his flesh was torn in many parts of his legs and buttocks. He was bloody from the waist down and in great pain when he reached Mr. Riddle's house, but there his wounds were washed with ammonia and he was allowed to sleep.

The next morning Thompson learned that the Mexican gamblers knew where he was staying. Evidently the savage dogs had marked his trail, though none of the Mexican owners of the dogs had chosen to wake up long enough to call off the animals. Before setting out again, Thompson sent a friend to ask Captain Carrington to ride with his men to a certain point on the river bank, so that when Thompson crossed he could be met by United States troops for his protection. Captain Carrington arrived exactly when needed, while Mexican troops watched, cheated of their quarry by only a few minutes.

However, Captain Carrington insisted that if Thompson were on the camp grounds when the Mexican officials requested that he be turned over, their request would be gratified. Thompson thereupon took several friends down the road along which they expected the Mexicans to pass, determined to kill as many of them as possible. But Captain Carrington, hearing of this plot, sent a messenger to notify the Mexicans, who avoided the ambush.

Thompson joined Capt. William Armstrong's company, but was not encouraged to stay, in view of the Mexican demand for his head. Therefore at three o'clock in the morning he hurried to join Capt. Robert Gardner, who was in charge of a train of artillery. After further suffering from the dog bites, the fugitive finally caught up with Captain Gardner, who set up cannon and prepared to fight the Mexicans rather than surrender Thompson.

Thompson arrived safely in Austin some time later and rested for a while with his family.

Colonel Ford detailed Thompson to raise a company and to join the regiment of Colonel Beard for operations against the Indians in the northwest. He started to sign up recruits, but the members of the home guard resented this. In a street brawl Thompson killed several of these local opponents. There was danger that a mob might storm his house during the night, so he stayed elsewhere until the following day. Then he refused to surrender to arrest but declared he was willing to stand trial if he were left free on his own recognizance until the trial was called. It was long delayed, and when it finally opened the jury acquitted him without leaving the box.

Thompson succeeded in raising a company of volunteers and joined Beard's regiment near the city of Waco, but by then the Indians had quieted down. Very soon the collapse of the Confederacy changed the situation, and thousands of disbanded soldiers flooded the state, desperate, defeated, and impoverished.

Early in June, 1865, Colonel Badger of the First Louisiana Cavalry arrived in Austin and issued an order for Thompson's arrest without making any specific charge. Thompson was placed in the Travis County jail and kept chained to the wall. But he made friends with his guards and planned an escape with them to Mexico, where they hoped to enter the service of the Emperor Maximilian.

Before long Thompson was in Mexico, marching into battle and receiving promotion for his bravery under fire. He was attached to a company which was besieged by a weak force, and frequently he broke through the lines with his men. On one occasion he intercepted a supply train and killed the soldiers in charge of it, commandeering the animals and the cargo.

Of course Thompson found, as usual, an opportunity to gamble, and his pistol remained his constant companion. After one long game there was a gunfight that drew the police. He was arrested and marched through the Mexican streets toward the city jail. But he was rescued by some Americans, and he killed a number of Mexican policemen while escaping. When the general under whom Thompson was serving asked for an explanation, he closed the interview by saying "Thompson, see that you don't let it happen again." No reference was made to the murders.

In battle the next day, eleven hundred out of fourteen hundred men on Thompson's side were killed. Thompson had gone into the fight with fifty-eight men. At the close he had only seventeen left, eight of them seriously injured.

Perhaps looking for consolation, he appeared at a gambling house but lost heavily and, disgruntled, went on to a dance hall. There between dances he had a fight with a Mexican whom he left dead on the floor before fleeing in the dark.

Once again Thompson had to explain to his general, who sighed and said: "Never mind. We shall soon be far from here."

At four o'clock the next morning the regiment marched to help Maximilian. They covered four hundred miles in ninety-six hours and entered Queretaro on the fourth night shortly after midnight. Accompanying his general, Thompson had audience with the Emperor, and was moved by his great dignity even in this hour of defeat.

At the close of the royal interview, the flag of Juarez was brought in with a demand for unconditional surrender. The Emperor thought surely he would be given time to reply, but an immediate assault was begun. He and his generals were surrounded and taken captive.

Thompson escaped from Queretaro and overtook a rider on a fresh mount, whom he forced to trade horses with him. He rode furiously over two hundred and eighty miles toward Vera Cruz, where he knew he could join the French commander, Bazaine. He told himself that now, with the war over, he would travel to the Pacific coast as quickly as possible, to try his luck in the goldfields of California.

But he was struck down by yellow fever, and for many months was nursed by Sisters of Charity. While he was convalescing a stray New York newspaper fell into his hands, and he read that civil government had been established in Texas under Governor J. W. Throckmorton. He was homesick, and took the first occasion to return to Austin. However, on arriving he discovered that the military still had plenty of power in the region, and that was not good news for him.

Because there were several indictments still pending against him in Austin, Thompson remained on the outskirts of the town at the home of a relative. But his handsome horse with its silver-mounted saddle, whose housings were of long black hair plaited into highly dressed leather, challenged the attention of the soldiers camped north of the capital. They learned the name of its owner and decided at their own discretion to arrest Thompson. However, the gambler suspected their plan when he saw a solider guarding his horse, which he had sent for shoeing.

He approached the horse. He was dressed like a young hidalgo, in blue trousers with silver cords down the seams, embroidered buckskin jacket, and a wide stiff-brimmed, low-crowned hat with a golden snake coiled around it as a band. About his waist he wore a red sash to cover his pistol. While he took hold of his horse's bridle rein with his left hand he grasped his pistol with his right.

The soldier was greatly surprised to be ordered to hand over his pistol, but he did so and stepped back when he found the muzzle of Thompson's gun at his nose. Thompson leaped into the saddle and rode off to the Cedar Mountains. A squad of troops almost captured him when his horse stumbled and fell, but he got away without being hit. He led his injured horse into a thicket and hid quietly until his pursuers were out of earshot.

After this incident Thompson consulted his attorneys and urged them to bring him to trial so that his innocence could be established, for he claimed that he had never killed except in self-defense. At the trial he was acquitted of all charges brought against him.

Thompson next turned to his favorite vocation, gambling, in the city of Bryan, a thriving town on the Houston and Texas Central Railway. A gigantic man named Big King, proprietor of the Blue Wing Saloon, one night lost heavily to him, but still did not want to quit. He offered to bet his saloon if Thompson would continue after daylight. Thompson was practically worn out, but agreed, and the two men played through that day and another night without rest. By daylight of the following day Big King had lost the Blue Wing and Thompson was installed as proprietor. He ordered champagne and treated all the men in the house.

He had the back room fitted up for gambling. A few nights later Thompson returned in time to find his dealer being threatened by some gamblers who had lost heavily. Practically everything in the Blue Wing was broken in the fight that ensued.

Thompson's brother Billy, during an argument in a house of prostitution, killed an army sergeant and went into hiding. Thompson was not able to go to his brother because he was constantly shadowed, but he managed to send provisions. As a rule, to prevent the army from discovering the boy's whereabouts, Thompson sent a messenger in the wrong direction with a note urging Billy to make a certain journey. This usually misled the patrol. But on one occasion the troops did learn where Billy was. Learning this, Thompson armed himself and rode swiftly to his brother, gave him his horse and directed him to a new shelter, then returned to the city by a roundabout route.

The sheriff and a big posse later found out where Billy was hiding while Thompson was in the same house with him. They surrounded the house and attacked at about one o'clock at night. They made a tremendous noise in trying to get through the bushes and vines and briars and prickly pears. Ben and Billy were both out of the house and gone long before the posse had reached the front door. Eighteen days later Billy arrived safely in the Indian Nations.

Once Thompson found himself in danger of using his pistol on a man who repeatedly annoyed him. For his own safety's sake he appealed to a magistrate for help, but was refused. The next time the man annoyed him Thompson shot him, inflicting a flesh wound that was not fatal. The gunman then returned to the magistrate and asked to be put under bond to appear to face an indictment on this count. The magistrate again refused. Presently Thompson heard that this same magistrate was preparing a warrant for his arrest by a military commission. Incensed, he again called at the magistrate's office.

"A short time ago," said Thompson, "you couldn't draw up

135

a warrant because you didn't know how, and now you are able to prepare this difficult document!"

He lost his temper and forced the magistrate to get out of his own office, saying: "If I ever see you playing officer again I'll kill you, if I hang for it."

The magistrate dodged away through an alley. In less than half an hour Ben Thompson was in the hands of the military, heavily ironed and enclosed in the "bull pen." This was a small space securely surrounded with broad walls upon which sentries walked with loaded rifles. When two drunken soldiers attacked another inmate Thompson, in a spirit of chivalry, hit one of them with his closed knife, driving it through the man's eyeball.

For this he was put in double irons and chains, and fastened to the ground so that he could not move from side to side nor lift his arms or legs. Thus he lay every night for nearly a month. The irons ate into his flesh, and because he endured this affliction courageously several of the guards expressed their sympathy—though they did not dare to show him any favors.

Thompson was finally arraigned, and the trial lasted for five weeks, costing the government $15,000. Each day of the trial Thompson was forced to walk to it, a distance of over one mile, carrying his fetters. The flesh of his ankles became lacerated, and his socks were saturated with blood.

When sentence was read Thompson and another prisoner, both emaciated by their prison treatment, were refused permission to see their families. They were escorted by two hundred and twelve men to the Huntsville penitentiary. Thompson was kept in solitary confinement until his wounds were sufficiently healed to permit him to do hard labor. After a couple of months he was assigned to the hair department, and became an expert in plaiting, twisting, and weaving hair into fashionable articles. He remained there for two years— until the military was transferred from this section of the country, at which time he was summarily dismissed.

Thompson returned to his family in Austin and also to gambling, for that was now his only means of earning a livelihood. When he had accumulated funds to enable him to travel he moved to Abilene, where Texas drovers congregated regularly and where he felt he would be operating among friends. After a long spell of bad luck he was at last able to quit with $2,583 in his pockets.

Just at this time Thompson's old friend Phil Coe arrived in Abilene with several thousand dollars of his own. Together they opened a saloon, making it the town's headquarters for gambling, and they prospered. Wild Bill Hickok became marshal, drawing fifty percent of all fines collected and also receiving regular cuts of profits from various gamblers. Thompson and Phil Coe refused to pay such protection money, and knew they had to be prepared for trouble.

Thompson sent for his wife and children now that he had enough money to give them a comfortable home, and on the first day of their reunion he took them on a buggy ride to show them the surrounding country. As they drove over an unexpected hole in the roadway the buggy was overturned, and they were all injured. Ben's leg was broken, his little boy's foot was crushed, and his wife's arms were shattered. They were picked up by strangers and carried to the Lindell Hotel in Kansas City, where they had to undergo medical treatment for three months. Thompson wrote Phil Coe about his difficulties, and Phil Coe telegraphed him $3,000. When they were able to travel the whole Thompson family set out for Austin, knowing that Thompson's mother would nurse them.

They were traveling by easy stages when they were overtaken by a party carrying a casket, and for the first time Thompson learned that Wild Bill Hickok had shot his best friend, Phil Coe, and had closed the prosperous saloon which he and Phil Coe had been operating. Thompson had thus lost everything.

It was a long time before he recovered his health. Then he went to Ellsworth, Kansas, where his brother Billy was one of the men delivering cattle on the hoof to the rail terminus. Together they collected enough money to set up gambling rooms.

During a fight with a man named Martin, who had refused to share his winnings, the whole town was aroused by Thompson's shooting in the street. Sheriff Whitney, a friend of Thompson, was anxious to avoid bloodshed, so he persuaded Thompson and Billy to go with him to the Grand Central Hotel. On the way there was another melee, and Billy, attempting to shoot a man who was aiming at Thompson, shot Sheriff Whitney. Thompson got his brother on to a fleet mount with some money and told him to ride for his life, but the boy was not exactly aware of his danger.

"I made up my mind," said Thompson later, "that if the mob should get hold of Billy I'd empty my gun and pistol into its ranks."

Billy got away, and Thompson saw a group of men with

137

drawn guns approaching him. To his surprise they did not see where he was leaning against a post, but marched beyond him, calling out to others: "Where are the those murderers, the Thompsons?"

Thompson was within ten feet of them, so he drew a bead on them and said quietly: "The man who moves I shall kill. Lay down your arms."

He held them at bay until Mayor Miller appeared, and then Thompson offered to surrender if the mayor would first disarm the hostile men. This was done, and Thompson went with the mayor to his office. Since it was too late in the day for a trial, the mayor asked some residents to post a $10,000 bond for Thompson, who was then released.

Thompson spent the evening at the theater, seeing *She Stoops to Conquer,* and during the performance a friend tapped his shoulder and whispered: "Billy's back in town."

Thompson knew that regular and special law-enforcement officers were scouring the country for his brother at that very moment, and he was shocked to hear of the boy's return. He found him in a small upstairs room, and Billy made him see his reason.

"The country for a long distance is full of officers," Billy explained, "and the authorities have telegraphed in all directions. It would be foolish for me to try to pass out of this locality now."

Thompson helped his brother disguise himself by cutting his long hair and then coloring his whole body, even between the toes, to make him look like a Mexican. He painted his teeth yellow to resemble the stain of tobacco juice. In Mexican boots and a cap and black clothes with a secondhand blue army blouse, Billy was soon ready to drive stock, as he had been doing before. He was even able to speak Spanish, so he continued at his job until he had a chance to leave for a safer region.

When Thompson appeared for his trial there were no witnesses against him, and the case was dismissed. Within a week he had left for Kansas City, whence he later went to St. Louis, then by boat to New Orleans, and so back home to Austin.

About this time the competition between the Atchison, Topeka, and Santa Fe Railroad and the Denver and Rio Grande had reached a danger point. The Atchison engaged Thompson for a bonus of $5,000 to protect their roundhouse until they should have time to appeal to the law. With a carefully worded agreement, to the effect that Thompson would be required to fight only against an unauthorized body of men if they should attack the roundhouse, the deal was concluded. Thompson took charge and barricaded the place.

The Denver and Rio Grande officials offered him $25,000 if he would surrender the roundhouse to them, but he replied: "I will die here unless the law relieves me." This of course was his own version of the episode, though there were currently other versions.

When Thompson was relieved by law-enforcement officers he returned home by way of St. Louis, this time with money for his family. He established a gambling house in the second story of a downtown building, but the work made him lose sleep. He became pale and was, in fact, not in his usual robust health. Some strangers who mistook him for a weakling once heckled him, and he let them continue with their insulting remarks out of curiosity. Suddenly he revealed his true identity and, too late, they tried to retreat. In their flight one of them caught two of Thompson's bullets.

Again he submitted to arrest and was bonded. Within the next two months he was indicted, tried, and acquitted of assault with intent to kill. He always had very persuasive lawyers to defend him, and his constant care to cooperate with officers won their cooperation in return.

One evening Thompson left his gambling rooms in the charge of his partner, Loraine. But he felt he had several grievances against Loraine. These developed greater proportions as he steadily drank champagne at dinner with his friend Bill Johnson. At length, in a terribly belligerent mood, he insisted on going back to have it out with Loraine. Bill Johnson went along, hoping to prevent trouble, and with this end in view he even searched Thompson and satisfied himself that the gambler was unarmed.

However, Thompson had secreted a pistol in his clothes, and he drew it out at the least expected moment. He shot the pile of chips and the dealer's box and the chandelier.

"Loraine," he said, "you can buy another set of tools and charge them to me. I don't like the ones you had."

The police whistle sounded, and Bill Johnson forced Thompson out the back door. They went down to the Iron-Front Saloon, where the keno rooms were being operated by a man named Simon. Thompson began shooting into the cylinder-shaped box holding the balls with which the game is played. At the first sound of shooting all the players and dealers and waiters, and indeed everyone else attached to the establishment, left through the doors and windows and up the

139

stairs and over the roofs of neighboring houses. Again the police congregated, but Thompson was no longer there.

Bill Johnson continued to remonstrate with him, but without any effect on Thompson, who by this time had worked up such momentum that nothing could stop him. He led the way to the First Ward and shot out the street lights and the lamps which marked the houses of prostitution. The police rushed toward the shooting, but by the time they arrived there was shooting in another district. Thompson led them on a wild chase through dark streets.

Usually, however, Ben Thompson was in a more sober mood. To the surprise of many citizens, he actually became a candidate for the office of marshal in Austin. The incumbent won the election, but 744 men voted for Thompson in spite of his unsavory reputation. After this defeat he went to Colorado and New Mexico for several months.

As soon as he had returned and started another gambling room, he met new trouble. He and several cronies late one night crossed the street to attend the Variety Theater, and Thompson roared with laughter when he saw one young man set off some firecrackers. Of course, anything that sounded like firearms started confusion in the audience. Mark Wilson, the stout, red-faced, impulsive proprietor, who had become a deputy sheriff especially so that he could keep order at the theater, rushed from behind the scenes to find out what was going on. A wag who had some lampblack leaned up to the stage and stroked Wilson's face with it, drawing a laugh from the audience.

Wilson cried: "Officer, arrest that man!" pointing to the man with the lampblack.

Thompson stood up at his table and called: "Officer, I'll be responsible for the prisoner. He was only trying to have a little fun and meant no harm. I'll have him at the mayor's office tomorrow morning. Don't lock him up for a harmless joke."

"Who is running this house—you or me?" cried Wilson, turning on Thompson in fury.

Thompson fingered his gun, a gesture which usually induced everybody present to let him lead the discussion his own way. But in this case Wilson was not intimidated, being an officer of the law in his own right and in his own premises.

"You're probably the one who instigated this disorderly conduct in the first place," he snapped.

It was later Thompson's claim that when he denied this

Wilson accused him of lying. At any rate, Thompson slapped Wilson's face.

Wilson chose not to reply in kind, but instead he walked down the aisle toward the bar where his firearms were hung. When he had a double-barreled shotgun in his hands he called out loudly: "Clear the way!" He cocked the gun and brought it to bear in the direction of Thompson.

Members of the audience darted, dodged, squatted, crawled, did everything to get out of the way. As soon as the aisle was clear the shooting began. Thompson claimed that Wilson fired first and tore a hole in his clothes above the hip, that only when Wilson was about to fire the second time did he himself fire. Thompson's first shot at Wilson crippled him, and then he shot him several times after he had fallen. When Thompson saw the bartender raising a gun he shot at him too. The bartender dodged behind the bar, but the shot went through the woodwork and broke his lower jaw. He died several weeks later.

Completely satisfied with his success over the impudent Wilson, Thompson immediately walked over to the sheriff's office and surrendered.

"Looks to me as though a mob is forming to attack you," said the sheriff.

Thompson answered: "Don't endanger yourself for my sake, Sheriff. Prepare me with a few good pistols, and I'll defend myself."

This time, however, the law was permitted to take its course. At the preliminary trial the judge committed Thompson to jail without bail. On a writ of *habeas corpus* the prisoner was taken to Galveston, where the Court of Appeals was in session, and he was released on a $5,000 bond. When an indictment had been prepared in Travis County, he was tried, and the jury, after deliberating for only a few minutes, returned with a verdict of "not guilty."

Because the Indians were becoming troublesome again, Thompson joined the Rangers, commanded by Capt. Ed Burleson, son of the honored General Burleson who had repelled the redskins a generation earlier. The company left for the headwaters of the Brazos River to drive the Indians from the border, but they were drawn farther and farther into the desert as the Indians retreated. Water was found only at great intervals and often was unfit to drink until it was filtered through sand to eliminate salt and other minerals. By the time the Rangers had kept up their pursuit as far as the Pecos and Canadian rivers, their horses had been galloping for forty days and the riders themselves were in need of rest. Consequently, Captain Burleson camped for ten days north of the Concho River and south of the Red Fork of the Colorado. At this place the water was good, the grass fine, and buffalo and elk abundant.

Of course Thompson had his monte cards along. As counters the men used pieces of copper ore which they found lying about on the ground. It was a profitable time of "rest" for the gambler.

After camp had been broken and the march resumed Captain Burleson detailed Thompson to scout ahead to make sure that no Indians were over the horizon. Thompson chose Buckskin Sam to ride with him, and they climbed a hill from which they could see for considerable distances in several directions.

As Thompson described it:

> The sun, descending through what seemed to be a yellowish haze, was red as blood, the air as still as death, save a dull, heavy, regular, distant sound. The earth trembled beneath us, the red, angry, avenging sun, the oppressive silence broken only by the strange sound. The quaking, shaking earth impressed me with an awful fear.

Thompson put spurs to his horse and rode rapidly to the crest of the next hill. There he saw, coming up the slope toward him, thousands of buffalo, making a noise like thunder. They were rushing madly ahead. But then he discovered that in the midst of the wild herd eighty or a hundred Comanches were riding. He could see their long black hair floating in the wind, their eagle-feather adornments waving from side to side as they swayed on their fast-moving horses. Their faces were disfigured with red and black warpaint. Their lances were held in one hand, and their bows and quivers full of arrows were slung across their shoulders.

Thompson and Buckskin Sam prepared to fly back to their detachment, but it seemed important to do something to slow down the redskins before they could advance much farther. In spite of the danger they were in, the two scouts checked their horses long enough to take aim and shoot. The two leaders of the Indians fell. While Thompson and Buckskin Sam were dashing off to save their lives, they once more checked their horses and fired. They were so well satisfied with the result of these tactics that they risked stopping and shooting even for a third time. Taking their courage in their hands when the whole buffalo herd with the Indian war party

142

seemed about to swoop down on them, they halted, took aim, and fired.

This time Thompson's horse was killed, and he rolled over the ground while a flight of arrows went over his head. Buckskin Sam flung himself to the ground and joined Thompson behind the prostrate horse, which they used as a barricade while they continued to shoot.

Fortunately for them, Captain Burleson on the other side of the rise had heard the shooting and had arrived with his entire contingent. The Rangers drove the confused Comanches back over the hill once more—and Thompson never did explain what happened to the herd of maddened buffalo.

Thompson returned to Austin with this story and several others, to enhance his pose of hero. Another election was in the offing, and once more he became a candidate. This time he won the marshalship. He enjoyed parading in his uniform and took pride in keeping the lawless element out of the city. At every hour of the day and night he was on duty, and it is claimed that during his period in office there was not a murder nor an assault with intent to kill within the limits of the city. Moreover, not a burglary or theft was committed but what the criminal was promptly brought to trial and punished.

In 1880 Thompson engaged one of his attorneys, William M. Walton, to write his life story. He felt this was called for because his belief in himself as a public figure had reached incredible dimensions. Besides, he was so powerful that everyone with whom he came in contact cheerfully verified his own opinion of himself. Dutifully, Walton wrote a paean of praise—but the tone of the last part of this book changed when Thompson was no longer able to supervise its preparation. Only after Thompson's death did Walton dare to admit that the gambler had sometimes used intoxicating liquor to excess, or even that at times he had acted unreasonably.

Friends had invited Thompson's little daughter and son to visit them in San Antonio, and the children had been begging their father to take them. At last he had time to do so, and after many preparations they left for the short ride by rail. On arrival in San Antonio Thompson telegraphed his wife: ARRIVED SAFE—ALL WELL—CHILDREN HAPPY—GOD BLESS YOU.

The children were handed over to the womenfolk, and the menfolk indulged in a social glass or two. During the confidences exchanged somebody said that in San Antonio there were some men, among them Jack Harris, who wanted to see Thompson assassinated.

Jack Harris was at the time conducting a gambling house in San Antonio, but he had once been a friend of Thompson. They had marched side by side in the army and had slept under a single blanket on the ground. But in the intervening years Jack Harris had forgotten the old friendship and had developed an enmity toward the more famous gambler. There is no record of the reason for this change on his part.

While in San Antonio on this visit with his children, Thompson stopped at Jack Harris's place, and was betting at the table where Joe Foster was the dealer. Thompson's wide experience with cards made it possible for him to detect that things were not exactly right. He therefore changed his tactics and played so recklessly that the dealer could not keep up with his turns in the way he had started out to do at the beginning of the game. As a result, although Thompson had at first lost heavily, now he won all his losses back, to Foster's consternation.

When Thompson rose to leave the table with his winnings, he loudly denounced Foster as a swindler, and Foster reached for his pistol. But Thompson had his own pistol at Foster's face instantly.

"Any movement on your part is death," he said carefully.

Foster remained rigid until Thompson, his pistol still pointing at him, had backed away and gone into the street.

When Harris, the owner of the place, heard this story, he naturally sided with Foster and said: "Oh, the time will come when we'll get Thompson in a tight spot. Just wait."

Thompson took his children back home, but he returned to San Antonio on an excursion to Laredo with the members of the Legislature and city officials. During their stop in San Antonio Thompson was told that Harris was in the street with a double-barreled gun, avowing his intention of shooting him on sight.

When the two men met Thompson called out: "Hello, Jack! Is it true you've been looking for me?"

"No," said Harris, "but if you come to my place I'll make you wish you hadn't!"

Thompson retorted: "Go and get your gang and arm them, and meet me out at the Main Plaza. Come out and fight like men."

Harris ignored this challenge, but at a number of places he talked freely about what he thought of Thompson. Gossip reached Thompson, of course, and he was informed that Harris had been threatening to kill him. This did nothing to calm him.

Harris was running the Vaudeville Variety Theater. It was his habit to go home at four o'clock in the afternoon, then return at eleven o'clock in the evening after the theater money had been collected. The ticket office was on the same floor as the bar, with swinging doors between the two, and he kept a double-barreled shotgun in his office.

Thompson with a friend entered the bar and ordered drinks. He said to the bartender: "Where's that shotgun brigade that's on the hunt for me?"

"Never heard of it," said the bartender tactfully.

Later it was reported that Thompson next said: "You tell Joe Foster he's a thief, and tell Jack Harris he's living off the labors of those poor variety women," but this was hardly in line with Thompson's jovial mood. He usually kept his comments for strategic moments.

Thompson and his friend swallowed their drinks and walked out, but all the employees felt that they had been in danger. They sent for Harris, and one of his partners handed him a pistol as he approached the building. Thompson, unaware of the stir his presence had caused, met a friend outside who wished to eat, so together they walked back into the bar.

One of the employees saw Harris entering a moment later and whispered: "Ben Thompson's here."

Thompson heard people muttering that Jack had got his shotgun, and he saw through the swinging doors that Harris was standing behind the wall of the doorway with his gun resting on his crippled left hand, ready to shoot with his right.

Although at the trial later Thompson claimed that he cried out: "Jack Harris, what are you doing with that gun?" and that Jack Harris had replied, adding some profanity: "It's to shoot you," that was too good a defense to be taken seriously after the event.

At any rate Thompson fired through the slats of the swinging door. The ball cut along the wall and passed into Harris near his heart. A second shot caught Harris as he fell, and a third was fired into the air to scare off any other conspirators. Thompson then stepped into the street among the hacks near the pavement, and he pointed his pistol at the band on the balcony. The musicians hurriedly went inside the building, and Thompson felt it was safe for him to turn his back and get away.

He went through several houses and over to the Menger

145

Hotel, where he remained during the rest of that night and most of the next day. He was in considerable mental turmoil, but he finally decided to send for the sheriff and surrender. He allowed himself to be jailed in a comfortable room with iron bars at the windows. Then in a grandiose show of caring more for the reputation of his home town than for his own interests, he publicly resigned his job as Austin's marshal, pending his discharge.

The trail was held in January, 1883, and lasted from Tuesday morning to Saturday night, with the courthouse crowded to capacity. The judge charged the jury at nightfall. At eight o'clock the next morning they brought in a verdict of "not guilty."

"At a reading of the verdict the applause was deafening and long continued," reads a report of that time.

Freed at last, Thompson with his wife and daughter returned by train to Austin, where a crowd of people greeted him. Enthusiastic young men unharnessed the horses and drew his carriage by hand along the principal street, to celebrate his vindication.

Gradually Thompson had taken to drinking more and more heavily, and frequently he was the cause of disturbances in various parts of the city. Even when he shot off blank cartridges for fun scores of people who did not know he wasn't in earnest were frightened. He suffered from insomnia and liked to spend the night roving from one quarter of the town to another, usually shooting playfully at anything he saw.

On March 10, 1884, Thompson met his old friend J. K. Fisher in Austin, and they spent several hours together. Late in the afternoon Fisher said he had to leave for Uvalde County, west of San Antonio, and he asked Thompson to go along with him. Reluctantly Thompson agreed to go part of the way, but it turned out that he stayed on the train as far as San Antonio. They arrived in that city, where Thompson had so frequently been in trouble, at about eight o'clock in the evening.

After several drinks the two went to the theater to see *East Lynne*, and, following the eleven o'clock curtain, they wandered over to the Variety Theater, where Jack Harris and his bartender had been killed. At the bar they met W. H. Sims, who was now running the place in partnership with Joe Foster. Thompson expressed a desire to see Foster so as to make friends with him again.

146

The old trouble is all forgotten, you know," said Thompson genially.

"Why don't you two go upstairs and watch the show?" said Sims.

While Thompson and Fisher were ordering drinks Sims joined them with Foster. Thompson lumbered to his feet and offered to shake hands, exclaiming: "Foster, suppose we let bygones be bygones?"

It was characteristic of Ben Thompson, who usually dictated the terms of any relationship, that he should expect Foster to accept his overtures the moment he was inclined to be friendly, in spite of his repeated claims that Foster had tried to swindle him.

Foster backed away, unwilling to shake hands with the murderer of Jack Harris, a man he had admired. It may be that it seemed to Thompson that Foster reached for his gun as he jerked his hand away.

Regardless of the contradictory testimony at the coroner's inquest—the main object of which was to save anyone from prosecution—the fact remains that suddenly guns were fired. Joe Foster was hit in the leg. Thompson and Fisher, who had been standing at his right, both fell dead. It was found that Fisher was shot thirteen times. Thompson received nine bullets, five in his head and four in his body, all entering from the left. Any one of the head wounds would have been fatal.

Thus, at the age of forty-one Ben Thompson's career was ended by the same method he had used to conclude the lives of many men before him. But his single-minded attitude toward accomplishing his own purpose at any given moment, plus his uncanny courage, have established him in the annals of the West as a remarkable gunfighter, and an even more remarkable person.

Probably the story of his life can be summed up in the tribute paid Ben by the famous Bat Masterson, who said of him, "It is doubtful if in his time there was another man living who equaled him with a pistol in a life-and-death struggle."

Colt's single-action .45-caliber Peacemaker (1873)

8   Clay Allison—Gunslinger

FRANCISCO (PANCHO) GRIEGO scratched his bewhiskered chin. Even for November it had been a warm and dusty day. He shaded his eyes with his hand as he watched the blazing sun flaming its last rays as it sunk behind Wheeler Peak in the Sangre de Cristos. Pancho had been acting marshal of Cimarron, New Mexico, for only a short time, and so far, the job had not appealed too greatly to him. He was used to gunfights and shootouts, having to his credit six men killed in fights—one way or another.

The evening hour seemed to have kept citizens off the streets; except for a lone cow-pony standing hipshot at the Lambert Saloon hitchrack, there was no sign of life around. It was also very quiet. Only the noise coming from the Maxwell corrals sprawled along Ute Creek, out past the James Hotel, could be heard.

The marshal wearily flicked the dust from his shirt, and decided to have a drink at Lambert's before checking in at the jail. Pancho stopped cold as he shouldered through the batwing doors. The only patron in the saloon stood at the bar—a tall cowman in dusty leather chaps. Pancho knew this man, this handsome hombre, six feet or more tall, with clear, keen, gray eyes, wearing dusty but quality clothes befitting those of a gentleman.

Pancho knew this man was Clay Allison, the gunman from the Palo Duro country of Texas, not far from Mobettie and

148

the Washita. The man standing at the bar was quiet, unassuming, with no element of the desperado about him. Pancho had heard that Allison never killed a man except in self-defense, but when drinking, anything could be expected from Clay.

A tied-down holster belted to his lean hips held a black-butted Navy Colt, and on his head he wore a gray hat, askew on his tousled black hair. The hat was unmistakably Confederate issue.

"Greetings, *amigo*," grinned Pancho. "Glad to see *Señor* Allison back again in Cimarron City."

"I'll just bet you-all are."

"Hear you had a run-in with a Mexican desperado over in Dodge City not long ago."

"Yep, at the Wright Hotel. He came in after me and I shot him right between the eyes."

Pancho gulped, visibly disturbed for some reason or another.

"Pancho," said Clay, "c'mon over here. I've something to ask you."

Allison motioned Pancho to step back in the corner of the saloon, as if he had something confidential to tell him. Then Lambert heard several pistol shots echo from the rear of the room. Looking back in the corner, he saw Pancho dead. It has never been determined just why Clay had killed the Mexican.

A detachment of Negro troops, under the command of Captain Francis S. Dodge, was dispatched from Santa Fe to arrest Allison for the murder of Pancho Griego.

It had been a long dry haul from Fort Union in the Turkey Mountains, up the Canadian to the swing-around on the famous Maxwell Grant property. Captain Dodge decided to billet his men at Cimarron, not thinking for a moment that Allison might be there. He told his men to take cover, while he went to the hotel for a hot bath.

But the big sergeant had other ideas. After his white officer left, he passed the buck to the corporal, and with two cronies, he headed for Lambert's Saloon. Clay Allison also was there.

It was evident that the black soldiers were taken aback by the man wearing a Confederate hat, but apparently they did not realize who he was. In that early postwar era trouble seemed to flare up when Confederate and Union veterans met face to face, even though ten years had passed since the close of the war.

"You-all come to arrest me, Yankees?" drawled Allison in a soft voice.

The sergeant was taken aback momentarily, but did not retreat. The three yellow chevrons on his sleeves represented the dignity of the United States Army; and pride in them forbade his losing face before privates.

"We don't know you, stranger," said the sergeant. "Step aside and let's not have any trouble."

Allison grinned.

"I'm Clay Allison, that mean anything to you?"

The man at the rail stiffened visibly as his eyes flashed. Livid anger flooded his swarthy face, and he spat out an oath.

"Easy now, Clay," cautioned the suddenly pale bartender.

Unheeding him, Allison turned. He was drunk ... very drunk. He even swayed against the bar. He cursed the soldiers, and his eyes were blue frost as he snarled: "Yankees! Damned stinking Yankees! Heah's yoah drinks!"

His right hand snaked down and came up working the deadly .45. The saloon rocked alive with its roar, and blood spurted from the dumbfounded sergeant's mouth as the first slug slammed him backward. Before he could fall, a second bullet killed a private bolting for the door. The third man was killed as he dived behind a card table.

Through the smoke haze the horrified bartender saw Allison toss off his drink and start reloading.

"My God, man, don't just stand there. You just murdered three United States soldiers. Get out of here *pronto*."

Holstering the Colt, Allison shoved his glass at the shaking man.

"Whiskey," he demanded curtly, a sardonic smirk twisting his mustache and chin whiskers. "They deserved killin'."

The bartender didn't argue. Colfax County's citizens had learned never to cross Clay Allison while he was in his cups. Not until he downed two slugs of liquor did the sneering gunman reel out to his pony. Nobody was about. Mounting up, he rode away slurring off-key "The Bonnie Blue Flag."

Only then did those who had heard the shots venture into the crimson-splashed saloon. Quickly Captain Dodge was notified.

There was no active law in Cimarron. A lesser man than Captain Dodge might have gone off half-cocked. In fact, his remaining twenty troopers angrily clamored for permission to ride out to Allison's ranch near Otero and arrest him or kill him.

Dodge refused. His fury no less because it was controlled,

150

he sent a courier to Taos for the sheriff. The trooper returned alone. The wily lawman wanted no part of the dreaded Allison. But he did send a warrant. If Dodge brought Clay in, then the sheriff would see that he stood trial.

At noon the following day Dodge rode up to the Allison ranchhouse with two sets-of-fours as escort. Throwing off, he strode boldly to the porch.

"Clay Allison!" he called out sharply. "I have a warrant for your arrest!"

The door creaked open, and the barrel of a Greener shotgun appeared. Behind it came Allison. He looked badly hung-over, but his eyes glinted.

Ignoring Dodge, he waved the shotgun at the mounted troopers. "You-all got ten seconds to high-tail it for town," he grated. "If you-all are still heah after that, I aim to use this shotgun on the lot of you."

"See here now," protested Dodge angrily, brandishing the warrant.

"Don't wave that papeh at me, Yankee, I ain't foolin'." Shotgun hammers clicked ominously, and Clay's face mirrored the cruelty and ferocity of which he was capable.

Captain Dodge was no coward. His bravery in the Indian wars proved that. Nor was he a fool. Side glances revealed Clay's brothers and over a dozen gunmen skulking in the corrals, waiting for the slightest pretext to allow them to bear down on the soldiers. To prevent needless slaughter on both sides, Dodge ordered the eight fuming troopers to leave.

Some writers insist that Clay alone bluffed Dodge; his two brothers said no.

"I'll ride into town with you-all, Cap'n," said Clay, "but I aim to keep my guns."

Captain Dodge did not press the issue.

Cimarron must have gaped in awe when the pair rode into town with Allison still fully armed. Even now it seems incredible. But that wasn't all. When Allison insisted they wash the dust from their throats, Dodge prudently posted sentries outside Henry Lambert's saloon. Whereupon Clay swore he'd kill the first man he saw leaving. So Captain Dodge had to drink alone with Clay until Sheriff Isaac Rinehart arrived, expecting to find a dead captain. When the amazed lawman rode out with his prisoner, Clay still wore his Colt revolver.

Most historians claim Sheriff Rinehart never made it across the Sangre de Cristos with the moody, tricky gunslinger. One says Clay found a foul-smelling water hole, where he forced the sheriff to soak his hat in it and wear it back to town.

Then he rode off, laughing. Another report claims that Captain Dodge's patrol of ten black soldiers followed closely behind the sheriff. The records indicate this did happen, and that in Palo Flechado Pass Allison suddenly leaped behind a large rock, yanked out his Colt, and forced the sheriff and the soldiers to head for Taos.

"If de sheriff don't want Mistah Allison, what use have we for him?" cried the soldiers. So Clay was left behind the rock.

Sheriff Rinehart had come to Cimarron originally at the invitation of Lucien Maxwell, who was looking for a good miller to run his grist mill. Maxwell later treated him coldly because he and his wife stood as witnesses for the marriage of Virginia Maxwell to Captain Keyes. As the ceremony was performed in the mill, Maxwell suspected Rinehart of protecting the elopement. General Keyes of World War I fame was a grandson of this union. Maxwell forgave his daughter before he died; it is doubtful whether he forgave the miller. Shortly following the sale of the Maxwell Grant, Rinehart sought the office of sheriff, rather reluctantly, according to some; because of the cut derived in collecting taxes, according to others. The law permitted the sheriff to retain 10 percent of all taxes collected. Rinehart's name is intimately connected with the history of the Washita country in Texas, Amarillo, and Tascosa. He later became successful in real estate and banking. He visited the Allisons often when he lived in Mobeetie, the humiliations suffered at the hands of Clay forgiven and forgotten.

Robert Clay Allison (commonly called Clay) was born in Wayne County, Tennessee, near Waynesboro, the son of Reverend and Mrs. John Allison, both from Sugar Creek, North Carolina.

Not long before the outbreak of the Civil War Reverend Allison died. He had grieved himself to death thinking of a war that would pit brother against brother, father against son. Mother Allison did her best to raise the five children in a way fitting to Tennessee farmers. Clay spent one term in school at the county seat of Waynesboro. During all that time he was a leader and outspoken advocate of the Southern cause.

When the Civil War broke out, Clay joined the raiding forces of Colonel Nathan Bedford Forrest, who was later to become one of the ablest generals of the Confederate cavalry. At their first meeting Forrest immediately saw in Clay a man he could like and could trust. Allison, slender, trim, and tough, was a perfect specimen of manhood as he stood gazing with his light, steely eyes into those of Colonel Forrest. From that day on their mutual respect and admiration was forever sealed.

Many stories became associated with Clay's life while he was a cavalryman. Mainly he acted as a messenger for Forrest and later as a spy. His keen memory for details and messages proved valuable to Forrest in that Clay could describe fortifications and troop locations almost to their exact dimensions. His suggested methods of attack in many instances were invaluable to his commander.

On the romantic side, it is said that he acted as a spy for General Fitzhugh Lee after serving with Confederate guerrilla forces. Some claimed he was captured at Murfreesboro by Michigan cavalry, and while being questioned, shot and killed a Union major with a hidden derringer. He was then sentenced to be hanged but managed to escape by brutally garroting a sentry and two sleeping guards.

Fact is, Clay Allison remained in the services of General Forrest until the close of the war, surrendering at Selma, Alabama. He then returned to his Tennessee home, where he was joyfully greeted by his sister Mary, now married to Lew Coleman, and his brothers, Monroe and John.

Appomattox left Clay nursing a hatred for Yankees. When drunk, this obsession became bloodlust, for although shootouts with peace officers and "treeing" towns on drunken sprees high-lighted his infamous career, Clay became kill-crazy if crossed by soldiers or Union veteran lawmen. Clay also felt he was appointed on this earth to kill all the gunslingers and badmen he could, especially those who needed killing.

Clay tramped the old homestead for days, but found no animals, chickens, or any living thing to disturb the deadly calm. Northern and Southern soldiers had crossed the farm repeatedly, clearing it of every live and edible thing. The only animals they had were the two horses Clay had brought with him and the saddle horses of John and Lew. There was only one thing to do. The family must move to Texas. They all agreed.

Early one daybreak, in a patched-up old wagon loaded with blacksmith and farm tools, they started for the Lone Star State. Mary and Lew Coleman and Monroe Allison riding in the wagon; Clay and John Allison riding to the front on their saddle horses. They headed due west for Memphis. A few days later they crossed the Mississippi River and headed south by west to Little Rock, Arkansas, and soon reached Texas soil at Texarkana.

The family soon reached the upper Brazos River, where they established a home on the east bank of the Brazos River. Clay made it his business to cultivate the friendship of other folks in the valley. There he met Colonel Charles Goodnight, the giant cattleman, who asked Clay to drive a herd of his cattle to Denver, Colorado. This was the drive which earned Clay Allison his reputation that kept him in constant demand for such work.

The spring following their arrival in Texas, Clay was asked to guide a number of families into the western Panhandle area. Comanches attacked at dawn one morning, badly scattering the livestock, killed many animals, and escaped. The fight with the Indians convinced Clay the area was unsafe, so he decided to discuss the matter of moving when he returned to his cabin on the Brazos. At that point he was still under contract to drive cattle to the markets at Abilene, Wichita, and Ellsworth, Kansas.

When Clay finally arrived home he found Lew Coleman and his partner, Issac (Ike) Lacy, waiting for him to discuss another move. They had been waiting for Clay to move the family to Cimarron, New Mexico, where they had acquired land from the Maxwell Grant Estate. Lew and Ike offered Clay one head of cattle for every ten delivered. Clay was thrilled with the prospects of becoming a cattleman. Lew and Mary Coleman chose a homesite close to Taos, and Clay and his brothers selected adjoining land to the south, near the head of the Cimarron River. There he built a large dugout as temporary living quarters. The brothers Allison used several cattle brands, and in 1880 Clay registered his brand in Texas as A C E on the left side, right ear cropped, slash bent under; left ear cropped near end, no slash.

While operating his ranch in Colfax County, New Mexico, Clay was accused of allowing his cattle to graze beyond his own property lines, south toward Fort Union and north on the ranges below Las Animas, Colorado, an area where Clay felt at home and where he had many run-ins with the law and other gunmen.

It was in Las Animas that Clay and his brother John became involved in a dancehall fight with Deputy Sheriff Charles Faber. Faber had no use for Clay and resented his actions in insulting anyone he saw fit to insult. On that particular Saturday night Clay apparently decided to reenact his nude ride through Old Mobeetie (not Canadian, as many say; that town was not there at the time) by removing his clothing in the center of the dance floor, punctuating his actions by

154

shooting into the wall with his pistol. At the same time he would make some luckless bystander kneel nearby, forcing the man to gulp all the whiskey he could while staring into the muzzle of Clay's six-gun. At that point someone sent for Faber.

At the entrance to the dance hall Faber yelled out: "Allison, you know you are not supposed to wear guns in here!"

"Hell with you!" cried Clay. "Your men got 'em and we'll just keep ours on."

Faber knew the situation was hopeless. He knew that it would be a bloodbath even with a number of his deputies behind him. He raised his shotgun and fired, aiming a little high but not high enough, for some of the buckshot hit John just off the right shoulder. It was a flesh wound, but all Clay saw was blood streaming down his brother's arm. His pistol roared, the first bullet killing Faber instantly. The rest of the officers, including Sheriff John Spear, dashed for the door. Clay ignored those about him as he dragged the dead deputy by the hair of his head to where John lay bleeding.

"Here's the son-of-a-bitch who shot you, John. Don't worry, everything's going to be all right. Don't you fret none."

At the same time Clay snatched up his clothing and tried to stop the flow of blood, crying all the time at the hurt caused his brother. He finally agreed to have John taken to Fort Lyon, where a doctor treated him. Clay was with him all the time. After Clay saw that his brother was safe he consented to being arrested with no trouble. He was released on a writ, and before the trial could be held, all witnesses had disappeared. Even so, at the trial, the judge and jury ruled self-defense since Faber had fired without notice of any kind and Allison had made no threats. One juryman recalled having heard Faber say he hoped to shoot it out with Allison for the distinction of being faster on the draw. So the Allisons went free.

Much has been said of how many men Clay Allison killed, the number is high. Yet courthouse records in Texas, New Mexico, and Colorado show that he was booked in seven slayings; one of these never even occurring, some said, and the six ruled as being in self-defense.

From Las Animas Clay brought his cattle to Cimarron or Dodge City, always accompanied by a number of hard-case Texas gunmen. With him also rode his equally noted brothers.

In order to get a picture of Dodge City as Clay saw it,

here is a description that appeared in the Topeka *Times* in 1878:

> During the year 1873 we roughed it in the West. Our first stopping place was the famous Dodge City, at that time a perfect paradise for gamblers, cutthroats and girls. On our first visit the buildings in the town were not buildings, with one or two exceptions, but tents and dugouts. Nearly everyone in town sold whiskey or kept a restaurant, perhaps both. The A.T. & S.F. railroad was just then working its way up the low-banked Arkansas, and Dodge was the frontier town. Its growth was rapid, and in a month from the time the railroad was completed to its borders, the place began to look like a city; frame houses, one-story high, sprang up; Dodge became noted as the headquarters for the buffalo hunters, and the old town was one of the busiest of trading points, and they were a jolly set of boys there. They carried a pair of Colt revolvers in their belts, and when they died, they did so generally with their boots on.
>
> It wasn't safe in those times to call a man a liar or intimate this his reputation for honesty was none of the best, unless you were spoiling for a fight. In those days Boot Hill was founded, and the way it grew was astonishing to newcomers and terrifying to tenderfeet. We all remember but now forget the date, when a party of Eastern capitalists came out to look around, with a view of locating. They were from Boston and wore diamonds and kid gloves. The music at one of the dance halls enticed the bald-headed old sinners thither, and what with wine and women, they became exceedingly gay. But in the midst of their sport a shot was fired, and another, and, in a little time the room gleamed with flashing pistols and angry eyes. This was enough. The Eastern capitalists hurried to the depot, where they remained until the first train bore them to the classic shades of Boston.

Some historians try to depict his two brothers as nursemaids to Clay when he was on one of his periodic drunks; recorded history refutes such claim. They were conspicuously absent when he killed the black soldiers, or during one particular case—the night Clay backed down the Commandant at Fort Union.

On one of his cattle jaunts Clay bedded his herd down near Las Animas. He needed a drink so he rode up Coyote Creek to the post suttler's store, where, after a few snorts, his hatred of the Yankees took over. He began to wreck the store until the colonel entered the room and ordered the drunken cattleman off the post, backing up his demand with a cocked .45 pistol.

Allison laughed aloud.

"Put thet cannon back in yore holster and give me an even break."

The colonel wisely refused. Whereupon, Clay labeled him a damned Yankee coward and a yellow-livered dog.

That did it. Blood drained from the furious colonel's face as his trigger finger whitened. But he did not fire. Clay's derisive sneer and his snake-poised hand turned the trick—the colonel broke and left the store. When Allison rode off loudly whistling "Dixie," no one bothered to try and stop him.

Maybe so. No official evidence of this incident exists to prove it really happened. But no post commander in field grade would personally try to stop a drunk from "hoorawing" a suttler's store. He'd have called the OD and gone on writing his memoirs. Yet in those days, men in high position and with high military rank did many things that would be impossible today.

United States troops still occupied forts in the region, and often furnished escorts for wagon trains and herds of mules needed in the operation of the mines. Clay resented the frequent use of Negro troops in the Southern and Western states.

One night Clay and several of his henchmen tried to stampede a herd of Union-owned mules from a corral near Cimarron City. One of the animals ran into Clay's horse in the rush, and Clay, with pistol in hand, reached to push the mule away. In so doing the pistol was discharged and Clay shot himself through the instep of his left foot. Many stories have been circulated that this wound was caused when Clay was just a boy and supposedly dropped a pistol which discharged.

Clay was taken to an abandoned nearby shack, where it was discovered that the wound was serious. Dr. Longwell was summoned. He instructed the men to take Clay to a spare room in his office in Cimarron City. Several days later Reverend Thomas Harwood and two young women called on Clay. He was informed this was part of their function, to call on the sick and to cheer them up.

Mrs. Longwell introduced the McCullough sisters, Dora and Kate, to Clay, and they remarked they were aware of the Allison brothers.

"John has often spoken of a lady friend by the name of Kate, I suppose that is you," said Clay.

"Yes, they are quite good friends," chimed in Dora.

157

The next day Clay told brother John of his interest in Dora McCullough.

"Don't you trifle with the heart of my sweetheart's sister, Clay; that is something I will not tolerate, even from you," said John.

Once John was convinced that Clay's intentions were honorable, they planned a course of action with regard to the courtship of the McCullough sisters. Dr. Longwell, on learning of their intention to marry the girls, stated he did not believe that the A.J. Youngs, with whom the girls lived, would consent to the marriages. Mrs. Young was an aunt of the girls. She had taken them into her home after the death of her parents at Sedalia, Missouri.

It was decided to perform the wedding ceremony without the knowledge of the Youngs, for fear they might object. As it was, when they learned that the weddings had been performed by Rev. Thomas Harwood, all was well.

Every man of note in those days must have tried once to tangle with Wyatt Earp—or at least have it said he had. Even Clay Allison has this rumor attached to his early life, but it was more than a rumor, for it has been substantiated by people who knew.

The trouble really started over a man named Bennington Du Pont, an easterner staying at the Wright House in Dodge City. He made an unfavorable impression with the people, and they nicknamed him the "Ground Owl."

"We called him that," said Cimarron Bill, "because even rattlesnakes don't kill ground owls and nobody knows wherefore."

When Clay, on a cattle-buying trip from Las Animas, stopped at the Wright House for a drink, he wanted a doughnut from the free lunch bowl. The Ground Owl was alone in the breakfast room of the hotel when Allison limped in. The Winchester he usually used as a cane was left at the hatrack, and his pistols were hidden beneath the tails of a clerical black coat. Clay's limp, due to the foot wounded during the mule stampede incident, never revealed itself while he sat handsomely in the saddle; only when afoot did he display the limp which seemed to embarrass him.

"Pard, pass me one of them fried holes," Clay remarked to the Ground Owl.

"Say, you limp in your talk like you do when you walk," laughed the Owl.

His grin frooze on his face when Clay's Colt pushed its way into his startled face.

In terror the Ground Owl cried: "Don't shoot! I ain't wearing iron."

"Then go heel yourself, varmint, and come a-shootin'!"

The Ground Owl ran into a stack of alfalfa hay behind the Trask Corral, and after dark he got away with his skin.

Clay rode up to the Alamo Saloon the next day and demanded the city give up the Ground Owl to him or he would tree the town.

Jack Webster, the owner of the saloon, hurried and got Bat Masterson out of bed.

"You got to do something, Bat. We cannot let him return to Las Animas and brag how he backed down the city of Dodge."

"I know, Jack, and it would be opening Dodge to all the trail drivers who came here, once the story got out."

"There he sits high and mighty in the saddle. Take your buffalo gun and send daylight plumb through him."

Masterson raised the Sharps and caught Clay directly in his sights. He could send a heavy slug into the gunman at any time. One detail stopped him. Clay's revolvers were still in his belt and his Winchester was still in the saddle scabbard. He must, according to all rules, wait until Allison drew a weapon.

"Jack, go and tell the others to keep out of Clay's sight," Masterson told Webster. "I can bowl him over any time."

When Jack was gone, Masterson again settled on his aim, picking a spot under the right shoulder of Allison wherein to plant the bullet.

Clay Allison continued his verbal denunciation of Dodge City and of all its citizens, but never once reached for his gun. Finally he yelled out: "Where's Masterson? He won't let no saloon clerk do me ambush dirt."

Masterson tossed the buffalo gun into the corner, buckled on his revolvers, and headed for the Alamo. In the saloon he found Clay telling Webster to seek out Masterson.

"What's wrong, Clay?" asked Bat.

"Oh, there you are. I've been looking all over for you. Where have you been the last hour?"

"Well, Clay, for the better part of it I was covering you with my Sharps," grinned Bat.

"Is that so?" exclaimed Clay. "You know, I had some kind of a feelin' that somebody had me bested. It was shore one of them gospel hunches yore told about at gospel or pra'r-meetin's."

Clay told Bat the story of the Ground Owl and said he did

159

not want to harrass Dodge, but he wanted to get the Owl. Masterson agreed with him. Later Bat stated that the Ground Owl, by stirring up Clay, could have been the cause of ten or more men getting killed, and himself getting off scot-free.

Another version is told of this same incident. It is said that Clay came into Dodge City looking for Wyatt Earp and not Bat Masterson. He rode into town alone that morning and was not backed up by a gang; he had come to kill Earp. Certain Texas cattlemen still fought the Lost Cause and were weary of Yankee badge-toters in their midst. Yet they feared to stand up against the fast-draw lawmen and had hired Allison's guns to do the work for them. But they promised to back Clay's actions when and if a showdown came.

Bat Masterson carried word to Earp as he ate his breakfast at the Dodge House.

"You'll need help this time, Wyatt," he commented.

Earp calmly offered his deputy some coffee.

"Why? I believe I can take Allison."

"Maybe so, but there'll be a dozen Texans hiding at Wright's place and I aim to even the odds."

As Wyatt Earp left the Dodge House, Masterson walked up Front Street to Second Street, where he pretended to examine horse brands at the hitch racks.

Wyatt stepped from the Dodge House, lighting a cigar, and strolled toward Second Street. Just as Earp neared Second, Allison turned the corner.

Both stopped warily and Allison asked: "You Wyatt Earp?"

"Yes, I'm Earp," said the marshal, cigar nudging his mustache.

Allison seemed confused. He flicked a glance at Wright's window, framing expectant Texan faces. Witnesses crowding batwing doors said Clay then accused Earp of killing his foreman, and began backing away.

There was a tense moment of utter silence. Then Allison went brick red under his tan. Growling something eager listeners could not understand, he turned and limped away. Shortly, Allison rode from the livery stable. Spurs raking, he tore furiously up Front Street. At Wright's store he slid to a dust-clouded stop.

"You damned sneaking coyotes! A hell of a backing-up job you did! Didn't you see Masterson ready to side Earp?" With that, Clay reined about and raced headlong out of town.

From all historical points and existing records, the first report seems to be the more accurate one.

But every Goliath has his David, and Allison was no exception.

A churlish young gunslinger named Buck Bowman returned to his home range during Cimarron's annual Mexican fiesta. Strutting about, flaunting twelve notches on his pistol butt, he quickly cowed the local talent.

Pushing his luck, he noisily bragged: "I hear some Johnny Reb named Allison is top gun hereabouts. I aim to make him thirteen on my pistol handle."

One of Clay's riders overheard the boastful remark. It did not take long for him to high-tail it to the ranch and tell Allison what he had heard. Soon Clay and his men were in town, but Allison was alone when he saw Buck emerge from Yee Fong's steak house.

"You Bowman?" he drawled. The hard-faced, black-garbed youth answered his rider's description, but he had to be certain. Not even Clay Allison could gun down some rancher's son in a fiesta crowd and laugh it off.

Buck's lip curled as he shoved back his hat.

"Sure am, hombre, and what about it?"

"I'm Allison. I hear you-all got a big mouth."

He backed off five short steps. Then Bowman crouched, his elbows crooked, and both clawed hands streaked for leather. Allison's gun hand blurred; the big Navy Colt bucked and roared. The heavy wallop of the .45 slug spun Bowman clear around. His guns spanged a vicious echo, and dust sprayed at Clay's boots. But it was just the reflex act of a dead man.

For once nobody blamed Clay. Folks agreed Buck got what he had asked for. And Clay got looped, unaware that he had fixed to meet his "David."

On Monday evening a burly stockman with drooping mustaches rode up to the Otero ranchhouse and was invited to supper. Afterward, he announced that he was Mason B. Bowman of the Rocking-B spread down near Tres Ritos.

"I'm Buck's uncle," he said quietly, "and I aim to even the score, but being a fair-minded man, I'll hear your side first."

Clay's face was impassive as he offered the rancher a drink. Mase Bowman was a man of ominous repute. As a gun-swift lawman of the Texas Ranger McNelly caliber, he had made cowtown Tascosa unhealthy for characters like Allison, until turning rancher. And Tascosa was Dodge City and Tombstone and Abilene tied together on a short, lighted fuse.

Clay Allison explained how Buck had forced the shoot-out.

Bowman listened. "Buck did have a mean streak in him. I suppose it was you or him." They drank and discussed calf crops until bedtime.

It should have ended so, but Clay awoke feeling he had been insulted. To his neurotic mind, Bowman would depart thinking he had feared a showdown. During breakfast he dropped sarcastic remarks about "has-been" lawmen.

"I'm warning you, Allison, take care. I'm no trigger-happy kid like Buck. Draw and you're dead."

Clay's features twisted in silent rage. But he did not draw and he let no rider interfere. His brothers were gone, having moved to Colorado. To save face he pretended that he had been joking, and said he would accompany Mase to Cimarron. Mase agreed. Knowing gunslingers, he rode behind Allison.

As they dismounted before Lambert's, Clay swiftly drew his pistol, but Bowman had his Walker Colt leveled and cocked before Allison could act. Clay sheepishly led the way inside. There he tried again to outdraw Mase, always meeting that icy, mocking grin across the .44 sights. Yet Mase did not pull the trigger. It seemed he enjoyed humiliating Clay before the other saloon patrons.

Livid with rage, Allison tried to get Bowman drunk. Several times Clay drew his pistol, and managed to equal Mase's fast draw several times; but Bowman's taunting grin said he'd get him anyway.

Bowman even out-drank Allison, who finally passed out cold. Amazed and joyful patrons loaded him onto his pony and headed it homeward.

Getting to the ridiculous side of Allison, we have it related that on one occasion he rode into town and stopped his horse at the top of College Hill, probably located at old Mobeetie. He removed all his clothes except his boots, then tied his clothes behind his saddle and rode through town on the run, shooting and yelling, and so proceeded with the exhibition until he had reached the outskirts of town. Clay was a tall man of striking proportions, so this ride was something of a sensation, even in those days.

In the fall of 1875 a murder took place between Taos and Cimarron. It excited Allison's anger and inspired many efforts on his part to get the killer. The Reverend F. J. Tolby, a Methodist minister, had been riding back to Cimarron when he was shot and killed for no apparent reason. He was not robbed and his horse was neatly tied to a tree not far from the body. The Reverend O. P. McMains wanted to clear up the matter. He carried Tolby's blood-stained saddle about with him, showing it to everybody and urging that something be done.

It was known that Tolby had written a letter to the *New York Sun* opposing the Santa Fe Ring which controlled elections and appointments in the New Mexico Territorial government. The first suspicion was against the Ring, and for several weeks Clay hunted for clues.

Finally Cruz Vega was implicated. On October 30, 1875, a mob dragged him from his hut and hanged him from a telegraph pole. Before he died, he stated Manuel Cardenas was the man who had pulled the trigger. Cardenas was soon arrested.

"We should turn him over to the law," said Reverend McMains.

"We are the law," Allison told him.

While Cardenas was being led to jail he was shot through the head by a group of self-appointed officers.

W. A. Marley, editor of the *Cimarron News*, took a dim view of how things were being handled, and, while usually siding with Allison in most of his doings, he now took an opposite stand and even connected the Santa Fe Ring with Clay. In fact, he dared to publicize certain decidedly incriminating facts about the Ring in the *News*. Then the Ring took drastic measures. They hired Clay.

The Marley home adjoined the *News* office. One night when Marley was in Taos, his wife heard strange noises in the office. She went to investigate. A shambles greeted her. Type and cases littered the floor; the press was a sledge-battered ruin; the newsprint had been smeared with sticky ink.

Cimarron seethed when the story became known. But nothing was done about it. It seemed unbelievable that a whole county could fear one man so much. But better times were coming. It was election year. At last, long-dominated Cimarron saw a chance to escape Allison's tyranny ... by running Mase Bowman for Sheriff of Colfax County. But Mase refused. Said he was through with being a lawman. Finally he gave in to the tearful pleas of the women in town.

It was a landslide. Now it was Allison's move. Mase had hardly pinned on his star when the gang rode yelping into town. Down the fear-emptied street they tore, to pull up in a swirling dust before Lambert's.

Just then Bowman stepped from the sheriff's office next door. Hip-high he held a sawed-off shotgun.

"Hold it, Allison. Take your men and leave town, *pronto*."

"Don't give me no ohdahs," Clay told him.

Bowman's eyes did not waver.

"Refuse, and I'll splatter your guts all over town."

Clay could see that the lawman meant every word he said. His words, like raw wind cutting, stiffened Allison in his saddle.

"Wal, boys, this beats all, let's mosey on home."

Without looking back they trotted up to the end of the street. Suddenly Clay wheeled about, firing in the air.

Bowman had learned a lot in Tascosa. Now he held a .44-.40 Henry rifle. The big gun boomed twice. One slug ripped off Clay's hat, the other seared his left side, almost knocking him from the saddle. Awed by such a turn of events Clay and his men left Cimarron, never to hurrah the town again.

Of course, law returning to Colfax County only shifted Clay's attention to other unfortunate locales. For a number of years he continued his arrogant gun-rule with a vengeance. Clay never did recover from the humiliation heaped upon him by Bowman.

In 1881 he settled in Washita, not far from Mobeetie in Hemphill County, Texas, where he was a member of the first grand jury ever appointed in Hemphill County. Although the foreman kept the jury together for twenty-eight days, all the jurors were too tipsy to turn in any indictment to the court. Clay Allison especially was hilarious the whole term.

About that time rustling on the Washita became a worse menace than usual, and the cattlemen called for a meeting one night to discuss what could be done about it.

Clay Allison said coolly: "Do you really want to know who the damned thieves are?"

"Yes!"

"Well, two of them are sitting among us. There they are."

The two men he pointed out pulled their guns and leaped for the doorway. They dashed around the corner of the house.

"Look out, Allison, or they'll shoot you through the window!" one man cried.

With both pistols drawn, Allison stood in the corner of the room and bellowed: "C'm back yar, you calf-stealing hypocrites!"

The two men were never seen again in that area.

From then on Clay Allison attended to his own business and enjoyed life with his family while raising his cattle. His next move was to a ranch in the Seven Rivers area of Southern New Mexico.

All the ranchers of the Seven Rivers district welcomed Clay Allison, for they knew of his business acumen, his love of cattle and horses, and they thought that he might be a help to the Justice of the Peace in establishing law and order. His word was his bond.

Allison sold his cattle in many towns. Once during the sale of cattle at Cheyenne, Wyoming, he entered a dentist's office to have a tooth looked after. Most writers claim this incident occurred at Las Vegas, New Mexico, because the reporter who got the story from Allison worked on the Las Vegas *Optic* and the story first appeared in that paper. The incident happened on June 6, 1886, but did not appear in the newspaper until July 3, 1886.

Clay Allison, who has just left this city for Lincoln County, is known as a holy terror when he is aroused, and although increasing years and different conditions have made him less vindictive, he still has a decided fondness for getting even with his enemies, and is pretty likely to do so as a general rule. Clay was in Cheyenne a few days ago with a bunch of steers, about fifteen hundred head in number, which he sold at a good profit, and as he was suffering from a toothache while there, he went to a dentist to get relief. The dentist who was "on the make" sized up the man as a cowman with plenty of cash and determined to make some money out of him. Instead of applying a little creosote to Clay's aching tooth he got him in his dental chair and proceeded to bore a hole in one of the cowman's best teeth for the purpose of filling it, which it didn't in the least need. He was a clumsy quack and he inadvertently broke about half the tooth off. Clay got mad and left and went to another dentist, who repaired the damage at the expense of twenty-five dollars, and told the victim he had been treated by an arrogant quack who evidently wanted to make money out of him. This fired the blood of Mr. Allison, who fairly thirsted for revenge, and he got it, too.

He proceeded to the quack's office, seized a pair of forceps, threw him down on the floor, and in spite of the yells of the victim, inserted the instrument in his mouth and drew out one of his best molars. Not content with this, he grabbed for another and caught one of the front teeth together with a large piece of the upper lip and was tugging away at it when the agonized shrieks and yells of the poor devil upon whose chest Allison was pressing his knee, drew a crowd and ended the matter. The story is said to be absolutely true and Allison admitted it.

In 1886, Seven Rivers suffered a drought which grew steadily worse in 1887 and 1888. Cattle died of hunger, thirst, and dust. The wars between the sheep men and cattlemen were renewed with increasing violence. Crowds were putting up huts in a place called Eddy, which was to emerge as the modern Carlsbad. Up the Panhandle, new counties were being cut from the vast trackless plains, sliced off like a side of beef. Buffalo hunters gave up dreaming and returned to Dodge City, Mobeetie, and other points when the skin and bone trade fell off. Some remained to work on the famous Turkey Track Ranch or the Rocking Chair spread.

John and Monroe Allison were aware of the changing times due to the coming of the railroad. They felt farming in Tennessee would not bring the same financial returns as did ranching in Texas, but when big-money interests took everything over, they would be back where they started. They sold their land and cattle interests and returned to Waynesboro. Clay decided to remain in the West. Seven Rivers slowed up. The town melted away. Today it is only a memory, added to the multitude of other ghost towns throughout New Mexico.

Across the Territorial line to the south another town shaped out of the void. Near the eastern boundry of Reeves County, on the Pecos River, the Texas and Pacific Railroad established itself with the name Pecos City—today simply called Pecos. Toyah, on the San Martin Draw, was platted in 1881. In four years it had a population of sixty. But, small as it was, wild and woolly days were to make it as notorious as Pecos. Here Sheriff J. T. Morris met his death. His successor, Sheriff L. S. Turbo, was a friend of the Allisons, often having dinner with them at their home.

The Toyah country and the Pecos country were the last that Clay Allison was to know. No doubt had he lived he might have moved again. No sooner settled at Seven Rivers, he was off again to the infant city south of there,

166

where Patsy—now aged five, and a cripple—would ready herself for school. Besides, Dora was expecting again.

People who knew Clay in Pecos described him as tall, slim, and seemingly dark complexioned, due perhaps to long exposure to the sun. Clay's Pecos ranch was just above Pope's Crossing on the Pecos River, in Texas, about one hundred yards east of the river, above a seep spring of fine water, just at the head of a little box canyon. It is now inundated by the Red Bluff Reservoir. It was about fifty-two miles north by west of Pecos. Clay probably reached there by going up the Pecos on the west side, then crossed the river at Pope's Crossing, then a short distance to the ranch house.

As the town of Pecos was close to his ranch, Clay decided to buy a house in town. He bought the J. J. McNally place at Fifth and Cypress. The population of Pecos at the time was one hundred and fifty people. The land was part of the Hudson & Great Northern survey and the New York & Texas Land Company, and sold for two dollars an acre. McNally, a native of Chicago, built a small one-room home on the corner lot. Close by lived Mark Mitchell. It was their daughter, eight years old at the time, who became the intimate friend of Patsy Allison, and their mothers were more like two sisters, so much were they in and out of each other's house. It was Mrs. Mark Mitchell who saw Dora Allison through the dark days following Clay's accident. The friendship continued even after Dora, as Mrs. Lee Johnson, moved to other parts.

The tiny town of Pecos held a special election to incorporate as a city several months before Clay moved his family from his adobe house camp on the ranch on the Pecos River. At one point W. D. "Woody" Johnson and his brother built a drift fence from the southwest corner of New Mexico west to the Pecos River in an effort to keep stock from drifting south to the river during severe storms. More often than not, cattle roamed south against the fence, breaking through, much to the disgust of Allison's cowboys, whose job it was to mend the breaks as well as cut out these cattle from the Allison brand in the spring. These Johnsons were brothers of J. Lee Johnson, the lumber and cattle man of Pecos, who married Dora Allison some time after Clay's death. Lee Johnson sold the Allison ranch to his brothers later on.

The last owner of the Allison home in Pecos was Buck

Jackson. He bought it from Sid Kyle. The original deed on file shows that on December 15, 1886, John J. McNally sold the house to R. C. Allison for the amount of $75. Recorded as Block number sixty-six, town of Pecos City in Reeves County, State of Texas, Vol. 2, pp. 284–85.

In July of 1887, Clay became angry at some cryptic remarks made about him by two of his cowboys. Some said the remarks had been made by Clay's foreman and brother-in-law, John McCullough. There seems to have been no bad blood between Clay and John, because one of John's grandsons was named Clay.

Clay ran into the owners of the McDonald and Laramore freight hauling business in Pecos one morning, and told them that he was going to work the range toward the Crossing and, while there, take care of two cowboys who were spreading lies about him. The freighters knew him well enough to understand that he would be drinking along the way, for he was sensitive about hurting anyone who worked for him. The liquor was not a booster but rather an effort to get something painful over with as fast as possible. Humoring him as the loaded their wagons, they all set out together. At nightfall they bedded down for the night on the open plain. Meantime Clay rode home and came back later driving the family buggy. He had a late supper with the two freighters. He was in an ugly mood, having worked his self-pity up to the pitch of seeing himself as a sadly abused person. He would have to kill those two cowboys.

Anxious to avert a catastrophe, Laramore invited Allison to stay at the camp that night, hoping by idle talk to divert his mind from the fixation that the two cowboys were a menace to society and had to be eliminated. After several hours Laramore and McDonald worked him into a better frame of mind, and agreeing that perhaps the boys meant nothing by their talk, Clay promised the freighters that he would not kill the cowboys provided they promised never to speak to him nor in any way mention his name when he was about. He would not fire them. McDonald and Laramore vouched for the fact that drunk or sober Allison kept his word. If these were the terms he laid down for sparing the lives of the two hands, these were the terms he would go by.

The freighters also counted the intended victims as friends. So pleased were they that Allison had had a change of heart that McDonald saddled one of the horses for an all-night ride to spread the good news to the two men. These, on their side, knowing Allison's reputation with a gun, had decided to lie in ambush. They had no intentions of being caught unprepared. Even an amubush, they admitted, would be rather risky, for Allison had a way of tracing a line of fire. He was uncanny when it came to guns and shooting. Glad to learn that Allison changed his mind about gunsmoke, they accepted the terms.

Meantime, Allison stayed in camp to await the success or failure of the mission of mercy. Allison insisted that Laramore sleep in his buggy while he made his bed on the ground. When McDonald returned, he asked him to sleep in the buggy because of the hard ride. As they had to move on, it was agreed that the buggy would be tied behind Laramore's freight wagon, McDonald stretching out in it for a most restful repose. Allison's team of horses was tied to the back of the other freight wagon, and Clay took his place in the driver's seat. The four-horse team headed for the Y crossing. The road, cut by ruts over the prairie, still had its quota of bunched sacatone grass, salt grass clusters, large pebbles, thick layers of dust.

Hoping to increase the speed of travel, Allison cracked the whip, causing one of the horses to lunge forward, bringing the left front wheel hard against a cluster of salt grass; this upset Allison, who was unprepared for the severe bump. He pitched forward, striking his head against the wheel with such impact that his skull was fractured. The fall proved fatal. McDonald awoke with a start. It was too late to render assistance. Again he saddled a horse and rode to Pecos, where he called upon Mrs. Mitchell to break the news to Dora.

The day was Sunday, July 3, 1887.

Mrs. Mitchell told her as gently as she could, hoping that the sad news would not cause another calamity. Dora, too, realized that she would have to take hold of herself for the sake of the child she was carrying.

The body was brought to the Newell Hotel. At three that afternoon the whole town assembled for the last rites. After services, the funeral procession wended its way to the cemetery just below the site of the packing house. Six graves were filled when the body of Clay Allison was taken there. It was raining that Sunday afternoon when the mortal remains of Clay Allison found rest in the soil near the Pecos River.

When Dora's second daughter was born, she was named

169

Clay in honor of her father. After Dora married Lee Johnson they moved to Fort Worth, where she died. Patsy (Patti) Allison later married Ed P. Byars of Fort Worth, Texas. Clay Allison later married J. Lloyd Parker of Houston, Texas.

Clay's grave was forgotten, resting in a cemetery vandalized for years, overgrown with weeds. The once-wooden headstone, long ago destroyed by the elements and by vandals, was replaced with a fitting marker which reads: "He Never Killed a Man Who Didn't Need Killing." Descendants of the famous gunman finally located and visited Clay's grave to have it properly cared for.

That was in 1971. On Thursday, August 28, 1975, the remains of Clay Allison were removed from the Gunfighters Cemetery north of Pecos to the West of the Pecos Park in the downtown section of that city. This was done to counteract the repeated acts of vandalism in the out-of-town cemetery.

The gentleman gunfighter was laid to rest the second time in a 25-×40-foot section of the new park in an area to be known officially as Old Gunfighter Graveyard. Reverend Ray Powell, pastor of St. Mark's Episcopal Church, conducted solemn but simple rites at the new gravesite.

Credit is due Barney Hubbs, President of the West of the Pecos Museum at Pecos, Texas, for his help in furnishing me with photos and authentic notes dealing with the life of Clay Allison. His research and study of the gunmen and lawmen of the West is indeed fantastic. I am indebted to him. I think he summed it up best when he said:

> The factual story of Clay Allison is that of a pioneer cattleman who fought for his rights and allowed no one to push him around. Times were rough and people had to be likewise. The six-shooter was useful, yet its use was abused in the name of the law. The fictional story of Clay Allison sometimes strayed from facts, but that is to be expected.

Colt's .45-caliber Peacemaker (1875)

9   "Buckskin" Frank Leslie

THE SOUND OF an open-hand slap across the face echoed from the walls of the Oriental Saloon like a peal of angry thunder. A young man, his face redder from embarrassment than from the slap, crouched back against a chair, his hand to his cheek.

"Damn you, Leslie, you'll regret that! You'd best get your gun and come a-runnin', 'cause I aim to shoot you full of holes for this insult, as well as for having a hand in the killing of my friend John Ringo."

"Go home and sleep it off, Billy. You're too drunk to think straight right now," said the mild-mannered man who had slapped the young man, and who also was the bartender at the Oriental. The slap had resulted from a dispute as to whether or not the young fellow should be served whiskey. The bartender did not believe he should be served, and his sentiments were the same as those of the lone customer who stood at the bar.

The outraged young speaker was Billy Claiborne, once a good-natured cowboy who had worked at the John Slaughter ranch in the San Pedro Valley, but who now thought that he was a gunfighter because he had slain a man over a trivial matter during a card game. On paydays he would ride into Galeyville, Charleston, or Tombstone, the places frequented by Curly Bill, the Clantons, and the McLoury boys. In a spirit of drunken fun Billy's wild associates

171

dubbed him "Billy the Kid." Of course, Billy's ego went hog-wild and he boasted that he would make Billy the Kid Bonney look like a Sunday school teacher insofar as his lawless deeds were concerned.

Billy Claiborne quit his job at the Slaughter ranch and joined Curly Bill and his band of bandits and cattle thieves. It was here that he also met that deadly gunfighter Johnny Ringo, whose background was as mysterious as that of any man who came West and wanted his past unknown. This writer has verified that Ringo once attended the famous theological college of William & Jewell at Liberty, Missouri. Also, that members of the Ringo family still reside in Missouri. It is believed that Ringo was born in California and was the grandson of Colonel Coleman Younger.

Billy and Ringo became as friendly as anyone could in such a group of robbers, and when Ringo's body was found under perculiar circumstances, and a rumor circulated that Frank Leslie had killed him, it preyed upon Billy's mind. He felt it was his duty to avenge Johnny. However, it became a known fact that Leslie had nothing to do with the demise of Ringo; many people believed that the famous gunman had committed suicide while on a drunken spree. Of course, this was just pure conjecture, for it later became known that Doc Holliday had actually killed Ringo.

His composure recovered, Billy strutted up to the bar and pounded his fist against the wood.

"I want whiskey, damn you, Leslie!"

Frank Leslie walked from behind the bar, caught Billy by the collar, and walked him to the batwings.

"Get out, Billy, come back when you're sober," said Leslie, as he turned away.

Billy left the saloon, his clouded mind still seething with rage over being insulted in such a manner. Suddenly he turned around and walked back into the building.

"You no-good bastard, Leslie, you can't insult me like this and get away with it!" Billy yelled out across the bar-room.

Frank Leslie ignored the insult, realizing whence it had come, left the bar, and, seizing Billy by the coat collar, pushed him into the street.

Claiborne glared, and he muttered: "I'll be back. Nobody shoves Billy the Kid around and gets away with it."

"Whenever you're ready, Billy," said the unarmed bartender.

At 7:30 that morning, November 14, 1882, a cowboy rushed into the Oriental, excitement beaming from his face.

"Frank, Claiborne's out in Allen Street; he's still all drunked up and carrying a rifle."

Leslie simply shrugged his shoulders as he waited on his customers. Many figured that Claiborne was just "shooting off his mouth" and would not dare tackle Leslie. Leslie was of the elite. Some even ranked him a shade faster than Doc Holliday, although he wasn't a deadly killer like Doc.

When patrons began kidding Leslie about the braggart near the saloon he replied: "I'll see what I can do to appease him. We've always been good friends and his attitude sure puzzles me. I'll just go see what he's shouting about."

Leslie leisurely removed his white apron, opened a drawer behind the bar, picked out his .45 Colt's Peacemaker, and walked to a side door leading into Fifth Avenue.

Billy Claiborne stood on the corner of Allen Street, his rifle cradled in his arms. Leslie silently approached him. When about thirty feet from the drunken youth, he covered him with his six-gun and called out: "Billy!"

The would-be gunslinger spun around, and when he saw Leslie, threw his rifle to his shoulder and pulled the trigger. At the same time Frank's big .45 boomed, the two shots sounding like one. Billy's shot missed its mark, while Leslie's heavy slug tore through the young man's chest, and he collapsed in the street and died.

As onlookers poured into the street, one guffawed: "He shore warn't no Billy the Kid. Missed with a saddlegun at thirty feet."

Leslie didn't join them. Without a further look, he spun around on his heel, stepped back into the saloon, and placed the revolver in the drawer. Tying his apron around him, he turned to a customer and asked: "What's yours, partner?"

Billy Claiborne's death apparently did not faze Leslie; he went about his work as unconcerned as if he had just swatted a fly instead of a former pal. Leslie was given a hearing, but was acquitted on a claim and proof of self-defense.

This was Tombstone, Arizona, in its heyday. Born of danger and necessity in June, 1879, on an arid mesa called Goose Flats, it had been named by its founder, Ed Schieffelin, an old army scout whose discovery of fabulous silver mines brought thousands of miners and gunmen into the territory.

United States Army Scout Al Sieber had warned Schieffelin that he would not find gold in the San Pedro Valley, but would find his tombstone instead.

"That's Geronimo county, Ed, and filled with Apaches," Sieber had told him.

Yet Ed refused to listen. He knew the danger when he rode his mule into those low, forbidding, almost naked hills in 1877. Ed was careful and ambitious. He found the mountain of silver from which was spawned the town of Tombstone.

Word of the fabulous riches to be mined in the hills spread. Men from every station of life flocked into the district, and the new town of Tombstone grew up. Ed Schieffelin lived in luxury and later traveled all over the world. He eventually tired of civilization and left his palatial Los Angeles home for a trip into the wilds of Oregon, to enjoy the freedoms of an outdoor man. There he suffered a stroke and died surrounded by loneliness.

His remains were shipped back to Tombstone. There he was laid to rest, dressed in a miner's corduroy breeches and red flannel shirt, and his old pick, shovel, and canteen were placed beside him in his coffin. A huge monument of rough stone was erected to mark his last resting place.

In 1886 the population of Tombstone was 15,000. Today only a sun-baked village remains, drowsily contemplating its past.

But what a past! Bloodier than Abilene and Dodge City. Wealthier than Virginia City and Leadville. The town where murder was a pastime, death a gruesome joke, and the six-shooter law. A hell-roaring Gomorrah of the Apache-infested Dragoons, where grisly humor produced a newspaper named *The Epitaph* and United States Marshals were ambushed by outlaws led by the sheriff.

It's all there on the weathered headboards in Boothill. *Conley—shot by Doc Holliday. Marshal White—shot by Curly Bill. Les Moor—shot with a .44. Black Jack—1881. George Johnson—hung by mistake.* Men too violent for other tough towns found men more violent in Tombstone.

And into Tombstone rode Frank Leslie. The claim staked by Leslie was rich in ore and would probably have made him a rich man, but he disliked work and left his mine to be run by hired help while he devoted his time to the lustful glamor of the painted Junos and the lure of the card games.

Who was this small and wiry man whose speed and accuracy with the six-gun could compete with any gunslinger of the day, and whose long-flowing mustache and wicked .45 Peacemaker caused comment wherever he went?

He was Frank Leslie, who, according to many reports, was born in Kentucky during the 1850's. Others have stated he was born in Galveston, Texas, in 1842, and that his real name was Kennedy. Leslie told friends his mother's maiden name was Leslie and that he took this name after he and his father had some personal differences. His early training on the raw frontier had apparently included the art of handling firearms. He was so fast on the draw that many old-timers said he was as good as or better than most of the gunfighters who roamed the West. Wyatt Earp, who claimed that Doc Holliday was the fastest gunman of the era, stated many times that Leslie was the only man who was near Doc's equal on the fast draw.

When Leslie rode into Tombstone in 1880 he was still wearing the fringed buckskin scout's jacket which he had worn when stationed at the San Carlos Indian Reservation in Arizona in 1877. His brown hair was shoulder-length, and he usually had two six-guns draped from his lean hips. Many of the men in town called him a "ham" and also dubbed him "Buckskin Frank." However, those who questioned his skill soon learned their mistake. Beneath the title of "Adonis of Tombstone" and that fetching smile and gaudy dress lay a vicious and passionate man, a man who could back up his hand with one of the fastest draws of any man in Tombstone.

Frank's later neglect of his mine proved disastrous. The large mining interests in Tombstone found a loophole concerning Leslie's mine and annexed his mine to their own. Legal action proved fruitless. Frank lost his holdings to the powerful mining combines. His loss did not seem to effect him greatly, for he soon opened the Cosmopolitan Hotel on Allen Street, in direct competition with the Commercial Hotel, the bartender of which was one Mike Killeen.

May Killeen, the raven-haired, blue-eyed estranged wife of Mike, was a maid at the Cosmopolitan Hotel, where Leslie struck up a close friendship with her. Mike Killeen had threatened to kill any man who dared show his wife any attention. It was apparent that Mrs. Killeen and Frank Leslie had fallen in love.

On the night of June 22, 1880, the trouble happened, with George Perine, a close friend of Frank, becoming involved in the romantic triangle. Perine and Leslie had gone to the dance being held at the Cook-Vizina Building, and May Killeen joined them when the dance was over. The trio walked to the Cosmopolitan Hotel, where Leslie and May sat down on the front porch, while Perine went into the bar for a drink. Perine saw Mike Killeen approaching and he yelled a warning to Leslie.

"Take that, you lousy son-of-a-bitch!" yelled Killeen, as he fired at Leslie.

His first shot grazed Frank's head; the second also grazed the top of his head. Leslie was not carrying his hip-gun at the time, only a small pocket revolver. Before he could draw his weapon, Killeen was upon him, beating him over the head with his heavy revolver. Leslie then grabbed his weapon from his hip pocket and shot his assailant twice. Killeen fell away, running into the hotel and down a hallway. Frank Leslie was arrested by Officer Bennett and Perine by City Marshal Fred White. Killeen died five days later after giving a statement to a male nurse named E. T. Packwood, who reported Killeen swore that it had been Perine who had fired the fatal shot. Therefore, no legal action was taken against Frank Leslie.

On August 6, Buckskin Frank Leslie and May Killeen were married by Judge Reilly at the Cosmopolitan Hotel. It was also about this time that one W. T. Lowry swore out a warrant for the arrest of George Perine, charging him with the murder of Mike Killeen. Judge Reilly heard all the testimony and decided to hold Perine over for the grand jury. Unable to raise the bail, Perine was taken to Tucson by Deputy Sheriff Wyatt Earp for safe keeping. However, he was released when the October grand jury failed to return an indictment against him.

In 1881 Leslie became head bartender at the Oriental Saloon, property of Billy Harris and Mike Joice. The upper floor of the building was devoted to gambling operated by Lou Rickabaugh and associates. There he met the Earps, Bat Masterson, and Luke Short, but he always managed to remain neutral and never did become a member of the Earp faction. When the clash finally came between the Earps and Sheriff Johnny Behan of Cochise County, he was not dragged into the affair, even though he was working in a pro-Earp saloon at the time and at times drinking with Earp's enemies.

Things changed in Tombstone after 1881. Leslie no longer wore his famous buckskins, but had resorted to wearing a Prince Albert coat. His famous Peacemaker no longer rested in his hip pocket, now his revolver was on the side of his hip, held in a fancy, silver, engraved clip on the side of his belt. The Battle at the O.K. Corral on October 26, 1881, had touched off the spark which brought the Behan-Earp feud to its climax. Wyatt Earp and his group left Tombstone on March 21, 1882; later Sheriff John Behan was removed from office.

The middle eighties saw the silver mines flooded, and an exodus of citizens, until only a few hundred remained. Among those who left Tombstone was Frank Leslie, who, in June of 1883 again joined the Apache Scouts. Later he joined with Milt Joyce in operating his Magnolia Ranch, twenty miles from Tombstone. They built up a large herd in the two years before Joyce sold his interest in the ranch to Leslie and moved to San Francisco.

In May, 1885, when Geronimo again led his braves off the reservation (the last time), Leslie again acted as a scout for General Gatewood until the end of June, after Geronimo had surrendered. Leslie then returned to the Magnolia Ranch in the Swisshelms Mountains, where he returned to build up his herd.

After seven years of married life with Frank Leslie, May started divorce proceedings against him. She alleged that he was unfaithful; that he had beaten her; that he had failed to provide for her, and that she was fearful for her life when he would place her against a wall and shoot her profile in bullets.

Judge William H. Barnes granted the divorce on September 3, 1887. Frank's wife later married a man named Alexander Durward in October, 1889, and they moved to California, where she died on March 27, 1947.

Not long afterward he proposed to Mollie Williams (or Bradshaw), also known as "Diamond Annie," a former "red-light district" siren and entertained at the Bird Cage Theater. (An interesting sidelight to the term "red light" is that it was so named because when the railroad workers visited the area of ill-repute they left their red lanterns standing on the porch.) Mollie and Frank lived at the Magnolia Ranch for two years; then on the night of July 10, 1889, he killed her.

They arrived home from Tombstone, where they had spent the day fighting. Both had been drinking heavily, and in the evening there was another fight. Leslie knocked Mollie down several times. He then mounted his horse and stated he was going to William Reynolds' ranch to kill him. But Reynolds was not at home.

When Leslie returned to his ranch he found Mollie seated on the porch with Jim Neal, a seventeen-year-old youth who had drifted into town and whom Leslie had hired as a ranch hand. Insanely jealous at the sight of his ranch hand and Mollie engaged in pleasant conversation, and suspecting they had had intimate relations, Leslie raced into the house, grabbed a revolver, and fired at Mollie. She staggered to her feet, tottered to the side of the house and fell dead at the back door.

Young Neal was petrified. Leslie jammed his pistol into the boy's ribs and fired again. The young man thought it was a make-believe incident, but when he felt the blood trickling down his side, he bolted and ran. Neal managed to escape in the darkness, making his way to the Reynolds' ranch. The rancher summoned Dr. Goodfellow from Tombstone to treat the wounded lad. Dr. Goodfellow later placed the boy in a spring wagon and started back to town on the morning of July 12. He informed Sheriff John Slaughter that he had seen Leslie at the Abbott ranch on the way in.

Four deputy sheriffs found Leslie near the Four Bar Ranch. He was riding toward Tombstone with two other men, telling them that Neal had raped and slain his wife and that he had to kill the boy. When he walked into the sheriff's office and saw the boy resting on a cot, he knew he had walked into a trap.

Leslie readily admitted that he had shot and killed his wife. Tried for this deed, he was found guilty and sentenced to serve a term of twenty-five years in the State Prison at Yuma, appropriately called "Hell Hole." He was received at the prison on December 10, 1889, and booked as Convict 632. He was five feet, seven inches tall, and weighed 135 pounds. When it came time for outfitting the prisoner in convict garb, it was found impossible to find shoes to fit his small feet, so Leslie was permitted to retain his own size-five boots. He was also given the privilege of retaining his luxuriant mustache instead of being clean-shaven, as was the prison rule. Frank Leslie found he was not the only former resident of Tombstone in the Yuma prison when he met Johnny Behan. Behan, however, was not serving time. He was the prison superintendent.

Frank Leslie proved a model prisoner, and was soon made a "trusty." Four years later he was instrumental in preventing a prison break. His action saved the lives of several prison guards. At one time a reporter from the *San Francisco Chronicle* visited Leslie for his story of the killing of Frank's wife. Leslie gave him an entirely different version, which appeared in the *Chronicle*. Mrs. Belle Stowell, after reading Leslie's story, started to write him and continued to do so until his release. In 1896 Leslie's case was brought up before the Territorial Governor, accompanied by a fat portfolio of letters of recommendation and petitions for his release. On November 17, 1896, Governor Franklin granted Leslie a full pardon.

On December 1, 1896, Leslie married his benefactor, the divorced Mrs. Stowell. He then took a job as a bodyguard to Professor Dumble, a geologist, who was going into Mexico to check the coal mines of the Southern Pacific Railroad. In 1899 he headed for the Klondike gold fields, and it was reported he made a small fortune there. Nothing more is heard of his wife, so apparently he discarded her somewhere along the way. Prior to 1911 Leslie had returned to San Francisco, where he displayed signs of success. He was also seen several times in Seattle, Washington, where he looked up some old friends who had known him in Tombstone.

Research reveals that Leslie did work in a saloon in California in 1924; also, that the bartender there was Jim Neal. He did not remain there long, however, and he stole the owner's revolver when he left. This was has been traced to the one found alongside a skeleton of a man found in the desert, and the bones were readily accepted as those of Frank Leslie. Some thought he had committed suicide where the pistol and bones were found.

In the middle 1930s this writer and a friend drifted into Ely, Nevada, and while in a saloon were waited on by a middle-aged bartender, a friendly person with a flare for conversation.

"Strangers in town?" he asked.

"Just riding through," I replied.

"It's a wide-open town, but not like some I've been in," said the bartender.

"Such as?" we naturally wanted to know.

"Well, Tombstone, for instance. It was a real tough town in its day."

"Were you there when such characters as Frank Leslie and Wyatt Earp were around?" we asked.

"Yes I was there. Funny thing about Leslie. After he

was released from prison he disappeared, and I saw him only once after that. I was tending bar in Oakland, California, when an old derelict drifted into the place and asked the boss for a job. He was such a pathetic-looking old man that the boss took him on as a swamper. Somehow he reminded me of someone I had met before, but it wasn't until the next day that I realized who he was. He was Frank Leslie."

"I don't see how you could recognize him after all those years," I said.

A strange look was mirrored on the man's face as he said: "How could I remember? A man doesn't forget someone who tried to kill him. I was the boy who worked for Leslie on his ranch when he killed his wife. I am Jim Neal!"

What really became of the once swashbuckling Buckskin Frank Leslie is a moot question. In 1948 a decrepit man was admitted to the hospital in San Diego, California, under the name of Barney McCoy. He appeared to be around ninety years old. Shortly afterwards the old man passed away, but before he died he stated that his real name was Frank Leslie.

Still untamed, Tombstone grew and prospered. After the flooding of the mines, it declined. By 1929 only a skeleton town crouched on Goose Flats. They moved the county seat to Bisbee. Conflagrations twice wiped out the entire business district. On June 22, 1881, a bartender forgot his cigar while checking a whiskey barrel. The second blaze came eleven months later, on May 25. It reduced the same area to ashes. This was followed by the 1887 earthquake which leveled several older buildings. The 1889 tornado ripped away roofs and false-fronts, and uprooted trees. A cloudburst, rare in Arizona, caused untold destruction in 1890.

Some said sinful Tombstone was being warned—like Gomorrah of old. Yet she lives on with her heritage. The O.K. Corral was made into a garage, the Birdcage Theater into a cocktail lounge and museum, and the Alhambra into a grocery store.

The town cannot die so long as the ghosts of Earp, Leslie, Behan, the Clantons, Curly Bill, Johnny Ringo, and other old gunfighters in black stalk shoulder-to-shoulder down Fremont Street.

The Gunfighter: Epilogue

Gunfighter! Gunfighter! Where do you roam?
    Always on the loose, no place to call home.
Dusty and forlorn; with not much pride;
    Two forty-fours hanging at your side.
Hitting the trail be it night or day,
    Looking for a fight to come your way.

From the Dakotas down to the Rio Grande
    You'll welcome a draw from any man.
Maybe you're right; maybe you're wrong;
    But your gun is fast and your will strong.
You ride into town so easy and slow—
    People gaze upon you—they want to know—

Where do you come from, who might you be?
    Just a tough gunfighter trying to stay free—
A time will come, perhaps you'll lose or win.
    Someone may be faster and check your guns in.
When the last fight is over and dust settles at your feet,
    It'll be too late, Mr. Gunfighter, will anyone weep?

C. W. B.

About the Author

Carl W. Breihan is a former St. Louis County Police Commissioner, Deputy Sheriff, and Deputy Marshal. Presently he is serving his third term on the St. Louis County Council. Mr. Breihan resides with his wife and daughter in a suburban area of St. Louis. He also has a son who lives in Chicago, and a married daughter whose family resides in Detroit.

Colonel Breihan is an historian of note and a universally recognized authority on the James and Younger Brothers. He knew the sons of Frank and Jesse James and Bill Doolin, as well as relatives of the Youngers. He has published fourteen books dealing with various outlaws, lawmen, and badmen of the old West, and hundreds of magazine articles. Some of his books were also published in England and in Germany. *The Day Jesse James Was Killed* was done in Braille for the Royal Academy for the Blind in London.